school subject
TEACHING

school subject
TEACHING

the ***history and future***
of the curriculum

edited by
ASHLEY KENT

**KOGAN
PAGE**

First published in 2000

Kogan Page Limited
120 Pentonville Road
London
N1 9JN
UK

Stylus Publishing Inc.
22883 Quicksilver Drive
Sterling
VA 20166-2012
USA

British Library Cataloguing in Publication Data

A CIP record for this book is available from the British Library.

ISBN 0 7494 3377 9

Typeset by JS Typesetting, Wellingborough, Northants
Printed and bound in Great Britain by Biddles Ltd, Guildford and King's Lynn

Contents

The contributors

Dr Tony Burgess is Reader in Education and Head of the English Academic Group at the Institute of Education, University of London. He taught English in secondary schools during the 1960s, and in the 1970s contributed to curriculum research in the development of writing abilities and language diversity. He has written on many different aspects of English teaching and of language across the curriculum, and has current research interests in the history of English teaching and in the teaching of grammar.

Alaric Dickinson was formerly Head of History and Chairperson of the Department of History and Humanities at the Institute of Education, University of London. He has worked as a teacher, teacher trainer and researcher. His main interests include children's thinking in history, assessment, and ICT in teaching and learning. He was co-director with Ashley Kent (1988–91) of Project HIT (Humanities and Information Technology) and of Project CHATA with Peter Lee (1991–97). He is currently Chief Examiner (History) for the International Baccalaureate (IB), member of the IB Curriculum and Assessment Committee, and one of the series editors of the *International Review of History Education*.

Dr Tony Dyson joined the Institute of Education in 1976, becoming Senior Lecturer and Tutor to the MA course in art and design in education. His doctorate in history of art led to his special interest in fostering historical and critical studies in schools. He left his full-time post in 1987 to make and publish prints and was in this connection elected Honorary Fellow of the Royal Society of Painter-Printmakers. He continues to write extensively on art and art education and to teach part time at the Institute.

John Hardcastle is a lecturer at the Institute of Education, University of London. He taught for 14 years in a comprehensive school in Hackney and subsequently he was an advisory teacher in East London. He is the author of *Piece of the Past*, a sociocultural account of a multicultural, inner-city classroom. He is a regular contributor to *Changing English*. His most recent work has been in developing European historical perspectives on classrooms today. His current research interests include neo-Vygotskian theory and sociocultural psychology.

Alan Hornsey was formerly Head of Modern Languages and Senior Lecturer in Education at the Institute of Education, University of London. His books and articles have been mainly concerned with literature teaching, dictionary reviews, classroom practice, structured oral presentation of language, and language-teaching policy and aims. For four years he was a chief examiner at GCE O level and has served on policy and advisory committees at ILEA, Institute of Linguists, CNAA, CILT and RSA. He is also a past president of the Association of Teachers of German.

Dr Ashley Kent is Reader in Education and Head of Geography and the Education, Environment and Economy Group at the Institute of Education, University of London. Having taught in secondary schools he became Associate Director of the Geography 16–19 Project. He is a long-standing member of the Geographical Association and was President in 1996/7. He is an active member of the International Geographical Union Commission on Geography Education. He has written widely on geographical education.

Professor Denis Lawton is Professor of Education and a member of the Curriculum Studies Academic Group at the Institute of Education, University of London. He is internationally known as an expert in the field of the curriculum. He has taught in secondary schools in the United Kingdom and was the Institute's Director from 1983 to 1989. He has published extensively and sits on the editorial board of major academic journals. He has acted as a consultant for UNESCO and OECD.

Ruth-Anne Lenga is Lecturer in Religious Education at the Institute of Education, University of London. She is Course Leader for the MA in religious education and Co-ordinator of Inset for religious education. She is also Senior Education Officer at the Jewish Museum, London. Her research interests include: religious and moral education, the search for pedagogy in Holocaust education and the role of museums in promoting moral and spiritual development.

Dr David Lines joined the Institute of Education in 1988, where he is now Subject Leader for Business and Economics Education, following a career teaching in schools and colleges and a period in industry. For 10 years he was an A level chief examiner and he has written a number of student texts. He was a co-director of the Nuffield Business and Economics Project and Assistant Director of the Cambridge Business Studies Trust. His main research interests are in the fields of assessment, values and maturation with a special focus on business and economics education.

Vanessa Ogden is Head of Humanities at Hurlingham and Chelsea School. She lectures in religious education on a variety of courses at the Institute of Education. Her research interests include religious education at post-16, religious education and school effectiveness, and the transition from Key Stages 2–3.

Dr Charles Plummeridge is Senior Lecturer in Education at the Institute of Education, University of London. Before being appointed to the Institute he taught in primary and secondary schools for a period of 15 years. His publications include books and articles on various aspects of music education. He is a conductor, organist and examiner and has lectured in Europe, South-East Asia, Africa and North America.

Roy Prentice is Head of Art and Design Education at the Institute of Education, University of London. Formerly he was the art adviser for East Sussex Education Authority and Head of Art and Design at a London comprehensive school. For six years he led the PGCE art and design course at the Institute and currently he is responsible for the MA programmes in art and design, and museums and galleries in education. He is a practising painter.

Clare Tikly has a BSc from St Andrews and an MA from the Institute of Education, University of London, where she now works as a tutor and lecturer on the mathematics PGCE course. The foundation for her work is secondary mathematics teaching, senior positions in schools in both pastoral and curriculum areas and public involvement in education. Her writing and research interests include the recruitment and retention of mathematics teachers and issues of interculturality.

Michael Totterdell is Assistant Dean of Initial Teacher Education and Head of CPD/Inset at the Institute of Education, University of London. Formerly a head of religious education and lecturer in the subject, his main research interest lies in the development of religious study in the public school sector of the USA.

Dr Sheila Turner is Reader in Education and Head of the Science and Technology Group at the Institute of Education, University of London. She is a biology graduate with many years' experience of teacher education and work in schools, as well as research in parasitology. Her professional interests cover both primary and secondary science and biology teaching. Her research, writing and teaching interests are in the field of science education in a multicultural society and nutritional education. Current research projects include collaboration with colleagues in Brazil and Greece. She has undertaken consultancies in several countries including Brazil, China, Indonesia, India and Kenya.

Dr Tony Turner was Senior Lecturer in Education at the Institute of Education, University of London until retirement in 2000, attached to the Science and Technology Group. His research interests included issues of equity in recruitment to initial teacher education. He is co-author of *Learning to Teach in Secondary Schools: A companion to school experience* (1999) and with Wendy DiMarco wrote the corresponding science text, *Learning to Teach Science in Secondary Schools* (1998). He is co-editor of the series of texts for student teachers – *Learning to Teach* (subject name) *in Secondary Schools: A companion to school experience*, published by Routledge.

Foreword

Professor Peter Mortimore

I am pleased to write the Foreword for this important collection of essays written by respected colleagues at the Institute of Education.

The chapters provide fascinating, often neglected, perspectives of the history and development of the subjects of the curriculum. They also display an appreciation of the interrelationships between the knowledge content of subjects and the wider cultural forces that shape them and, to paraphrase Burgess and Hardcastle, 'the passions at their hearts'.

As we enter the 21st century, the debates about what we should teach our young people continue unabated. What values and attitudes should we instil in them? What core knowledge is essential? What skills and competencies do young people need to master? In short, how best can we prepare the next generation for life in a participative democracy?

In teacher education, shifting views on the balance between theory and practice, the centrality or marginality of subject knowledge, and the importance that should be attached to research, all continue to pose dilemmas and excite comment.

Despite the near-continuous change that has followed the Education Reform Act of 1988, opinions still differ about the breadth, depth and ideological underpinnings of the current curriculum. Many questions remain unresolved. This book promises to be a major contribution to these important arguments.

Professor Peter Mortimore
Institute of Education
University of London

Preface

The post-war era has been one of significant changes in the English educational system. Legislative highlights have been the 1944 and 1988 Education Acts, bringing about large-scale structural changes. Since the 1988 Education Reform Act, governments have made a major political commitment to educational reform and the latest and third version of the National Curriculum, *Curriculum 2000*, has been constructed. Consequently, it is argued here that it is time to take stock of these momentous changes in the system but unusually and probably uniquely from the perspective of the subjects making up the curriculum. The 1988 Act after all did reinforce the role of the subject in a rethought National Curriculum. Curiously, subject specialisms and distinctiveness are often undervalued and at risk of being lost, almost overpowered by generic 'trends'.

This book reflects on curriculum change, particularly from the perspectives of the major subjects in the English 5–18 but especially the 11–18 curriculum.

The Institute of Education, the largest and most successful (judged by research assessment exercises, OFSTED inspections of its PGCE courses, and scale and quality of externally funded research) postgraduate university school of education in the country, has always been known for its expertise in the subjects of the curriculum. The tradition of some subjects (for example art and design, and geography) goes back as far as the early history of the Institute, yet others such as business and economics have but a relatively recent track record. Because of the size of the Institute, subject teams exist allowing for specialization, not least in research terms. These experts have therefore been very much involved in the development of their subjects at regional, national and international levels. They have had major roles in developments of the curriculum, research, teacher education, subject associations and international initiatives and are consequently in a privileged position to reflect on subject developments during a period of intensive educational change. The intention here is to reflect on these developments, but most importantly to identify the latest challenges facing their subjects and informed by this reflection to consider ways forward. Too often, as we so often hear about in other walks of life, political decisions are taken without learning the (significant) lessons of the past.

The authors are amongst the most experienced of the Institute's staff and are well known in their respective fields.

Various meetings were held with contributors at which were discussed the 'framing' of chapters. Consensus was reached that for reasons of consistency and readability each chapter would follow a common framework of 'themes'. However authors agreed that it was not desirable to force each subject history into an overly inflexible template that would fail to take into account subject-specific nuances. The conclusion was that where appropriate the following major themes would be considered: curriculum development; research directions and messages; the wider subject community including subject associations; teacher education; international developments; and ongoing challenges and ways forward for the subject.

There was to be a clear recognition of the Institute's leading role but to tell the subject stories from a wider perspective. The intention is for each chapter to aim to be a definitive review of its subject to date exploring ongoing challenges and future developments.

This subject collection is complete except for a chapter on social science and integrated humanities. Its omission is unfortunate and is not an intended slight but was unavoidable through staffing changes here. Professor Lawton comments on this omission in his postscript.

The book represents a fascinating collection of histories with inevitable variations in emphasis, concern and challenge. Not surprisingly, however, shared and changing political, social and economic environments have led to elements of commonality in these stories, for instance the role of the Schools Council in generating curriculum innovation and debate; the tightening grip of central government in a myriad of ways including the National Curriculum; the rich history of research undertaken by higher degree students and the research elements of curriculum development projects; the increasingly politicized developments in initial teacher education; the existence of international research and collegiate networks; and the constant repositioning and rethinking of all subjects in the face of particularly dynamic recent political environments.

The reader will no doubt find other similarities and differences in these compelling and up-to-date subject biographies.

Dr Ashley Kent
Institute of Education
University of London

Chapter 1

Englishes and English: Schooling and the making of the school subject

Tony Burgess and John Hardcastle

Introduction

A history of English is too bold an undertaking to be attempted in a short compass. The issue is one of scale. English has been developed as a subject, in different ways and with different purposes in different sectors of British education, across two centuries. Something of this scale and of these different courses of development needs to be retained in understanding the evolution of the subject. The problem is how much. Our focus here is on curriculum development and research in post-war years, against the wider background of the 19th century foundation of the subject. The price is some omission of detail in describing recent changes. But we hope that our approach provides a context for understanding issues presently facing English teaching, and contributes a perspective that emphasizes the importance of curriculum-oriented research.

Foundations of the school subject

From as far back as the Middle Ages, attention has been paid to learning to read and write. An education in Latin and in the classical trivium, for centuries the curriculum of the grammar school, also involved the art of composition and provided wider understandings about language. The calls for teaching English took a new turn from the 18th century onward. They posed the need for new kinds of schooling for those not served by the existing endowed secondary schools, as well as for a new subject. The energy came from the nonconformists, from the academies that educated Keats and Hazlitt, from those concerned with girls' education and from the workers' education movements and university extension classes that developed in the 19th century. These wider movements and initiatives accompanied Matthew Arnold's loftier vision of disinterested culture and his arguments, as school inspector, for poetry in the elementary schools. In the arguments for English, the educational hopes of groups disenfranchised in 19th-century society came together with claims for literature and language, as worthy of serious study.

The knowledge that began to form the field of literary and language studies reflected 19th-century preoccupations and scholarship. In the early stages, it was developed for the most part outside universities. A powerful influence was supplied by the example of German philology. Philology had been central in the formation of the German universities – a study of both literature and language, against the background of idealist philosophy and an idealist sense of history – and had opened up new horizons for intellectual exploration. In the British setting, scholars such as F J Furnivall, Archbishop Richard Chevenix Trench and James Murray worked on Anglo-Saxon and on the history of English, in the Philological Society (1840), from the mid-century onwards. Murray's *New Oxford English Dictionary*, published between 1888 and 1933, became the major project. Meanwhile, from the 1860s, the Early English Texts Society, the New Shakespeare Society, and other societies devoted to particular authors provided the editions that were to form the basis of university study. Against this background, the study of English made its way slowly in the universities, initially in London and the civic colleges, reaching Oxford and Cambridge in the 1890s.

In the schools, as education expanded and diversified, the highest-ranking public schools preserved their classical curriculum, as a mark of their distinction, through to the 20th century. However, English was increasingly offered as a school subject within the second and third ranks of Taunton's (1868) classification and in the preparatory schools that served them. From the 1850s, both literature and language could be taken in the Oxford and Cambridge and Durham universities' local examinations. In the elementary schools, a basic education in literacy was offered, which had been begun in the monitorial schools and was continued in the era of the school boards and the Revised Code. Compounded by examinations, these divisions supplied the ground-plan for the early development of English teaching. English in the grammar school was set off from elementary literacy, almost as two systems, as the 1902 Education Act reorganized the schools and set the pattern for development in the 20th century.

English was inserted very differently into the different levels and expectations for education, descending from the 19th century. For those concerned with English in the universities, the task was to evolve a serious and coherent set of studies from the disparate literary and linguistic aims within the philological project. The story cannot be told in detail. Broadly, though, Victorian criticism and interpretation, alongside biography, literary history and editorial work, evolved as 20th-century literary studies. There have been notable revolutions and individual projects since, and recurrent periods of crisis. Cambridge English, and what has been called the moment of 'Scrutiny', were influential from the 1930s onwards. In post-war years, there came the further impact of literary theory and cultural studies. To put it simply and too boldly, literary studies have developed as a set of different, often contending, approaches, against the background of more workaday historical and biographical concerns. The early missionary hopes for literary studies have largely been abandoned. In their place have come wide-ranging interests in texts and textuality.

As literary studies developed, language separated out from literature as a subject of university study. Although there have been patterns of interaction since, developed from both sides, the notion of a fundamental link within a unified historical study disappeared. Language had led literature, in the vision of philology. A history of the language might be supported by the recovery and editing of literary texts, and it was possible to see the two concerns as complementary in a common purpose. Yet clearly they were also rivals. The study of literature tended towards criticism and biography and history. Language looked toward science. For those who saw the future of the subject in enterprises such as the Shakespearean criticism of Dowson and Bradley, or in the attention to the lives of the poets in George Saintsbury's writings, literature sat awkwardly with Anglo-Saxon and with the study of the language. Philology lost impetus following the First World War, and the study of language was transformed by the European and American science of linguistics. Literature was ascendant in the early 20th century, and the early 20th-century arguments for English reflected this, as did the shape of university departments. If linguistics grew more slowly as a discipline in this country, it has emerged in post-war years as a powerful and separate set of enquiries. Insights from linguistics have come increasingly to shape educational understandings concerning language.

The task confronting those concerned with English in the schools was to construct a curriculum and an appropriate pedagogy for the teaching of a living language. Nineteenth-century educational traditions were in the teaching of the classics. English teaching needed to be won from pedagogies formed within the grammar and translation of Latin – from the study of rhetorical figures and grammatical constructions and from excessive textual erudition applied within the study of literature. In the secondary schools, grammar, composition, spelling, reading, literature might be on offer. But often, these elements of the subject would be taught as separate components, by teachers reliant on an apparatus of textbooks and on endless exercises. Literature syllabuses were overloaded, such that biographical information, quotation from memory and a little knowledge about a lot, predominated over reading. Works of literature in the classroom came scored with notes and textual commentaries. In the elementary schools, the diet was reductive. Instruction in reading was through the 'readers', graded sets of extracts, and learning to master a reading passage was the relevant transaction for judgement at the annual inspection. Students' writing was understood as copying or as the imitation of models. Robert Lowe's Revised Code was ended in the 1990s, but instructional habits persisted and were the target for the 20th-century reformers.

Through to the Second World War, it was elementary education that proved to be the central focus. As elementary educators hammered out a new picture of active learning, in English there was a new attention paid to oral work, to poetry, to composition and to children's creativity in language. Within this many-sided development English inspectors such as George Sampson and P C Ballard made important contributions. Their arguments for the importance of creative non-vocational teaching of English were supported by progressive educators such as Caldwell Cook and E A Greening Lamborn. There were changes too in secondary schools. In teaching literature, the encyclopaedic courses and massive apparatuses accompanying studied texts were gradually replaced by a priority for reading and appreciation. The teaching of composition was gradually remodelled towards a picture of the pupil as a writer, with something definite to say. A major stimulus came with the development of Cambridge English in the 1930s. The call to criticism and close reading, and the argument for the seriousness of literature, were an influence on generations of English teachers. Developments were gradual. Arguments were joined concerning the teaching of grammar and the emphasis on children's creativity. Of fundamental importance, the continuing separation of the grammar schools from the senior forms and middle schools providing education until 14 for the majority, entailed that developments were uneven. In essence, literature was developed as a grammar school study, a pattern reinforced by examinations. From 1917, the School Certificate examinations replaced the Oxford and Cambridge locals. The separation between language and literature in these examinations shaped the secondary curriculum, and throughout the period of the Certificate on through GCE in post-war years the forms of examining in English showed little change, for more than 40 years.

The broader picture for the schools was the devolved framework for educational provision introduced in the 1902 Education Act. Central government maintained an overall control, and this was exercised in various ways, including the Board of Education's Inspectorate and examinations. Explicit regulation of the curriculum by government eased as the century progressed. Handbooks of suggestions gradually replaced the more explicit 'codes', and for English these suggestions increasingly reflected the more pupil-centred set of educational understandings developing in the schools. Further influences on English came from local authorities and from teacher training. Both Ballard and Sampson, whom we mentioned as contributing to elementary education, were LCC inspectors, and through their inspectors, and subsequently through advisers and advisory teachers, LEAs helped to maintain and to develop the subject. In the post-war era, LEAs played a key role in disseminating good practice. The entry of the universities into teacher training, from the last decades of the 19th century, was also important for English teaching. Perspectives from child development and psychology were central to developing understandings in the elementary school in pre-war years. As secondary training developed, methods tutors in the university departments of education (UDEs) contributed increasingly to the methodological writing in the subject. Major initiatives in developing the rationale for English, and in deepening pedagogical understandings, came from methodological enquiries of this kind, as teacher training expanded in the McNair era (1944), following the Second World War.

The changing influences on English can be illustrated by comparing the (1921) Newbolt Report on English teaching with Sir Alan Bullock's Inquiry into English teaching, the principal report on English in the post-war years. The Newbolt Commission brought together the literary professors of the recently formed English Association (1907), headteachers and inspectors, such as Sampson, concerned with elementary education. The thinking looks back to Arnold. The passion of the Report lies in its advocacy for teaching literature, directed especially towards the secondary sector, and in the argument against the narrowing of English to teaching vocationally useful basic skills. Bullock reflects a different educational culture. Arising from concerns for literacy standards, Bullock makes its central case the argument for language and learning – and for attention to language across the curriculum. Newbolt, following George Sampson, had also famously declared that 'every teacher is an English teacher'. However, what has been evolved across the interval between the two reports is a broader sense of language and languages, and of the role of language in education, supported by the new research perspectives of the post-war years.

Curriculum and examinations in post-war years

In coming directly to these post-war years, we need to highlight at the outset
the major developments of the period. It is one in which there has been both
continuity and major change. From the 1970s onwards, there was gathering
impetus for increased government intervention leading to the major changes
of the 1988 Education Reform Act and of the succeeding acts in 1993 and
1998. However, in the years before these organizational changes, there was
a vigorous development of the subject. The impact of secondary expansion
resulted in a widespread impetus for curriculum development and in pressures
to reform public examinations. Much of the resulting work was relatively
local, involving the development of initiatives taken in classrooms and close
relations between schools and local authorities and/or a local university
education department. More sustained contributions were possible, as funding
for curriculum-oriented research became available through the Schools
Council for Curriculum and Examinations, formed in 1964. In many ways
continuous with patterns of development in pre-war years, this work made
possible a unified vision of the subject, which underpinned in turn the
movement to a national curriculum in the closing decade of the century.

A major stimulus came with the formation of the Schools Council. This
offered opportunities for funded curriculum research and in due course
gave a national focus for the rich work that had developed locally. We follow
these research directions in a subsequent section. Here, we make a general
point. The work of the Schools Council has had its critics. Some thought
that too little attention was paid to dissemination. Its independence did not
please the politicians. In English teaching, the impact of the opportunities
it offered was decisive for the development of the subject. No other organization has matched the encouragement given for research that bridged curriculum and fundamental perspectives. There has been no substitute, since. The
projects funded by the Schools Council in its 20-year existence sketched
out the shape of the contemporary understandings in the subject.

Accompanying the Schools Council work were local processes of curriculum development. In English teaching, the basis for this had been set before
the war. Denys Thompson had established *Use of English* groups from Yeovil
School, with other former pupils of F R Leavis and Cambridge English,
such as Boris Ford, subsequently Professor of Literature at Sussex University.
In post-war years, there was a gradual amalgamation of *Use of English* groups
with newly forming, more broadly based local associations for the teaching
of English, which were usually supported by the presence of a local UDE.
Formed in 1947, the London Association for the Teaching of English (LATE)
pioneered these developments, leading to the development of a National

Association (NATE) in 1964. Guided by James Britton and Nancy Martin, at the London Institute of Education, building on the work of their former colleague Dr Percy Gurrey, the association drew together the work of teachers in a pattern of conferences. Comprehension, teaching grammar, the GCE examination, pupils' talk were themes they turned to in the 1950s. The emphasis of the work was study, gathering evidence from practice and investigating points for English teaching thrown up by teachers' work. Primary teachers worked alongside secondary teachers. Teachers in the grammar schools came into touch with colleagues in secondary schools more generally, especially in the newly forming comprehensives. One of the best-known concepts of these years – language across the curriculum – was originated at a LATE conference (Barnes, Britton and Rosen, 1969).

Other associations followed London's lead, and in other areas and other UDEs a post-war generation of English methods writers and researchers shared in this pattern of development. Different interests formed, as the style of work was taken up more widely. Language and writing was pursued in London. Andrew Wilkinson studied oracy and spoken language, in Birmingham. Other themes included linguistics in English teaching, the teaching of English as a second language, literature and reading. It was the scale of these developments that was significant, and the articulation of work in classrooms, study and research. Through the routes established, English teachers were able to connect their work at classroom level with wider interests. Without the local momentum for ideas, supported also by developments in local authorities, Schools Council work would not have made the impact that it did. At the same time, the themes identified at local level contributed to developments more widely, and underpinned in due course the richness of the Bullock Report.

Balancing curriculum development, reforms to public examinations were also accelerated in this period. We have already noted the origins of public examining in the local examinations introduced in 1858 by Oxford, Cambridge and Durham universities. A 'Higher Local' was instituted in 1869. As secondary education expanded, government co-ordination of examinations followed. In 1917, a Secondary Schools Examination Council was established, composed of representatives of university examining bodies, teachers and local authorities. Two levels of examination were consolidated, following the pattern of the locals: the General School Certificate to test a five-year grammar school course and the Higher School Certificate to be taken two years later in the sixth form. In 1951, the General Certificate of Education at Ordinary and Advanced levels replaced the Certificate examinations, but without significant alteration to the intended constituency for the examination.

Throughout the various changes, including the replacement of the School Certificate, the pattern of examining in English remained astonishingly similar. As one historian of English, David Shayer, comments, 'an "O" level English candidate of the early 1960s would find the papers for the twenties almost unremarkable in their familiarity. He might find the grammar questions were a little more pedantic, the questions on the set books tending to the biographical-historical rather than to the critical, but the general pattern, content, and feel of the papers would be the same' (Shayer, 1972: 112). Shayer follows up his general comment with an investigation of Certificate and O level papers. In the first Certificate literature papers, the same set books, the same kinds of questions, the same general approach to the subject matter appear with unfailing regularity. There is even less change, if anything, in the language papers. The basic pattern was established as the essay and summary (or précis), with additional tests of paraphrase, letter writing, vocabulary, correction of sentences, clause analysis, identification of figures of speech. In the summer of 1926 the joint Oxford and Cambridge Board set essay, précis and such questions as 'Write a letter'; 'Paraphrase'; 'Distinguish between the following pairs – judicious/judicial...'; 'Correct the following incorrect sentences...'; 'Explain: Crossing the Rubicon, Gordian Knot'; 'Explain: alliteration, bathos...'. The format was still unchanged in 1952, in the joint board's O level language paper (see Shayer, 1972: 112–17).

From the 1920s onwards, there was a constant flow of criticism of examinations from those concerned with English teaching, most especially of the examining of literature. Such criticism was echoed in the reports made by the Board of Education's most prestigious advisory committee, The Consultative Committee (*The Education of the Adolescent* – The Hadow Report, 1926; *Grammar and the Technical High Schools* – The Spens Report, 1938). The report by Sir Cyril Norwood on *Curriculum and Examinations in Secondary Schools* (1943) followed lines of criticism made by both the Hadow and the Spens committees that the first School Certificate Examination dominated and distorted the curriculum. He concluded that examinations should play only a limited role in the assessment of secondary pupils. Norwood looked towards a time when all syllabuses and examination papers would be devised and marked by teachers, thus making formal assessment the servant not the master of the curriculum. This line of argument foundered on university opposition. The emphasis on teacher involvement, however, was taken up by the Beloe Committee (1960) and informed the development of the Certificate of Secondary Examinations (CSE), introduced in 1966.

The introduction of the CSE brought fresh momentum to examining, and this was followed by the development of the General Certificate (GCSE) in the 1970s and 1980s. Through the CSE, long-overdue opportunities for certification were offered to the populations not previously recognized within the examination system. The management of the examination, which was locally administered, permitted various examining modes. This articulated with the traditions of local curriculum development formed in the post-war years. The procedures of CSE examining gave many teachers an experience of assessment, wider than their own classroom. This was arguably a powerful form of professional development, which has contributed to subsequent developments in GCSE and National Curriculum assessment. The CSE, however, never commanded adequate public credibility and assent, within a framework dominated by O level, and for all the ingenuity of English teachers in devising patterns of common courses, the dual system was not a satisfactory arrangement.

In the early days of teaching English in the schools, as we have noted, different components of English – composition, spelling, reading, grammar, literature – would often be taught separately, frequently by different teachers. The separation of language and literature in the local examinations in many ways reflected the different bases of 19th-century scholarship in the grammar school curriculum. The ending of the dual system of examinations – and its replacement by the GCSE – also indirectly helped to bring about an ending of the division between literature and language. For while the central concept of the CSE was a unified English, O level literature and language papers preserved the division. This in turn helped to perpetuate the old fault line in the subject, where literature was only offered to a specialist minority. The coming of a common examination was also instrumental then in the development of a unified subject.

The climax of this period of curriculum development came with the report of the Committee of Inquiry into 'the teaching of reading in the schools and the other uses of English', chaired by Sir Alan Bullock – the Bullock Report (HMSO, 1975). The Committee's substantial achievement was to weave together, in its central statement, the confidence in a 'new English' won in everyday classroom teaching and the literary, linguistic and educational strands of thought that had underwritten the researches of the 1960s and early 1970s. Initiated amid the criticisms being made of English teaching by the writers of the Black Papers (1968–77), the Report may be read, in some ways, as 'new English teaching's reply'. The central rationale for theorizing English as 'language and learning' reflects the hand of James Britton (see Britton, 1970), whom we have already mentioned. The recent work on oracy, linguistics and language study, writing development, English second-language teaching and language across the curriculum all received support.

The close of Chapter 4 of the Bullock Report offers the most cogent statement of the Committee's central position. Three propositions are briefly stated. They are inferences, in the Committee's view, to be drawn from a study of the relationship of language and learning. They powerfully capture the heart of the Committee's approach to English:

> All genuine learning involves discovery, and it is as ridiculous to suppose that teaching begins and ends with 'instruction' as it is to suppose that 'learning by discovery' means leaving children to their own resources; language has a heuristic function: that is to say a child can learn by talking and writing as certainly as he can by listening and reading; to exploit the process of discovery through language in all its uses is the surest means of enabling a child to master his mother tongue.
>
> (The Bullock Report, 1975: 50)

The thinking here is Britton's. A major influence on school English teaching in post-war years, Britton sought for more than three decades to draw together the disparate activities of English within a unifying account of language's role in learning. Britton's work had at its centre a long engagement with Vygotskyan thought, to which he added a notion of representation developed from an account of symbolizing given by Ernst Cassirer and Susanne Langer. This perception of the fundamental role of language, in Britton's work and in the Bullock Report, gave English teaching in the schools its unifying rationale.

Wider developments: teacher training, subject associations and the international dimension

Developments in teacher training, together with the formation of the English subject associations, accompanied, and partly shaped, the new moves in curriculum. The educational historian Harold Dent describes as 'massive' the expansion undertaken in teacher training to meet the increased birth-rate, following the war. 'By 1951,' he notes, 'there were nearly 25,000 students in training, more than twice as many as in 1939' (Dent, 1977: 130). As we have already mentioned, this expansion contributed to the development of methods work in UDEs and colleges. The reorganization of teacher training into Area Training Organisations (ATOs), following the findings of the McNair Committee (1944), also contributed to the dissemination of new work in the subject, bringing colleges and universities into closer contact. The training of teachers for secondary schools shared in this expansion, as qualified teacher status was increasingly expected for teaching in all state-funded secondary schools, as well as in the primary schools, where this had long been the case. Significant as these developments were, the goal remained a long way off, for English teaching to be undertaken wholly by teachers qualified and trained in the subject. A survey of secondary schools, which was conducted by Sir Alan Bullock's Inquiry, found that 'no fewer than a third of all secondary teachers engaged in the teaching of English have no qualifications in the subject' (The Bullock Report, 1975: 8), a finding described by the Committee as disturbing.

New perspectives in English teaching, teacher education, local development of the subject by teachers and by local authorities, and research reinforced one another, as the post-war period developed. Diploma and MA courses for serving teachers expanded from the 1970s, complementing PGCE work and the BEd courses, developed after the Robbins Report on Higher Education (1963). Courses at this level were supported by the 'pool' arrangement with the DES, whereby local authorities could recoup 75 per cent of the cost of paying for a seconded teacher, and were hard hit by the ending of this provision in 1986. The impetus for research was similarly affected by the ending of the Schools Council in 1984. However, traditions of collaboration were established between teacher education and serving teachers and LEAs, which fed the newer partnership arrangements in teacher training that followed. Stronger government control of teacher education developed from the 1980s, and passed through various phases to the present Teacher Training Agency (TTA), and its training standards and initial training curriculum for English (and for mathematics and for science).

The growth of English teaching's subject associations also served to bring together universities, local authorities and schools. The first association in English teaching was the English Association, formed in 1907, which still continues, with a predominantly university-oriented membership. *Use of English* groups were formed from the late 1930s onwards, as we have described. While these groups were absorbed by the post-war local and national associations for the teaching of English, the journal still continues to command a wide readership. Formed in 1972, the more recent Queen's English Society has been an active campaigner in the causes of phonics teaching, Standard English and improved communications skills. The National Association for the Teaching of English (NATE) has been the central association for English teachers, since its foundation in 1964, building on the work of local associations that have continued to develop and expand. NATE's administration and central organization has been tiny, compared with other subject associations, and it is only recently that NATE has afforded even one paid officer. Teachers and educators on a voluntary, part-time basis have performed the work of the Association's committees, and of its executive and council. None the less, the shaping influence of NATE on post-war

English teaching has been profound. Annual conferences bring together the work of branches and of individual teachers. The journal, *English in Education*, is widely read. A publishing arm developed, as the Association expanded, and a number of influential texts in English teaching have followed.

In 1966, delegates from NATE and from the American subject association, National Council for Teachers of English (NCTE), held a celebrated joint seminar in Dartmouth, New Hampshire, leading to the formation of the International Federation for Teachers of English (IFTE). Further conferences have followed at five-year intervals, with membership expanding to include all English-speaking countries. Various anthologies and collections have been published under IFTE auspices. With improved communications and with an expanding, world-wide market for publishers, English has grown international. Arising from the original seminar at Dartmouth, John Dixon's *Growth through English* (1967) was published as the British version of the proceedings. The book has been widely influential. It should be added, though, that Dixon's proposal for a new growth model for English teaching was never intended as the naming of a movement, a status that has sometimes been attributed to it in later commentary.

The contribution of research

By 1965, the Schools Council had recognized the need for a 'major initiative in the field of English teaching' and had produced its *Working Paper No 3: English – a programme for research and development in English teaching* (Schools Council, 1965). Following this, in 1966, several new researches were initiated. Oracy was to be studied in Birmingham, continuing work already funded by Gulbenkian (Wilkinson, 1965). A project on writing, *The Development of Writing Abilities, 11–18*, was set up by James Britton in London (Britton *et al*, 1975). A survey of approaches to English was to be undertaken by Bill Mittins, in Newcastle. Themes in teaching literature were taken up by Frank Whitehead, in Sheffield, who was to pay special attention to patterns of reading (Whitehead, Capey and Maddren, 1974). Douglas Barnes, at Leeds, set out to look at children as readers (1967–73), in a project to be developed in conjunction with NATE. There was also to be an investigation of relations between linguistics and English teaching, work that had already been begun by Michael Halliday, and that was transferred from Nuffield to Schools Council funding (see Doughty, Pearce and Thornton, 1972). The Council also took some steps towards developing the teaching of English as a second language.

We pause then on these main lines of English curriculum work and outline the major projects and directions taken, through to the present day.

What will be apparent will be the scale. What cannot wholly be conveyed within this compass are the broader movements of ideas arising from major disciplinary influences, which have entered into contemporary projects. We concentrate on the evolution of curriculum work, in what were to emerge as English teaching's shaping interests.

Oracy and spoken language

Some of the most effective studies of pupils' talk were conducted in the 1960s, with teachers recording lessons, staggering into classrooms carrying cumbersome and less than hidden reel-to-reel tape recorders. Typically, this work contrasted talk in formal lessons managed by the teachers with what pupils were able to achieve on their own in small groups. As just one example, the supportive spiralling talk of the Norwood girls in South London discussing Yevtoshenko's poem 'The Companion', which can be found in Nancy Martin's *Understanding Children Talking* (1976), plainly takes their learning further than the question-and-answer format of the contrasting teacher-led lesson. Douglas Barnes's larger-scale investigation of talk in different curriculum subjects, reported in *Language, the Learner and the School* (Barnes, Britton and Rosen, 1969), hypothesized 'a language of secondary education', which was at odds with the informal discussion needed when encountering new concepts. With Frankie Todd, he went on to study pupil groups (Barnes and Todd, 1977). This later work contained the demonstration of what can be achieved by pupils working on their own, and also developed the helpful analytic concepts of 'cognitive and interaction frames'.

Work of this kind – small-scale, focused on pupil learning, attentive to group processes – has continued fruitfully, facilitated by more manageable equipment and providing a point of entry into studying classroom language that can be powerful in generating language policies. Predominantly the focus has been Vygotskyan, influenced by James Britton's (1970) account of language and learning, already mentioned; and Britton himself contributed to the developing analysis in his *Talking and Writing* (1967) and in his chapter in *Language, the Learner and the School* (Barnes, Britton and Rosen, 1969). Other perspectives were added in the 1970s and 1980s. Harold Rosen's work on language and class (1972; and see also the journal *Language and Class*, 1972–74, occasional) added a sociolinguistic dimension to investigations of informal pupil language. This was followed in John Richmond's work in Vauxhall Manor School in the early 1980s (1982), investigating pupil dialect and their switching between different codes. Accounts of talk in multilingual classrooms, and proposals for managing jointly the development of bilingual and monolingual pupils, can be found in Neil Mercer's *Language in School and*

Community (1981). Feminist work explored the interaction between girls and boys, showing the usual dominance of boys in formal classroom settings but also the different and successful classroom strategies pursued by girls (Swann and Graddol, 1988; Bousted, 1989; Maybin, 1991).

A further stimulus came from the National Oracy Project, administered by the then newly formed National Curriculum Council (NCC), from 1987–1993. Like its companion project of the 1980s, the National Writing Programme, the aims of this project were more concerned with development and dissemination than with fundamental, investigative research. The work was conducted by a small central team, supported by local co-ordinators, with a brief for enhancing the role of speech in the learning process and for developing the skills of teachers and their methods of assessment. Much of this development work, however, took the form of initiating small-scale research, and Kate Norman's (1992) edited account is alive with transcripts, conversations and dialogues, and studies of pupils working.

Writing

The major study of children's writing was Britton's (1975) account of the development of writing abilities from 11 to 18. This described development in writing as becoming progressively more able to write in different functions for different audiences, outlining the threefold division into expressive, transactional and poetic functions that has influenced much subsequent work. The awareness that different audiences pose different problems for the writer also has its origin in Britton's work. Britton sampled the written output of pupils of four different age groups (Years 7, 9, 11 and 13, in contemporary descriptions) in different subjects, in 65 secondary schools. With minor variations, informative writing, usually for an examining audience, accounted for around 80 per cent of the writing produced in every year in all curriculum subjects, except English. The level of abstraction moved slowly up from report to classification and stayed there. This finding about the narrow range of secondary writing lay behind the attention to language across the curriculum that was subsequently called for in the Bullock Report. Subsequent work in writing across the curriculum, together with that of the National Writing Programme, referred to below, has taken its cue from Britton in emphasizing variety and the role that writing plays in learning.

Work from other perspectives included rethinking the American rhetorical tradition, and work on process writing and on children's developing mastery of the systems of written language. James Moffett's (1968) account of the 'universe of discourse' and James Kinneavy's (1971) development of rhetoric originated in the United States but the approaches were also influential in the UK. Andrew Wilkinson's Crediton Project provided a different, wider approach to the study of development in writing (Wilkinson, 1987). Gunther Kress's study of *Learning to Write* (1982) showed children gradually differentiating written from spoken grammar, and had something in common with Katherine Perera's *Children Writing and Reading* (1984), though this was written from a different grammatical perspective. Kress also introduced the notion of 'genre' in written language, which had been widely influential in other Australian work. Marie Clay's 'developmental writing' (1975) offered a coherent way of working in the teaching of writing in the early years, reconciling the claims of development with the need for children to master the grammar, orthography and spellings of the written system. Donald Graves's approach to drafting and peer editing became influential in both the USA and the UK from the late 1970s onwards (see Graves, 1983). In the USA, also, what began as the Bay Area Project evolved into a National Writing Programme and provided a successful model for in-service education and for the development of writing practices.

Like the Oracy Project, the UK's National Writing Programme was initiated with the aim of enhancing practice and disseminating understanding. Again, much of the best work of this project was undertaken locally, and its success is to be judged by the engagement of teachers in development work rather than in published outcomes. Measured by these criteria, the several booklets, produced in the closing stages of the project (1989–90), provide evidence of powerful and successful work.

Reading

The classic study of young people's choice in reading was A P Jenkinson's *What do Boys and Girls Read?* (1940). This was followed up in Frank Whitehead's work for the Schools Council (Whitehead, Capey and Maddren, 1974) and has been replicated again in recent years by Peter Benton (1996). An interest in what is read – and what it's for – might be expected from English teachers, and indeed has been distinctive. Benton's study also broke new ground by treating viewing choices alongside reading, a further point in understanding literacy in which English teachers have been interested.

Trends in reading standards have been a major thread in national educational debate, ever since the National Foundation for Educational Research (NFER) Report of Start and Wells (1972) suggested evidence of possible decline. The issues were discussed in the Bullock Report, which was set up shortly after the NFER review. Bullock made proposals for a rolling programme of national monitoring to be undertaken by the newly formed Assessment and Performance Unit (APU) (1974) and questioned the validity of evidence drawn from existing forms of testing. The APU subsequently conducted national surveys in English, science and maths between 1978 and 1984, and again in 1988. As it happens, it seems that there was little evidence of change in either direction. The APU was subsequently disbanded during the move to national testing, but the pattern of argument and counter-argument continued. Recent work includes Martin Turner's *Sponsored Reading Failure* (1990), which sought to link changes in methods of teaching to a decline in standards, based on results of tests administered in nine local authorities. This has been followed up by a substantial NFER survey (1991) and HMI reports on the teaching of reading in both primary and secondary schools (DES, 1990, 1992). A good discussion of these more recent surveys can be found in Reed, Webster and Beveridge (1995). We note this back-ground out of interest, but cannot here pursue the issues in detail.

More illuminating for English teachers have been the continuing explorations of how children learn to read, new accounts of reading process, and specific examinations of causes of reading failure. Themes such as these have been pursued in English teaching and in psychology. Accounts of learning to read, with summaries of research, included Meek (1982), Clark (1985), Beard (1987, 1990) and Oakhill and Garnham (1988). Reading theory was influenced in the 1970s by accounts of reading process developed in the USA by Frank Smith (1972) and Kenneth and Yetta Goodman (Goodman, 1982). Balancing their account of what it is that fluent readers do, there has been a continuing examination of children's reading problems (see Bryant and Bradley, 1985). Among possible variables leading to 'backwardness', Bryant and Bradley proposed as most important 'that backward readers tend to find it difficult to disentangle the sounds in words'. Other influential work on reading difficulties included that by Marie Clay (1979a, 1979b, 1982).

While studies of initial literacy predominated in research in reading, there was some influential work on reading at higher age levels and on developing skills. Two major Schools Council projects were Southgate *et al*, *Extending Beginner Reading* (1981), and Lunzer and Gardner's work, *The Effective Use of Reading* (1979; and see also Lunzer and Gardner, 1984). Drawing on a wide set of fact-finding investigations, Southgate's special recommendations concerned the resourcing of books for the 7–9 age group and the effective use of teacher time. Lunzer and Gardner opened up a range of issues concerning comprehension, reading strategies and coming to read new and more complex texts, and their proposals included the influential 'directed activities related to texts' (DARTs). Their studies of reading across the curriculum parallel those made for talk and writing, with findings, not dissimilar to those for writing, concerning the limited extent of sustained, silent reading in the secondary curriculum. A generation of teachers has been influenced by Margaret Meek's concern to bring research in reading more closely together with the insights from the tradition of language and learning. Meek's own writings have always made subtle connections between reading, development and the part played in this by story telling and by children's literature (Meek, Warlow and Barton, 1977; Meek with Armstrong *et al*, 1983); and these links are to be found explored in other work of this kind. Notable studies have been those by Henrietta Dombey (1992) and Carole Fox (1992); and also by Eve Gregory (1992), where special attention is paid to bilingual literacy, investigated in the classroom setting.

Teaching of literature

The new criticism of I A Richards, F R Leavis and others in the *Scrutiny* in the 1920s and 1930s remains the starting-point for work on the teaching of literature. Cambridge English rediscovered literature, transforming an earlier generation's biographical and textual scholarship and substituting the aim of alert and critical reading. Drawing on this inheritance, educational work in English sought a general account of literature and its purposes, with a view to bridging specialist and developmental concerns. James Britton's account (1970) combined a view of literature and language within a general theory of the role of symbols in forming a representation of experience. His theory of the spectator role saw the making and reading of stories and poems as continuous, and he also links gossip and reflection on one's picture of the world with the work of the literary artist. In the USA, Louise Rosenblatt's *Literature as Exploration* (1938) placed a similar emphasis on the reader. Rosenblatt studies the 'transactions' between works and readers, distinguishing between types of readings. She argues for a case study method in investigating literary response. In her later (1978) work on poetry she distinguishes between 'text' and 'reader' and 'poem'. The poem is the event that happens in the transaction between the reader and the text. This phenomenological perspective has made its way more slowly in the UK, but has become more influential, as the theoretical turn in literary studies has gained wider currency.

Emphases on reading and the reader – and on the role of narrative in everyday life – were brought together in Margaret Meek's *The Cool Web* (Meek, Warlow and Barton, 1977), an important collection of themes in post-war British work. Several excellent books have followed, written in the light of these concerns for reading and the reader (Benton and Fox, 1985; Griffith, 1987; Stibbs, 1991; Benton, 1992). Each of these draws also on more recent literary theory, offering a restatement of English-teaching approaches and illustrative accounts of classroom work. Collections of articles and essays, similarly exploring new forms of work with literature, include Miller (1984), Corcoran and Evans (1987), Lee (1987) and Hayhoe and Parker (1990). As yet, though, there has been no sustained empirical research study of children's development as readers of literary texts. Robert Protherough's *Developing Response to Fiction* (1983) moves in this direction. The work is based on a number of 'linked, small-scale classroom investigations', carried out from Hull University over a number of years, involving local teachers and research students. A four-stage model of development in response is suggested and five case studies are reported. Other work by Protherough (1986) includes investigations of teaching literature at A level and enquiries into children's developing sense of stories. There is a need for a larger-scale investigation, as Protherough himself noted, one that crosses educational phases and combines case studies with a broad, developmental enquiry.

Influenced by literary theory, contemporary English practice regularly juxtaposes literary texts with texts of other kinds, in ways that are ahead of both full theoretical description and research study. Andrew Stibbs's (1991) work on narrative drew at points on film as well as literary text; and Michael Benton's work (1992) broke new ground in integrating painting and the visual image into teaching literature. Meanwhile, there has been a developing tradition of media studies teaching in schools and of school-focused research studies of this (Bazalgette, 1988; Buckingham, 1990). Studies of children's development as television viewers, ethnographies of classroom teaching of cultural studies and accounts of the construction of TV audiences have been developing lines of work.

Language study and knowledge about language

What should be taught about language, and more specifically about grammar, has been a controversial issue in English teaching throughout the century. The 1911 report of the Joint Committee on Grammatical Terminology did not resolve competing approaches in modern languages, classics and English. Evidence to the Newbolt Committee (1921) was divided about whether grammar should be taught at all. From the 1930s onwards, what troubled writers such as Gurrey (1961) was the reductiveness and poor quality of much of what was taught. Widespread dissatisfaction with the approach to grammar in the first Certificate examinations was also a concern. Many in the 1950s looked to the developing study of linguistics to renew the study of language, within a framework of contemporary understandings; and this has been at the centre of a serious post-war exploration, notwithstanding the often stormy nature of public debate, in recent years.

Looking towards linguistics entailed the recognition that grammar constitutes a level in the language, one among a number of others, and that wider understandings concerning purpose, function, style, variety, context have also to be included in a picture of how language works. Increasingly, 'language awareness', or 'knowledge about language', came to seem the appropriate unifying concept for English teaching, one in which attention was paid to grammar but in which it was related to other linguistic concepts and understandings. Grammar, then, has been a changing issue, as linguists' understandings of the formal aspects of language have been reshaped by influences from sociolinguistics, by study of the differences between spoken and written language, and by a new awareness of text and discourse. Various projects and writers took steps towards establishing a new consensus, in the post-war years.

Michael Halliday's 'Programme in English Teaching and Linguistics', funded by the Schools Council, issued in the 'Language in Use' (1971) materials produced for schools, and covered a range of linguistic topics. This was followed in the 1970s and 1980s by a wide-ranging exploration of language awareness, from many sides. Eric Hawkins, supported by the newly formed National Congress for Languages in Education, took initiatives in modern foreign language teaching (see Hawkins, 1984). Language awareness courses were developed in schools. A steady stream of books disseminated linguistic knowledge, including new approaches to teaching grammar (Crystal, 1976/86; Gannon and Czerniewska, 1980; Perera, 1984). Work on language diversity contributed to increased awareness of bilingualism and dialect and Standard English (Rosen and Burgess, 1980; Linguistic Minorities Project, 1985). Language awareness featured in both the Oracy and National Writing projects. Meanwhile, an increasingly sharp public debate about the teaching of grammar also played its part in taking the issues forward. From the late 1960s, Black Paper writers urged a return to formal and explicit grammar teaching, and a line of new argument and polemic developed. In several influential books, the linguist, John Honey (1983), also criticized descriptivist assumptions in contemporary linguistics. Within a general movement towards curriculum review in the 1980s, HMI raised the issue of teaching *about* language (*English 5–16: Curriculum matters*, 1984). A Committee of Inquiry into the teaching of the English language was set up under Sir John Kingman (1987/88), shortly afterwards.

This Inquiry contributed also to National Curriculum discussions, and we shall return to it in our final section on recent developments of this kind. Here, we note the report's contributions to the development of language awareness, as a topic within English teaching. The Committee's brief was 'to recommend a model of the English language, as a basis for teacher training and professional discussion' and also to 'consider how far and in what ways that model should be made explicit to pupils'. The resulting model drew on language awareness from the preceding years. It did not find universal acceptance, though it has influenced developments subsequently. Where Kingman did achieve some resolution of the issues was in settling unambiguously for an approach to language structure based in wider knowledge of language, and in explicitly ruling out a return to traditional grammar teaching. The subsequent National Curriculum working party, chaired by Brian Cox, pursued a similar line of argument.

The issue has been developed subsequently, within the different policy context of implementing the National Curriculum and of stronger government intervention, exercised through the various agencies that have been formed in the period following the 1988 Education Act. A major in-service initiative was the Language in the National Curriculum Project (1989–92), set up to implement the findings of the Kingman and Cox committees concerning knowledge about language. Supported by both government and LEA funding, this project accomplished much useful work at local level, and produced two useful publications (Bain, Fitzgerald and Taylor, 1992; Carter, 1990). Unfortunately, government refused the publication of the central materials, such were the political sensitivities of the times. Work, however, has continued. Published by NATE, Richard and Elspeth Bain's *The Grammar Book* (1996) offers materials for a new approach to grammar teaching, based in the wider sociolinguistic and textual understandings to which we have referred. Very recent work by the government's curriculum agency, the Qualifications and Curriculum Authority, is also taking matters forward.

The wider significance of research in English teaching

Before the coming of the Schools Council, methods writing and the development of textbooks formed the major means of intellectual exchange around school English teaching. In educational studies, more broadly, notable research fields developed from the 1880s in the history and philosophy of education, psychology and child development. Impacts on English teaching came from child development's focus on the child, and more specifically from concentrations in psychology on the teaching of initial reading and on vocabulary development. But research in methods work was undeveloped in comparison with these broader disciplinary fields. The post-war movement toward curriculum research affected English teaching profoundly. Central interests developed in oracy and spoken language, in writing, in reading and the teaching of literature, and in language study. Already apparent in the Schools Council's early list of projects, these themes continued to shape English teaching. They also opened English teaching to wider influences from national and international research. Fundamental perspectives from cognitive psychology, language acquisition studies, sociolinguistics, and British literary and cultural studies became available in English teaching, as the curriculum-oriented work proceeded.

The coming of the National Curriculum: future directions for English teaching

The local development of English as a subject, together with curriculum research, continued to inform English teaching, within the changes to the organization of education emerging from the 1970s. The Schools Council was ended in 1984, but development work in oracy and in writing was funded by the National Curriculum Council in the 1980s, in an essential continuity. Increasingly, however, the expectation of development and research as fundamental to the work of English teaching was redefined within a new expectation. This was that government should have a stronger role in providing direction in curriculum matters and should be able to identify and implement priorities. The twists and turns in the development of the National Curriculum in English reflect the evolution of this principle. There has been a transition from the consultative frame of reference behind the HMI *Curriculum Matters* series (1984) to the new, government-led order of the 1990s, in developing the National Curriculum. Marked in English teaching by the deliberations of the Kingman Committee (1988) and the Cox working party (1989), and by subsequent National Curriculum developments, it may well be that the wider organizational changes in this period of adjustment will carry most significance for the future development of the subject.

We will not dwell on the events in detail, but some chronology may be helpful. As other writers have noted, the movement towards greater government intervention began with James Callaghan's speech at Ruskin College and with the subsequent educational debate. This led to the neglect of the Bullock Report, whose substantial proposals for raising standards in literacy were never acted on by government. The new themes of the (1977) Green Paper were reassurance about curriculum, assessment, links with industry and raising standards. The Department for Education and HMI work on curriculum followed in the early 1980s, and issues for English were raised in HMI's report on English (1984) in the *Curriculum Matters* series. Subsequently, the sequence of events is complex. Disagreements over language study, which were noted in the report by HMI, resulted in the formation of the Kingman Committee (1988). The formation of this committee, however, anticipated the further curriculum initiatives and formation of subject working parties, arising from the movement towards the (1988) Education Act. Chaired by Brian Cox, the English working party made an interim report in 1989, with a final report in 1990, which was co-ordinated with the Kingman recommendations. The 1990 standing orders for English thus reflected the work of both committees. In a troubled story subsequently, changes to this curriculum were proposed by a (1993) NCC working party, following an internal document on *The Case for Revising the Standing Order*. This revised curriculum, though never implemented in standing orders, formed the basis for the (1995) Dearing Review, and with the adjustments made by Dearing supplied the National Curriculum in English until the present Curriculum 2000.

The evolution of assessment and accreditation has accompanied curriculum changes. The first GCSE examination was held in 1988, and National Curriculum assessment was introduced within a recently reformed pattern of public examinations, initially without much recognition of the implications. Subsequently, National Curriculum assessment has been confined to Key Stages 1–3, with GCSE fulfilling both functions at Key Stage 4. Adjustments have been made to both systems in the 1990s. SATs have been transformed and act as end-of-key-stage tests, revising their original design as flexible assessment probes, which had been intended by the (1988) TGAT working party. GCSE has progressed through several changes of syllabus, following adjustments to the National Curriculum. The coursework element of the examination has been reduced, the notion of different examining modes abandoned. The pattern settled, as the 1990s unfolded, with end-of-key-stage assessment becoming a recurrent feature of school life. In secondary schools, the end of Key Stage 3 now marks the transition towards public examinations and initiates what is increasingly spoken of as the 14–19 curriculum.

Reflecting on the position reached by English, it is important to note continuities. Least observed perhaps, the National Curriculum is predicated on a single, relatively unified framework of national schooling. In English, as we have seen, the formulation of English as unified subject was something that had to be achieved. The history has been one of different Englishes for different outcomes, and of seeking to overcome divisions. As recently as O level, the structure of examining tended to preserve literature as a minority specialism, intended for the grammar school and not for wider consumption. Behind the National Curriculum's perception of the complementary importance of both literature and language, there lies the work of elementary school reformers and of post-war secondary teachers. If the schooling framework is one precondition, others are the widening of public examinations and the sense of a common educational trajectory from 5 to 16.

Matching these wider preconditions is the more specific curriculum inheritance of English as a subject, which has been the achievement principally of post-war years. The selection as attainment targets of 'speaking and listening', 'reading' and 'writing' is a matter for comment, here. With this selection, it is processes of using language that have been made the organizing principles of curriculum. To see this choice historically is to see how far the subject has been shaped by a priority for the living language and escaped its earlier inheritance from the classics. We may contrast with it such earlier organizing topics of English as composition, spelling, grammar, comprehension, dictation, recitation, in order to appreciate the significance. More specifically still, insights from post-war curriculum work inform the framing of these language processes and the knowledge, skills and understandings related to them. Spoken language is given importance equal to literacy. Goals for writing reflect an understanding of different purposes and functions and of the shaping influence of audiences. There is recognition of higher-order skills in reading. Two general emphases are especially pertinent: interaction between different language modes is stressed; the need for skills to be deployed in different contexts is also recognized, a matter variously represented as 'range' (Dearing) or 'breadth' (Curriculum 2000).

It may be that English has not changed enough, within its current National Curriculum presentation. The unsettled issue in British education is still the balance between academic and vocational orientations. In its formulation as a subject English did not escape the influence of 19th-century hierarchies of knowledge and patterns of selection for higher education. The English curriculum still points skywards to the university rather than fanning out into a range of options, though patterns here are changing. The evolution of the 14–19 curriculum will no doubt call again for different Englishes, but hopefully within a framework of principle concerning language use and language development. Considering other points, perhaps the present literary component in secondary schools, and the requirement for set books, may overload the curriculum and lean too far towards traditionalist and 19th-century assumptions about literary study. Opportunities for ICT and for studying contemporary media may also be too limited. We indicate directions in current debate, in saying so. Yet a strength of Curriculum 2000 is the recognition that schools not governments make curricula. This, together with the greatly improved (and less contentious) quality of the drafting, looks like assuring a platform for the continuing development of English teaching, and for continuing government initiatives, such as those begun in literacy and numeracy.

How the subject will develop in the schools in future looks presently to lie with government, rather than with universities, or local processes, or research. Our stress within this chapter has been on the local development of English and on the part played by curriculum-oriented research, since this has been the history for most of the 20th century. There seems to us to be no necessary contradiction between a government acting to secure standards and contributions made from other quarters. But the way in which this balance will develop does not seem at the moment entirely clear. We hope for more encouragement for curriculum-oriented research, since the shuttle between practice and fundamental ideas has underpinned so much of what in our view has been best in English teaching, and research of this kind clearly has lost ground in recent years. But our final comment is more general. At the beginning of this chapter, we recalled the social hopes invested in the serious study of language and literature, arising in the 19th century. No one can understand the arguments and ideals in English teaching, who does not also appreciate the passions at its heart. How these social hopes and their equivalents evolve within the 21st century will no doubt be the final arbiter for the direction of the subject in the schools.

References

Bain, R and Bain, E (1996) *The Grammar Book*, NATE, Sheffield

Bain, R, Fitzgerald, B and Taylor, M (eds) (1992) *Looking into Language: Classroom approaches to KAL*, Hodder & Stoughton, London

Barnes, D, Britton, J and Rosen, H (1969) *Language, the Learner and the School*, Penguin, Harmondsworth

Barnes, D and Todd, F (1977) *Communication and Learning in Small Groups*, Routledge & Kegan Paul, London

Bazalgette, C (1988) They changed the picture in the middle of the fight: new kinds of literacy, in *Language and Literacy in the Primary School,* ed M Meek and C Mills, Falmer Press, Lewes

Beard, R (1987) *Developing Reading 3–13*, Hodder & Stoughton, London

Beard, R (1990) *Reading: 3–13*, Hodder & Stoughton, London

Benton, M (1992) *Secondary Worlds: Literature teaching and the visual arts,* Open University Press, Buckingham

Benton, M and Fox, G (1985) *Teaching Literature, Nine to Fourteen*, OUP, Oxford

Benton, P (1996) Children's reading and viewing in the nineties, in *What is English Teaching?*, ed Chris Davies, Open University Press, Milton Keynes

Bousted, M (1989) Who talks? in *English in Education*, **23** (3), pp 41–51

Britton, J (ed) (1967) *Talking and Writing*, Methuen, London

Britton, J (1970) *Language and Learning*, Allen Lane, London

Britton, J et al (1975) *The Development of Writing Abilities, 11–18*, Macmillan, London

Bryant, M and Bradley, L (1985) *Children's Reading Problems*, Basil Blackwell, Oxford

Buckingham, D (ed) (1990) *Watching Media Learning: Making sense of media education*, Falmer, London

Carter, R (ed) (1990) *Knowledge about Language and the Curriculum: The LINC reader*, Hodder & Stoughton, London

Clark, M (ed) (1985) *New Directions in the Study of Reading*, Falmer Press, Lewes

Clay, M (1975) *What Did I Write?*, Heinemann, Auckland, New Zealand

Clay, M (1979a) *Reading: The patterning of complex behaviour*, 2nd edition, Heinemann Educational, London

Clay, M (1979b) *The Early Detection of Reading Difficulties*, Heinemann Educational, London

Clay, M (1982) *Observing Young Readers: Selected papers,* Heinemann Educational, Exeter, New Hampshire

Corcoran, W and Evans, E (eds) (1987) *Readers, Texts, Teachers*, Boynon/Cook, Upper Montclair, NJ

Crystal, D (1976) *Child Language, Learning and Linguistics*, Arnold, London

Crystal, D (1986) *Child Language, Learning and Linguistics*, 2nd edn, Arnold, London

Dent, H C (1977) *The Training of Teachers in England and Wales 1800–1975*, Hodder & Stoughton, London

Dixon, J (1967) *Growth through English*, OUP, Oxford

Dombey, H (1992) Lessons learnt at bed-time, in *New Readings: Contributions to an understanding of literacy*, ed K Kimberley, M Meek and J Miller, A & C Black, London

Doughty, P, Pearce, J and Thornton, G (1972) *Language in Use*, Arnold, London

Fox, C (1992) You sing so merry those tunes: oral storytelling as a window on young children's language learning, in *New Readings: Contributions to an understanding of literacy*, ed K Kimberley, M Meek and J Miller, A & C Black, London

Gannon, P and Czerniewska, P (1980) *Using Linguistics, Art Educational Focus*, Arnold, London

Goodman, K S (1982) *Language and Literacy: The selected writings of Kenneth S. Goodman*, ed F V Gollasch, vols 1 and 2, Routledge & Kegan Paul, London

Graves, D H (1986) *Writing: Teachers and children at work*, Heinemann, New Hampshire

Gregory, E (1992) Learning codes and contexts: a psychosemiotic approach to beginning reading in school, in *New Readings: Contributions to an understanding of literacy*, ed K Kimberley, M Meek and J Miller, A & C Black, London

Griffith, P (1987) *Literary Theory and English Teaching*, Open University Press, Milton Keynes

Gurrey, P (1961) *Teaching English Grammar*, Longmans, London

Hawkins, E (1984) *Awareness of Language: An introduction*, CUP, Cambridge

Hayhoe, M and Parker, S (1990) *Reading and Response*, Open University Press, Milton Keynes

Honey, J (1983) *The Language Trap: Race, class and the 'standard language' issue in British schools*, National Council for Educational Standards, London

Jenkinson, A P (1940) *What Do Boys and Girls Read?*, Methuen, London

Kinneavy, J (1971) *A Theory of Discourse*, Prentice Hall, New York

Kress, G (1982) *Learning to Write*, Routledge & Kegan Paul, London

Lee,V (ed) (1987) *English Literature in Schools*, Open University Press, Milton Keynes

Linguistic Minorities Project (1985) *The Other Languages of England*, Routledge, London

Lunzer, E and Gardner, K (eds) (1979) *The Effective Use of Reading*, Heinemann/ Schools Council, London

Lunzer, E and Gardner, K (1984) *Learning from the Written Word*, Oliver & Boyd, Edinburgh

Martin, N (ed) (1976) *Understanding Children Talking*, Penguin, London

Maybin, J (1991) Children's informal talk and the construction of meaning, in *English in Education*, **25** (2), pp 34–49

Meek, M (1982) *Learning to Read*, The Bodley Head, London

Meek, M with Armstrong, S *et al* (1983) *Achieving Literacy: Longitudinal case studies of adolescents learning to read*, Routledge & Kegan Paul, London

Meek, M, Warlow, A and Barton, G (eds) (1977) *The Cool Web*, The Bodley Head, Oxford

Mercer, N (ed) (1981) *Language in School and Community*, Edward Arnold, London

Miller, J (ed) (1984) *Eccentric Propositions: Essays on literature and the curriculum*, Routledge & Kegan Paul, London

Moffett, J (1968) *Teaching the Universe of Discourse*, Houghton-Mifflin, Boston

Norman, Kate (ed) (1992) *Thinking Voices: The work of the National Oracy Project*, Hodder & Stoughton, London

Oakhill, J and Garnham, A (1988) *Becoming a Skilled Reader*, Basil Blackwell, Oxford

Perera, K (1984) *Children Writing and Reading*, Blackwell, Oxford

Protherough, R (1983) *Developing Response to Fiction*, Open University Press, Milton Keynes

Protherough, R (1986) *Teaching Literature for Examinations*, Open University Press, Milton Keynes

Reed, M, Webster, A and Beveridge, M (1995) The conceptual basis for a literacy curriculum, in *Children Learning to Read: International concerns*, vol 1 (*Emergent and Developing Readings: Messages for teachers*), ed P Owen and P Pumphrey, Falmer Press, London

Richmond, J (ed) (1982) *Becoming Our Own Experts: Studies in language and learning made by the Talk Workshop Group at Vauxhall Manor School*, ILEA English Centre, London

Rosen, H (1972) *Language and Class*, Failing Wall Press, Bristol

Rosen, H and Burgess, T (1980) *The Languages and Dialects of London Schoolchildren*, Ward Lock, London

Rosenblatt, L (1938) *Literature as Exploration*, Modern Language Association, New York

Rosenblatt, L (1978) *The Reader, the Text, the Poem: The transactional theory of the literary work*, Southern Illinois University Press, Carbondale, IL

Shayer, D (1972) *The Teaching of English in Schools 1900–1970*, Routledge & Kegan Paul, London

Smith, F (1972) *Understanding Reading*, Holt, Rhinehart & Winston, New York

Southgate, V *et al* (1981) *Extending Beginner Reading*, Heinemann Educational, London, for the Schools Council

Start, K B and Wells, B K (1972) *The Trend of Reading Standards*, NFER, Windsor
Stibbs, A (1991) *Reading Narrative as Literature: Signs of life*, Open University Press, Buckingham
Swann, J and Graddol, D (1988) Gender inequalities in classroom talk, *English in Education*, **22** (1), pp 48–65
Turner, M (1990) *Sponsored Reading Failure*, Education Unit, Warlingham
Whitehead, F, Capey, A C and Maddren, W (1974) *Children's Reading Interests*, The Schools Council, London
Wilkinson, A (1965) *Spoken English*, Educational Review Occasional Publications (2), University of Birmingham School of Education, Birmingham
Wilkinson, A (1987) *The Writing of Writing*, Open University Press, Milton Keynes

Further reading

Barnes, D (1976) *From Communication to Curriculum*, Penguin, Harmondsworth
Barnes, Dorothy and Barnes, Douglas (1984) *Versions of English*, Heinemann Educational Books, London
Benton, M *et al* (1988) *Young Readers Responding to Poems*, Routledge, London
Britton, J (1982) *Prospect and Retrospect: Selected essays of James Britton*, ed G Pradl, Heinemann, London
Brumfit, C, Ellis, R and Levine, J (1985) *ESI in the UK: Educational and linguistic perspectives*, ELT document 121, Pergamon, Oxford
Cato, V and Whetton, C (1991) *An Enquiry into LEA Evidence on Standards of Reading of Seven-Year-Old Children*, NFER, Windsor
Chall, J (1967) *Learning to Read: The great debate* (2nd edn 1983), McGraw-Hill, New York
Creber, J P (1965) *Sense and Sensitivity*, ULP, London
Czemiewska, P (1992) *Learning about Writing: The early years*, Blackwell, Oxford
Davies, C (ed) (1996) *What is English Teaching?*, Open University Press, Milton Keynes
Dixon, J (1991) *A Schooling in 'English'*, Open University Press, Milton Keynes
Goody, J and Watt, I (1972) The consequences of literacy, in *Language and Social Context*, ed P Giglioli, Penguin, Harmondsworth
Halliday, M (1973) *Explorations in the Functions of Language,* Arnold, London
Halliday, M (1975) *Learning How to Mean,* Arnold, London
Halliday, M (1978) *Language as a Social Semiotic*, Arnold, London
Halliday, M (1985) *An Introduction to Functional Grammar,* Arnold, London
Halliday, M, McIntosh, A and Strevens, P (1964) *The Linguistic Sciences and Language Teaching,* Arnold, London
Leavis, F R (1930) *Mass Civilisation and Minority Culture*, CUP, Cambridge
Leavis, F R and Thompson, D (1933) *Culture and Environment*, Chatto & Windus, London
Levine, J (ed) (1990) *Bilingual Learners and the Mainstream Curriculum*, Falmer, London
Levine, L with Hester, H and Skirrow, G (1972) *Scope: Stage 2*, Longman, for the Schools Council, London

Maybin, J, Mercer, N and Stierer, B (1992) 'Scaffolding' learning in the classroom, in *Thinking Voices*, ed K Norman, Hodder & Stoughton, London

Meek, M (1988) *How Texts Teach What Readers Learn*, Thimble Press, Stroud

Minns, H (1990) *Read It To Me Now!*, Virago, London

Morris, J M (1966) *Standards in Reading*, NFER, London

Moss, G (1989) *Unpopular Fictions*, Virago, London

National Writing Project (1989–1990) *Issues from the National Writing Project*, Nelson, London (see booklets published in this series)

Richards, I A (1929) *Practical Criticism*, Routledge, London

Rosen, C and Rosen, H (1973) *The Language of Primary School Children*, Penguin, Harmondsworth

Sarland, C (1992) *Young People Reading*, Open University Press, Buckingham

Scafe, S (1989) *Teaching Black Literature*, Virago, London

Sinclair, J and Coulthard, M (1975) *Towards an Analysis of Discourse: The language of teachers and pupils*, Oxford University Press, London

Smith, F (1982) *Writing and the Writer*, Heinemann, London

Street, B (1984) *Literacy in Theory and Practice*, CUP, Cambridge

Vygotskyan, L (1986) *Thought and Language*, ed L Kozulin, Harvard University Press, Cambridge, MA

Whitehead, F (1966) *The Disappearing Dais*, Chatto, London

Wilkinson, A (1971) *The Foundations of Language*, OUP, Oxford

Reports

1921: *The Teaching of English in England* (The Newbolt Report), HMSO

1944: *Report of Committee to Consider the Supply, Recruitment and Training of Teachers and Youth Leaders* (McNair)

1954: *Language*, HMSO

1959: 15–18 (The Crowther Report), HMSO

1963: *Secondary School Examination Council: Final report*, HMSO

1963: *Report of the Committee on Higher Education* (Robbins), HMSO

1964: *Half Our Future* (The Newsom Report), HMSO

1965: *Working Paper No 3: English*, Schools Council, HMSO

1975: *A Language for Life* (The Bullock Report), HMSO

1984: *Education for All* (The Swann Report), HMSO

1984: *English 5–16: Curriculum matters*, HMSO

1988: *Report of the Task Group on Assessment and Testing* (The TGAT Report), HMSO

1988: *Report of the Committee of Inquiry into the Teaching of English Language* (The Kingman Report), HMSO

1989: *English from 5–16: Report of the English working party* (The Cox Report), HMSO

1990: *The Teaching and Learning of Reading in Primary Schools: A report by HMI*, DES

1992: *The Teaching and Learning of Reading in Primary Schools 1991*, DES

1995: *English in the National Curriculum*, SCAA

1999: *English: The National Curriculum for England*, DfEE/QCA

Chapter 2

Continuity and change in school mathematics since 1945

Clare Tikly

Curriculum

The centre of mathematical activity within most secondary schools is the shared resources or common room where the maths teachers meet, prepare lessons and mark pupils' work, store books and equipment and discuss ideas and experiences. Children come and go with requests, information and materials. Visitors to the department are introduced here and may perceive the scope of the mathematics curriculum displayed on notices, timetables and computer screens. It is evident in the way that schemes of work and shared resources are organized. The ethos of mathematics within the school emanates from this room along corridors to classrooms and, more frequently nowadays, to computer resource areas. It is usual for displays of children's mathematics, puzzles, posters and information to line the walls of the corridors and add colour to the teaching rooms. This brightness may be a pale shadow of the atmosphere in the best primary schools but the notions of teaching and learning mathematics that underpin the activities are now common to both sectors. This chapter looks at the development of school mathematics since 1945. The era following the Second World War heralded several decades of increasing access to a mathematical education for all children. The nature of that mathematics is still an issue of considerable controversy.

Access and differentiation

Access to a mathematical education is multidimensional. It is concerned with the availability of courses but also with their content. Its continuation is heavily influenced by examination outcomes so that the relationship between curriculum and public assessment is a major consideration. Finally, mathematics education in England and Wales has always been characterized by differential provision between and within schools. This subsection gives an overview of how developments in the structure of schooling and in the systems of public examination since 1945 have influenced school mathematics. It is very much an overview in which generalities obscure significant regional and local differences such as, for example, the existence of middle schools in some areas since 1965.

Pre-war developments in teacher education in training colleges and university departments had placed mathematics education on a professional footing. However, significant changes did not take place on a large scale until post-war reorganizations had become established. Until the expansion of the comprehensive secondary sector in the 1960s most primary school mathematics was restrained by the demands of the 11+ examination with its narrow focus on numerical calculation. This emphasis on arithmetic continued for some time in many secondary modern schools. This was particularly acute for girls as exemplified by a statistic published in the Newsom Report (DES, 1963) and quoted in Howson (1982): 'In the girls' secondary modern schools sampled, 31% of all forms still learned only arithmetic. The average number of minutes per week devoted to mathematics was 260 in boys' schools, 215 in co-educational schools and 180 in girls' schools.'

Until 1965 the only public examinations available were the General Certificate of Education (GCE) O and A levels, which had replaced the School Certificate and the Higher School Certificate in 1951 and shared their features of university-based examination boards. Their mathematical content and methods were accessible to a limited range of children, a percentage that varied considerably between socio-economic groups and between girls and boys. GCE O levels were taken by 15–16-year-olds in selective schools and in the higher mathematics sets in comprehensive schools. In some secondary modern schools and middle-attaining classes in comprehensive schools there were attempts to modify O level mathematics courses to give wider access to the examination but the greater challenge was in the design of curricula for the majority independently of public examination requirements, and to provide a mathematical foundation for those who would leave school at 15. However, following the Beloe Report (DES, 1960), the Certificate of Secondary Education (CSE) was introduced from 1965 and developed in several modes over the following 20 years. By the time the minimum leaving age was raised to 16 in 1972 it was a minority, albeit a significant minority, of 16-year-olds who left school with no formal qualification in mathematics.

There was a wide choice of examination boards and, in the case of Mode 3 CSEs, the opportunity was taken by many teachers to design syllabuses and mark their pupils' examination scripts, with moderation by the Board. This was inhibited to an extent by the wish to run parallel and combined courses that could lead to either CSE or O level entry and inevitably followed, as far as possible, the GCE syllabus. Autonomy was more widespread for the non-examination classes resulting in the provision of several interesting alternative courses, some of which led to accreditation. Issues of access centred on the distinctions between CSE and O level and the attempts to achieve parity of esteem between a CSE Grade 1 and an O level C grade. When GCSE replaced the dual examination system in 1986 it provided a single scale of grades, A* to G, and a common certificate, for all but a small percentage of 15–16-year-olds. Mathematics in the final two years of compulsory schooling had become completely tied into a public examination system working to common criteria, provided through examination boards that were by the 1990s to be reduced in number to three. GCSE was considered suitable as the basis for programmes of study and assessment at Key Stage 4 of the National Curriculum, which began its phased implementation in 1989.

Several important principles underpin the GCSE system in general but of particular significance in mathematics education is the existence of differentiated levels, known as 'tiers'. Pupils are assigned to courses that lead to Higher, Intermediate or Foundation examination entry and some grades are awarded through examination at more than one level. For example, it has been possible, since 1994, to achieve a B grade through either the Higher or Intermediate examination. Only for an A or A* grade is it necessary to study the Higher level syllabus. Wolf (2000) has demonstrated how this grading overlap has had the effect of reducing the percentage of entries to the Higher tier examination and, as a consequence, the level of mathematical knowledge among the post-16 population. This prevents and inhibits many individuals from studying mathematics beyond GCSE and, since the key skills component, 'application of number', in post-compulsory education such as GNVQ courses is both poorly implemented and at a low mathematical level, they are unlikely to enter adult life with the mathematical understanding required for skilled employment in an increasing number of fields.

The rationale for the revised National Curriculum makes explicit the principles of access and entitlement: 'The National Curriculum secures for all pupils, irrespective of social background, culture, race, gender, differences in ability and disabilities, an entitlement to a number of areas of learning' (QCA, 1999).

It will be important to evaluate the 21st-century curriculum with reference to aims such as these. It needs to be borne in mind that the National Curriculum itself came as part of a package of educational change following the 1988 Act. The in-built assessment, in the form of Standard Attainment Tasks (SATs), has the potential to make a valuable contribution to both diagnostic and formative assessment. However, they are more publicly perceived as tools for accountability in the core subjects of English, mathematics and science. This is why mathematics teachers are cautious about levels of entry to all the end-of-key-stage examinations, including GCSE. Preparation for SATs examinations has become a regular feature of the patterns of tests within schools, partly to guide teacher assessment but also to familiarize pupils with the types of questions in the national tests. The National Curriculum is intended as a framework but, in a very real sense, constraints of time, tests and resources may be limiting school mathematics to the content listed in the official publications. Targets, now statutory, are set and sometimes become an artificial ceiling for the mathematical knowledge of classes and of individuals throughout the period to which they pertain. It is by no means clear that pupils' mathematical understanding will increase because of targets set in general terms (see Tikly, Noss and Goldstein, 2000). Reforms intended to raise standards may be failing to address very real deficiencies such as those identified in the influential 1995 report by the London Mathematical Society, the Institute of Mathematics and its Applications, and the Royal Statistical Society.

Content and pedagogy

Primary school mathematics

The post-war primary sector was formed when developments towards activity-based, child-centred learning had already begun in some elementary schools. Theories such as those of Froebel and Montessori had indicated how practical work might enable young children to acquire a more conceptual understanding of number before learning procedures for calculation. Piagetian theory provided a structure for planning schemes of work based on stages of development, a basis used by publishers of teaching schemes in the 1970s. The Mathematical Association report of 1955 endorsed the value of experiential learning and also suggested thematic, investigative approaches to develop mathematical thinking. However, the report recognized the need for children to discuss and reflect upon their activities and, after understanding, to consolidate what they had learnt:

Practice without the power of mathematical thinking leads nowhere; the power of mathematical thinking without practice is like knowing what to do without having the skills or tools to do it; but the power of mathematical thinking supported by practice and rote-learning will give the best opportunity for all children to enjoy and pursue Mathematics as far as their individual abilities allow.

(MA, 1955, quoted in Howson, 1982)

As long as selection for secondary education continued (there were regional variations in the extent and pace of change) the demands of the 11+ examination ensured that children spent time consolidating their knowledge of number and practising procedures for calculation. The balance within the mathematics curriculum was individual to each school and the time spent on mathematics was at the discretion of each teacher although auton- omy would be moderated by school and local education authority (LEA) policies. The Plowden Report of 1967 (Central Advisory Council for Education) gave an additional boost to the new pedagogies of experiential and thematic learning and encouraged their more widespread application through the support of teacher educators, local authority advisers and inspectors. Restraints on implementation, as was the case with similar curriculum developments in secondary schools, included insecurities among teachers about some of the modern mathematical content. When published schemes of work, such as those of the Nuffield Foundation Project, became available in the 1970s many teachers were to rely too heavily on them; the crucial learning stages of reflection and consolidation did not always take place. Within the same decade the Department of Education and Science (DES) began to monitor standards and also set up the Cockcroft Enquiry, with a wide brief that included looking into the mathematical needs and attainment of school leavers particularly in the area of computational skills. However, when the Cockcroft Committee reported in 1982 it recommended the continuation and extension of breadth in school mathematics at all levels. Brown (1999b) notes the Report's positive assessment about teaching and learning: 'We believe that this broadening of the curriculum has had a beneficial effect both in improving children's attitudes to mathematics and also in laying the foundations of better understanding' (DES, 1982, quoted in Brown, 1999b).

Here was a clear brief for the inclusion of topics about shape and space, data handling and some pre-algebraic activities in the coming National Curriculum at primary level. This breadth has been maintained but several other factors require consideration. A broad curriculum may facilitate the transfer of ideas and techniques across topics if the processes of thinking mathematically are integrated with the learning of content, but such coherence will be impeded in circumstances where the curriculum is viewed as a series of skills and where drill and practice methods predominate. The non-statutory guidance that accompanied the 1989 version of the National Curriculum (NCC, 1989) gave examples of investigative approaches to topics but left choices of methods to teachers. This guidance was not reissued in 1995 and the National Numeracy Strategy (DfEE, 1999) advocates very specific ways of introducing procedures and conducting lessons in primary schools.

The implementation of the suggested methods of teaching and learning will have to be carefully evaluated, not merely through assessment, which concentrates on a narrow range of skills, but against the wider aims of mathematics education. When teachers plan lessons they should continue to exercise their judgement about the most suitable teaching methods for their class and for the mathematics in the lesson. Sutherland writes about the dangers of advocating general teaching strategies irrespective of the nature of the mathematics to be learnt: 'It leads to a reification of methods, such as individualized learning, group work, and interactive teaching as opposed to an unpacking of the complexity of teaching and learning mathematics' (Sutherland, 2000).

Secondary school mathematics

Until the 1970s there were few changes in the examination syllabuses that defined the GCE O level curriculum for children in selective schools and the higher-level sets of non-selective schools. Innovations first proposed in the 1920s, such as the introduction of 'modern' topics (eg set theory, probability) and the unification of the separate arithmetic, algebra and geometry courses, were delayed until the university-based examination boards agreed to them. In addition, the inadequate supply of well-qualified teachers was a conservative influence since many felt too insecure with their own subject knowledge to relinquish their reliance on familiar standard procedures. When change did begin it lacked an overall rationale. New topics introduced greater curriculum breadth but essential mathematical processes, such as deductive reasoning and proof, were given considerably less emphasis. Dean (1982) provides a clear account of the shift from Euclidean geometry to the less formal methods of transformation geometry.

After the introduction of GCSE formal algebraic content became largely confined to the Higher tier syllabuses and, even there, provided an insufficient basis for progress to traditional A level courses. Sutherland (2000) analyses the ways in which curriculum change has resulted in seriously reduced facilities with algebra, which, in turn, is having grave repercussions in higher education. Furthermore, when the proportion of Higher level GCSE entries reduced after 1994, a much smaller proportion of students was equipped for A level studies in mathematics. Changes at A level have included the introduction of investigative coursework and a modular structure. Throughout the 1990s there were significant reductions in the percentages of all A level students who studied even one mathematics A level and an even greater decline, particularly in the state system, of students of two mathematics A levels (Wolf, 2000). This was a marked change from the situation in the two or three post-war decades when almost all undergraduates in mathematics, physical sciences or engineering would have had a double mathematics A level.

Since the mathematical needs of industry and the economy remained undefined the public perception that arithmetic remained the key to economic progress continued. Pupils in secondary moderns and the lower sets of comprehensive schools studied a disproportionate amount of arithmetic until the advent of CSE examinations in 1965 and the growing prevalence of published schemes of work in the 1970s. When the minimum school-leaving age was raised to 16 in 1972 curriculum change for all 11–16-year-olds became extensive. An immediate necessity was to provide courses for all pupils that would lead to external accreditation at 16+.

Research in mathematics education and in developmental psychology seemed to support the value of working in groups, discussion and mixed-ability classes. The challenge of providing differentiated materials that took different approaches to the same topics was taken up by publishers. The most widely used mixed-ability scheme from the mid-1970s was SMP 11–16. It was designed and published by the Schools Mathematics Project (SMP), which had been set up following meetings between mathematicians from industry and teachers from schools and universities between 1957 and 1961, the year the project began. Initially the aim was to address the need for a modern and unified academic curriculum (see Thwaites, 1972). SMP 11–16, which followed in the 1970s, consisted of mixed-ability materials (booklets, worksheets, tests, practical equipment and computer software) for the first two secondary years and different textbooks for setted classes up to 16+. For non-examination classes there was the SMP Graduated Assessment Scheme, which led to accreditation by continuous assessment with a link to CSE and, later, to GCSE grades. By the mid-1980s mathematics teachers had begun to supplement the materials to include more investigative work and many organized the booklets into modules to allow for some pupil–pupil discussion in groups and whole-class teaching. There was also some criticism emerging about the linguistic demands of the materials and a social-class bias in some of the contexts (see Dowling, 1991).

A particularly innovative individualized learning programme was initiated in 1970 at the Ladbroke Mathematics Centre in London: the School Mathematics Individualised Learning Experiment (SMILE). The written materials, in the form of work cards and books of tests, are remarkable for the accessibility of their content and the care taken over issues of multiculturalism, class and gender within the contexts. Workshops and courses for teachers were, and continue to be, run at the SMILE centre as part of the objectives about teacher involvement (see Gibbons, 1975). Although the full SMILE scheme is less commonly used now, the computer software and individual cards are often integrated into schools' own schemes of work.

SMILE, SMP 11–16 and other individualized schemes provided valuable curriculum development and opportunities for teachers and LEA advisers to discuss mathematics education. However, as with similar innovations in primary schools they were not always implemented in ways that provided the full range of mathematical experiences, partly because of complexities of management but also because of teacher shortage and turnover. Senior managers observing an SMP or SMILE class were prone to think that it could be managed by cover teachers, gravely underestimating the role of the teacher in individualized lessons.

Another major influence on secondary, and to a lesser extent primary, mathematics was the aim that mathematics education should be more investigative. There was considerable writing and research, both here and in the USA, about problem solving and its benefits. This was accompanied by research evidence (see Schoenfeld, 1985) about the inability of students who had attained highly in traditional school mathematics to apply their knowledge in higher education. Lerman expressed the similarity between the growth of knowledge within mathematics and the way that individuals construct knowledge for themselves: 'The problem-solving approach to mathematics… reflects both the conceptual growth view of mathematical knowledge and also the nature of the learning process' (Lerman, 1983).

It became clearer to many teachers that 'mathematics has two faces' (Polya, 1957), that it is both a changing body of knowledge organized into formal systems and also a field of enquiry. It became established that school mathematics would aim to induct children into both aspects of the subject. Investigative approaches were endorsed by the Cockcroft Report and became established in some form through GCSE coursework and Attainment Target 1 in the National Curriculum. The aim is that many mathematical topics should be approached in investigative ways but in reality there are schools where children have a narrow range of mathematical experiences – taking notes and following worked examples. Ruthven (1999) quotes an HMI report of 1992, which estimated that one-third of school mathematics departments made no provision for the 'using and applying' components of the National Curriculum.

The framework of mathematics attainment targets was simplified in 1995 following the Dearing Review. The revised National Curriculum (QCA, 1999) provides considerably more detail within the programmes of study for mathematics and, at 14+, there are two separate programmes of study, Foundation and Higher, to be implemented from 2001. The increased detail includes more algebra and also explicit references to proof, a change that reflects the views of many concerned with the mathematical needs of industry and higher education.

Some research directions

Research in many areas is required to keep the mathematics curriculum under review. The expert analysis and interpretation of data, including data within the system as a whole, depends on developments in statistics. Ways of learning mathematics are being altered through the use of new technologies. The mathematical requirements of industry and higher education are not static. Teacher education must include an understanding of all those developments and establish means of achieving this aim through partnerships between HEIs and schools. Much research that has influenced mathematics teaching has been psychological in basis, carried out within theoretical frameworks such as those of Piaget, Bruner, Vygotsky or the constructivists. Considerable research has been empirical and classroom-based, often in the form of research and development.

There was a large body of research evidence submitted to the Cockcroft Committee in the late 1970s. Bell, Costello and Kuchemann (1983) reviewed aspects, largely from the UK and the USA, relating most directly to classroom practice and their work provides a useful starting-point for tracking developments in methodologies and outcomes. The selection presented here may seem to be particularly relevant at the present time since it reveals early concerns of contemporary significance.

The teaching of facts and skills

Since the 1920s there has been evidence that rote learning of facts and skills, appropriate for the purposes of immediate recall, needs to be accompanied by teaching to develop meaning if the knowledge is to be retained or applied. In the 1970s the research extended to computer-assisted learning of skills and pointed to the significance of factors such as context and differentiated feedback.

It was during the 1970s and 1980s that research began to reveal discrepancies between children's abilities with their own informal methods of calculation and their abilities with procedures taught in school. One such study was that of Carraher and Schliemann (1988) in which the differences between mental and written calculation methods were explored. During mental calculation the meanings of numbers remain intact and held holistically in the mind. During written algorithms numbers sometimes seem fragmented and confusing as the child considers place value. Their meaning can be lost.

Process aspects

A review of research (Bell, Costello and Kuchemann, 1983) analyses teaching experiments carried out in the 1960s and 1970s that were designed to identify and improve children's selection and use of problem-solving strategies. The outcomes identified some strategies that were easier to apply than others and found that the most effective approaches use long-term explicit teaching of a few general strategies.

There are tensions between the aims for pupils to select their own strategies and the teaching of a limited range of process skills, like pattern spotting. Investigative school mathematics in this country developed throughout the 1980s and 1990s, with initial in-service training from LEA advisory teachers and experts employed by the GCSE boards. This led to the examination coursework component and the 'using and applying' attainment target in the National Curriculum. Investigative school mathematics was a stimulus for considerable pedagogical research, much of it discussed by Morgan (1998) from the standpoint of teachers' assessment of pupils' written reports of investigations.

There was research in the USA in the 1970s that looked at children's approaches to proof in mathematics and suggested strategies for making some of the processes more explicit. In the UK, processes of justification and proof are embedded within investigative activity. In the late 1990s Hoyles and Healy (1999a) conducted a nationwide survey amongst pupils being prepared for the Higher level GCSE examination, in the year prior to the examination. The survey, followed by an analysis of the contexts and practices within participating schools, and by qualitative data from interviews, led to the following interpretation:

> Students' responses are a reflection of the curriculum they follow as much as any measure of their mathematical abilities. Those who are given early opportunities to make simple inferences, and who are explicitly introduced to the

ideas of using one set of mathematical properties as tools to deduce others, may well go on to experience more success with proving than those whose experiences are limited to endless production of evidence.

(Hoyles and Healy, 1999b)

Attitudes

Research into children's attitudes to mathematics reported from the 1960s and 1970s was significant in terms of both results and methodologies. Children were found to either strongly like or strongly dislike mathematics from ages as young as 11, and that more developed negative attitudes during secondary school. Whether the content was traditional or modern appeared to have no effect. Children were found to have different beliefs about mathematics. Considerable curriculum development followed, including the extended range of experiences recommended in the Cockcroft Report.

There was research in the 1980s into beliefs, expectations and attitudes especially in relation to the underachievement, as noted over several decades, of girls compared with boys. Joffe and Foxman (1986) give a clear account of gender-related outcomes from their analysis of surveys carried out by the Assessment of Performance Unit (APU). Qualitative research, such as that reported by Walden and Walkerdine (1985), provided insights into girls' underachievement. The ensuing changes, supported by many LEAs, included a shift in classroom culture towards more discursive practice and co-operative group work. By the early 1990s girls were outperforming boys at GCSE level but whether this significant development is related more closely to changes in school mathematics or to the improved employment expectations for women is debatable.

Evaluation and assessment

Assessment methods diversified throughout the 1960s and 1970s and it came to be better understood how the tools of assessment need to match the objectives being assessed, and how outcomes are related to styles of questioning. For example, it became recognized that multiple-choice tests, in which the candidate chooses between four or five suggested answers and ticks a box, without any explanation, is only suitable for assessing knowledge of a limited range of facts and skills. The assessment of higher-order thinking skills, such as problem solving, began to be carried out through the medium of coursework projects. The process of teacher assessment, moderated by examination boards, provided opportunities for discussion about mathematics and the learning of mathematics. Children's oral responses were seen to have value over and above their written mathematics. Early examples of diagnostic guides for teachers led to increasingly extensive graduated assessment schemes, such as the 'Graded Assessment in Mathematics' (ULEAC, 1992) project set up to introduce continuous assessment into normal classroom practice.

Early attempts to evaluate learning and teaching at national level began in the USA in the 1970s and revealed methodological problems. In this country diagnostic surveys of children's performance were carried out annually by the APU amongst large samples of 11- and 16-year-olds between 1977 and 1982. The assessment methods were varied and innovative and teacher involvement, through LEAs, was extensive. The survey items covered concepts and skills, problem solving, practical tasks and attitudes. Details of design, methodology, outcomes and evaluation can be found in APU (1985). Recommendations about assessment methods were made to the Cockcroft Committee and five further annual surveys were commissioned. Teacher participation included training in the oral assessment methods used.

The monitoring of performance since 1989 includes all children, as compared with the in-depth assessment of the understanding of random samples of children in the APU surveys, and the emphasis has shifted from designing questions for diagnostic purposes to assessing children's attainment of National Curriculum objectives. Test results are also used in attempts to assess the effectiveness of LEAs, schools and individual teachers. This raises the issue of controlling for other variables. The difficulties of tracking standards longitudinally need to be understood if the test results are to be used to evaluate curriculum change.

Electronic calculators

Failing to control for other classroom variables has invalidated much of the early research into the use of calculators in mathematics lessons. However, a Schools Council Project (County of Durham Education Committee, 1976) identified areas of the secondary curriculum where calculator use had positive learning outcomes. It was also found that weaker pupils made more progress with their mathematics when calculators were available.

In contrast to earlier research the Calculator Aware Number (CAN) Project (Shuard et al, 1991) was based on an awareness that mathematical experience is altered when calculators are used. Children in four trial primary schools followed a mathematics programme around practical and investigative activities. Calculations were carried out mentally using the children's own methods and, where this was not possible, a calculator was used. Written algorithms were not encouraged. The trial ran from 1986 to 1989 when the National Curriculum was introduced. Although it was not possible to draw conclusions from the pilot scheme, subsequent observations of the same children gave some positive indications of benefits derived from such a mathematics curriculum. Walsh (1991) writes about her observations of beneficial effects of calculator use by seven-year-olds in the CAN project, but also on the reluctance of other primary teachers to introduce them.

Wider research

For many decades there has been considerable concern at local and national levels about perceived differences in school effectiveness and qualitative judgements would be made about factors affecting examination results. They would include teachers' assessments about pupils' prior attainment, crude measures of socio-economic factors (such as the numbers of pupils entitled to free school meals), pupil attendance and turnover rates and the reliability as assessment tools of the examinations themselves. Qualified in this way, public examination results would contribute to evaluations of whole-school and departmental effectiveness, in any one year and longitudinally over time. LEAs and parents would have some idea about the relative effectiveness of schools in the area for different groups of pupils. Reviews of curriculum or resourcing might follow.

Throughout the 1980s there were initial attempts to provide a quantitative basis for comparisons between schools, leading in the 1990s to the use of SATs and GCSE results for the purposes of public accountability. Statistical modelling techniques were applied by researchers to the analysis of the considerable amount of data generated and to the complexities in the patterns of variation between schools. Woodhouse and Goldstein (1996) write about the difficulties encountered when attempts to compare school outcomes are provided with a sound statistical basis. Multi-level modelling theory, developed in the 1980s, reveals the limitations of using examination results as one of the measures of comparative school effectiveness and of the impossibility of providing a simple measurement of a school's contribution to pupils' progress ('value-added' measures). They conclude that the majority of schools cannot be separated statistically from one another on the basis of their examination results. However, measures of achievement can, and should, be used for diagnostic purposes and to define areas for research into factors associated with achievement.

The nature of mathematics in the workplace is often concealed because it is bound up in established procedures, particularly through the use of computers. In order to function flexibly, to be able to adapt procedures creatively and to recognize malfunction, workers have to be more than mere operators. The underlying mathematical relationships need to be explicit and understood. Hoyles, Noss and Pozzi (1999) describe the research they carried out to identify the mathematics implicit in two sets of working practices and how they used computational modelling to reveal the underlying mathematical structures and make them visible to the practitioners. Their research methodology will have application in the future.

For many children mathematics appears to be divorced from their culture, sidelining the informal mathematical activity that they observe outside school. There have been studies of 'ethnomathematics' (D'Ambrosio, 1984) and they are reviewed by Nunes (1992). She places them within a theoretical framework and provides insights that have relevance for the design of more inclusive curricula in the UK as well as in developing countries.

Research in mathematics education, initiated in the early 20th century in training colleges and university departments of education, is really necessary to inform meaningful curriculum development. Evaluation of teaching programmes must take place with reference to substantial aims and not be confined to the inconclusive tracking of public examination results over time.

Subject associations and journals

National

Developments in school mathematics in England and Wales are mirrored in the reports and publications of two long-standing organizations, the Mathematical Association (MA) and the Association of Teachers of Mathematics (ATM). They provide a forum for discussion about research and practice between teachers and educators, many of whom are members of both associations.

The MA and its journal, the *Mathematical Gazette*, date from the final decade of the 19th century. Until the 1930s the Association was concerned predominantly with the mathematics taught in boys' selective secondary schools. The early reformers in the MA were behind the drive to create unified examination courses from the separate components of arithmetic, algebra and geometry. They had already been instrumental in broadening the traditional content of algebra and devising geometry courses in which formal Euclidean geometry was preceded for younger boys (and, later, girls) with practical and more intuitive work. There was also a developing interest in teaching approaches particularly as education expanded and diversified.

From the late 1930s some members of the MA extended their research and writing to elementary school teaching. Although their report, *The Teaching of Mathematics in Primary Schools*, was not published until 1955, its impact was considerable. Four years later another committee of the MA produced *Mathematics in Secondary Modern Schools* (1959), which produced guidelines for general secondary mathematics. It proposed a breadth of mathematical content beyond arithmetic and developed themes of 'utility' and 'reality' that had been discussed within the MA 50 years before. This report was not so influential because of constraints on the progress of secondary school mathematics.

The MA also collaborated with other professional associations. In 1963, in conjunction with the mathematics group within the Association of Teachers in Colleges and Departments of Education (ATCDE), the MA published *The Supply and Training of Teachers of Mathematics*, which discussed issues of teacher supply and mathematical subject knowledge that are still relevant today. In 1995 the London Mathematical Society, a branch of the MA, together with the Institute of Mathematics and its Applications and the Royal Statistical Society published *Tackling the Mathematics Problem*, a very influential report that added weight to protests from higher education that school mathematics, even A level, was not equipping undergraduates to cope with the mathematics within a wide range of degree courses. It made far-reaching recommendations ranging from primary school mathematics to in-service mathematics courses for practising teachers. In 1971 the Association published the first edition of *Mathematics in School*, in which practising teachers write about their ongoing work and research.

During the period of post-war expansion and diversification many teachers in primary and secondary modern schools looked for support and ideas in the design of their curricula and development of resources. The Association for Teaching Aids in Mathematics, later renamed the ATM, was formed in the mid-1950s and the first edition of its journal, *Mathematics Teaching*, was published in 1955. Membership grew rapidly with active participation by practising teachers at conferences and in writing for the journal. There are regular publications of classroom resources that correspond to the priorities of teachers at that time and are often written by teams of teachers formed into working groups. An example from 1993 is *Talking Maths, Talking Languages* (Association of Teachers of Mathematics), which looked at the issues and practices associated with working in multilingual mathematics classrooms. The use of such resources within schools promotes discussion about research, policy and practice. For some time now the quarterly, *Micromath*, has been published alongside *Mathematics Teaching* and has become a focal point for research into the use of computers in mathematics education.

As active professional associations the ATM and the MA have been able to work influentially within the wider community of those concerned with mathematics education teaching or research. Two such associations are the British Society for Research into the Learning of Mathematics (BSRLM) and the Association of Mathematics Education Teachers (AMET), both of which have the active support of teachers and teacher educators. However, it is less common for other than informal contact to take place between teachers and mathematicians in university departments or in industry, yet the profession would benefit from a coherent understanding of developments in mathematics and its applications. The aims of the Joint Mathematical Council of the United Kingdom, formed in 1963, and of which the AMET, the ATM, the BSRLM and the MA are among the constituent societies, include the principle of coherence between mathematics and the teaching of mathematics, its objective is to coordinate some of the work of constituent societies, to generally promote the advancement of mathematics and the improvement of the teaching of mathematics.

In 1997 a working group formed from members of the Royal Society and the Joint Mathematical Council produced a significant report on the teaching and learning of algebra (Royal Society, 1997).

The mathematics education community extends beyond membership of associations, however. The 1960s to1980s saw the formation of groups of teachers around specific issues or curriculum schemes. For example, the issue of the underachievement of girls prompted research and teaching experiments and an association, GAMMA, which held regular conferences (to which schoolgirls were invited) and produced a journal. LEA teachers' centres and advisory teachers were frequently involved in this aspect of professional activity. It was a role in sharp contrast to the one they have now been allocated by the DfEE to implement policies such as performance monitoring, target setting and teacher appraisal.

International

The International Congress of Mathematicians (ICM) was already in existence in the early 20th century and its education branch organized surveys and held meetings about school mathematics in several countries. After interruptions caused by the two world wars its activities as an international forum for mathematics educators were revived by means of the publication of *Educational Studies in Mathematics* from 1968 and the first of its conferences in 1969. Since then the International Congress on Mathematics Education (ICME) has met every four years in a different city.

The 1960s saw the involvement of the Organisation for European Economic Co-operation in school mathematics, largely through the publication of two reports about general secondary school mathematics, anticipating the need to consider the mathematics required in the workplace to contribute to economic growth. The United Nations Educational, Scientific and Cultural Organisation (UNESCO) has had an educational department since the 1960s and has published many books of relevance to school mathematics, not just in industrially developed countries, but world-wide.

Another important and influential association is the International Study Group for the Psychology of Mathematics Education (PME), which holds annual conferences in different cities. The conference proceedings are a rich source of knowledge about factors affecting the learning of mathematics in the contexts of schooling throughout the world.

International comparisons

Since the 1960s the International Association for the Evaluation of Educational Achievement (IEA) has been collecting data by means of written tests and questionnaires among samples of children in varying numbers of countries. English children often performed relatively poorly in written numerical calculations. Mathematics curricula vary considerably from one country to another and, until 1989, between schools in England and Wales. The variation covers aspects of access, content and pedagogy. International tests have only recently begun to be used to survey attainment across a broad range of mathematical activities. The results provide snapshots of what some children can or cannot do under particular circumstances at a particular time. The value of the surveys lies in identifying international research directions, and in refining methods of test design and interpretation. Two international surveys of children's achievements with mathematical and scientific tasks have been influential in the 1990s.

In 1990 the International Association for the Evaluation of Educational Progress organized the IAEP(2) tests in mathematics and science for 9- and 13-year-olds. English children performed relatively well in data handling and geometry but relatively badly in numerical calculations. Problem solving was not assessed. In 1994 the Third International Mathematics and Science Study (TIMSS) surveyed the achievement among samples of children from 19 countries. As well as written tests there were six mathematics and six science tasks. Problem-solving as well as procedural skills were assessed. Harris, Keys and Fernandes (1997) point to some significant results. The mean scores of English children were lower than the international average in the written mathematics tests but higher in five out of the six mathematics tasks. In the contexts of the six tasks the English means were higher than the international average in both procedural skills and problem solving. There were no statistically significant gender differences. Reynolds and Muijs (1999) argue that the significantly better achievement of the English children in science as compared with mathematics in TIMSS signifies that a complex set of educational, rather than socio-economic, factors are contributing to the relatively poor mathematical performance of English children in some areas of mathematics. They write about the evidence base behind the National Numeracy Strategy and refer to research into effective mathematics teaching in several countries. Distinguishing between methods for teaching facts and skills and for developing abilities to reason and solve problems, they put the case for a combination of whole-class interactive teaching and co-operative group work.

The surveys have produced different concerns depending on national outcomes. For example, in response to perceptions of underachievement in problem-solving tasks among children from Korea and Taiwan, both countries are revising the content and methods of mathematics teaching with the aim of encouraging creativity: 'It is felt that the direction of the mathematics curriculum in Korea should change from an emphasis on computational skills and the "snapshot" application of fragmentary knowledge to emphasis on problem-solving and thinking abilities.' (Lew, 1999.)

Curriculum change requires to be carried out on the basis of reliable and consistent information to which international comparisons make a contribution. Partially informed change is unlikely to suit the unique contexts of the national systems on to which it will be grafted and there may well be losses as well as gains.

Teacher education

The professional education of mathematics teachers has its origins in the 19th century when day training colleges were established in several cities. Nunn, who became the first director of the London Day Training College (later the Institute of Education) in 1922, was one of a number of early mathematics educators who contributed to public policy. Writing in a Board of Education Report he raised issues about subject knowledge and professional training that are still under discussion today:

> It is now beginning to be recognised generally that a knowledge of Mathematics is not by itself a sufficient equipment for the business of teaching the subject in a school... The change of opinion... implies the recognition that

'training' is concerned with something more than the tricks of management needed to keep a class… in order on a hot afternoon, and that method is not merely a system of devices for insinuating unwelcome facts into dull minds.

(Nunn, 1912, quoted in Howson, 1982)

The full extent of the necessary initial and in-service requirements for the professional development of mathematics teachers became increasingly obvious throughout the 20th century.

In the immediate post-war years school experience was affected by the reorganization of schooling into primary and secondary sectors with large classes often in unsuitable buildings. Wartime losses and expansion of provision, particularly after the minimum leaving age was raised to 15 in 1947, led to a serious shortage of qualified teachers and many practising teachers changed sectors and had to devise new curricula. For example, many of the mathematics graduates who had been teaching 11–14-year-olds in higher elementary schools found employment in the expanded grammar school sector. There was an increased need for NQTs throughout the system. Initial teacher education (ITE) continued as in the 1930s with colleges of education offering both the two-year Certificate in Education and the one-year postgraduate certificate, the PGCE. The majority of mathematics teachers in primary and secondary modern schools were qualified by virtue of their achievements at Higher School Certificate level followed by a Certificate in Education with mathematics as a main subject. Many such NQTs would be just 20 years old, unless they were ex-service personnel who had undergone an intensive one-year teacher training course when the war ended. Shortages of mathematics and physics teachers were particularly acute since many colleges of education had no departments in those subjects, on account of their pre-war focus on the training of women teachers, many of whom had a limited mathematical background.

Changes in ITE

The McNair Report (1944) recognized the need for longer courses of professional training to provide more time for both subject and professional studies. However, the recommendation of the Report to extend the Certificate in Education course to three years was not implemented until 1960. Teacher educators, such as Williams and Daltry, had long appreciated the value of a combination of theory and practice in ITE. Speaking of the benefits of a three-year course Williams referred to the need for student teachers to develop their mathematics as well as their teaching of mathematics: 'It was possible to base formal studies on practical experience, observation and experiment both in a student's own learning and in teaching practice' (Williams, quoted in Howson, 1982).

Such approaches became normal in the three-year courses, which in 1965 achieved recognition as the BEd degree.

There continued to be a shortage of mathematics teachers in secondary schools, a situation that was analysed in the joint MA/ATCDE report referred to in the previous section. Despite the post-war expansion in higher education considerably fewer mathematics graduates were going into teaching. They were finding employment in industry or mathematics departments in higher education or in colleges of education. It was a situation that was to become considerably worse throughout the following decades, culminating in the present shortfall where, despite incentives, recruitment to ITE courses is almost 50 per cent below target. Concern was also expressed about the mathematics subject knowledge of some graduates. University mathematics courses were changing with many more degrees combining mathematics with other subjects. Courses that would have provided useful background knowledge for school mathematics became optional or were replaced by 'modern' mathematics topics, which were not presented at degree level in ways that made the content easy to adapt to the school curriculum.

Developments in in-service teacher education

In-service teacher education increased during the 1960s and 1970s and was given impetus by the James Report (DES, 1972). However, many of the far-reaching James recommendations were never implemented. This was a period characterized by rapid development in curriculum and examinations, when innovations were implemented with the support of LEAs and when independent projects such as Nuffield, SMP and SMILE produced teaching schemes accompanied by in-service support for teachers. It was also a period when many teachers were involved in trials of new courses, in the development of new assessment methods and in research surveys. However, by the 1980s resources began to be channelled into government-sponsored innovations with in-service teacher education funded to support centralized curriculum change. Inspectors and advisers increasingly provided training in techniques that had been approved at government level, such as those stemming from the Cockcroft Report of 1982.

Partnership between schools and HEIs

There were variations in postgraduate ITE provision prior to the government regulations introduced in 1992. The proportion of time that student teachers spent in schools and the balance in theoretical input between subject and professional studies differed between PGCE courses. There was always a problem in relating theory and practice. Currently, in the partnership model where responsibility is shared between HEI and school-based tutors, the student teachers are in schools for 24 weeks out of 36. The remaining 12 weeks are divided between mathematics curriculum studies, wider educational studies and the students' private academic study for their assignments. The inadequacy of this time allocation is quite clear, especially when the diversity in the students' backgrounds is taken into account. Familiarity with contemporary British schooling is a necessary prerequisite for successful practical teaching experiences during the PGCE year. Several categories of potential teachers are likely to require an induction period: those whose own secondary education was outside the UK, those who are older (in their 40s or 50s) and those whose secondary education was in selective schools. Many PGCE students are insecure with their mathematical knowledge and find it difficult to develop this during the course, indicating a need to build in time for directed self-study.

Statutory requirements have increased since the introduction of the TTA Standards for Qualified Teacher Status (QTS) in 1998 and the National Curriculum for initial teacher education in mathematics and in ICT in 1999. It is acknowledged that the student teacher may gain QTS but still have areas for development and that the induction NQT year will provide opportunities for further support and progress. A consideration of just one of the QTS standards must bring into question the adequacy of the 10-month PGCE course:

> Those to be awarded QTS must, when assessed, demonstrate that they use teaching methods which sustain the momentum of pupils' work and keep all pupils engaged through setting high expectations for all pupils notwithstanding individual differences, including gender, cultural and linguistic backgrounds.

> (TTA, 1998: 4k (xiii))

Partnership between HEIs and schools has the potential to provide for initial and in-service teacher education of the type envisaged by Ruthven (1999) who referred to the formation of 'multi-faceted partnerships... committed to not just improving their practice, but to developing a qualitatively different basis for it'.

Challenges and ways forward

This section discusses the aims of mathematics education from the inter-connected perspectives of the needs of working life and the development of values.

Employment, mathematics and the new technologies

One challenge is to interpret trends in the nature of employment and to design curricula that will enable young people to take up the opportunities and responsibilities of work. Considering an example from the electronics industry, Clayton (1999) writes about the mathematical principles and techniques that underpin the development and application of computer software tools. Even although most employees, some temporary and others more permanent, are not involved in the design of the software, they use it for constructing their own models and refining them for specific applications. This requires judgement about the quantities concerned and about the relationships between them. It involves mathematical knowledge and under-standing developed in school. The basic curriculum needs to be enhanced by investigative modelling activities in which complexities are handled through the use of computers: 'In this type of learning, IT, with its power to produce graphical images and manipulate symbols, objects or numbers, has an important role as a tutorial assistant: illustrating mathematical concepts, encouraging directed investigations, and aiding visualisation in the explora-tion and transformation of data' (Clayton, 1999).

The computer as 'tutorial assistant' centralizes the human role while acknowledging that so much more can be done, and so much more under-stood, through the use of computers. An understanding of the power of ICT, which goes far beyond providing information, needs to begin in school.

A framework for post-16 progression

Another challenge lies in the development of a framework for post-compulsory mathematics for those who specialize in other subjects or study for vocational qualifications. Present arrangements lack rigour and progression and do not provide alternative pathways towards higher education in courses with mathematical content. For a detailed critique of the mathematics in non-specialist post-16 courses, see Wolf and Steadman (1998) and Wolf (2000). Participation in post-compulsory mathematics continues to decline relative to other subjects. Research about contributory factors has been discussed already but a transparent framework for progression, tailored to individual needs, would be a more attractive prospect for most 16-year-olds than a choice between A/AS level or 'application of number' tied to a vocational context. Sutherland (2000) analyses the inadequacies of the prior mathematical knowledge among many undergraduates in subjects such as earth sciences and physics, and the consequences for teaching and learning at degree level. The deficit is particularly noticeable in mathematical areas that were traditionally studied by double mathematics A level students, a proportion of the total A level population that has fallen rapidly in recent years. Brown (1999a) recognizes the 'tension between the interests of those university teachers who wish for more technical and specialist mathematics course content at A level, and schools who want courses to attract and be appropriate for the wider range of students who are keen to study mathematics'. She suggests that the greater flexibility within the revised post-16 curriculum (QCA, 1999) might enable broad A level courses to be complemented by AS studies of more specialist mathematical topics by those students who are aiming for degrees requiring such knowledge. Brown also points out that there is a need for university departments to review the essential prior knowledge required of undergraduates.

Mathematics and culture

Participation in post-compulsory mathematics is connected with attitudes and beliefs. Recent research indicates that not all groups in society are equally likely to study mathematics beyond GCSE. Woodrow (1996) discusses observed ethnically related differentiated choices and suggests further study to reveal strategies for attracting more people into careers in mathematics and science. Kitchen (1999) has evidence that many pupils who have high GCSE grades do not choose to study mathematics at A level and that this is especially true of girls. However, school experiences also contribute to attitudes and beliefs. Self-belief in one's own mathematical capabilities must be nurtured in every phase of schooling.

There is now greater understanding of how 'reality' and 'utility' are embedded in cultures, and that the diversity amongst children must make us wary of the contexts in which we present mathematical ideas. The statutory framework that includes the National Curriculum encourages schools to 'develop a distinctive character and ethos rooted in their local communities' (QCA, 1999). Bishop (1988) writes about ways of connecting children with their local mathematical cultures, with 'the procedures, knowledge and values that have grown from tradition and social practices'. Community projects, some with industrial sponsorship, are providing some children with insight into the uses of mathematics. School mathematics should consist of culturally significant and mathematically meaningful activities in which a sense of purpose is present and in which there are choices of strategies to be made.

Only through experiences of mathematics in school that are alive with cultural resonance and that draw children into the endeavour to extend their own knowledge will more young adults willingly volunteer to continue with the subject. Only then will there be a sufficient pool of graduates who, if rewards match their needs, will wish to become mathematics teachers.

Acknowledgements

My perspectives on the issues raised in this chapter are based on my experiences as a teacher since 1961 but have been developed through my collaborative work since 1992 with colleagues in the Mathematical Sciences Group at the University of London Institute of Education. In particular I would like to acknowledge the help received through specific discussions with Professor Alan Bishop (Monash University, Australia), Derek Foxman (Mathematics Education Consultant, Visiting Fellow, University of London Institute of Education) and Professors Celia Hoyles, Harvey Goldstein, Richard Noss and Alison Wolf (University of London Institute of Education).

References

Assessment of Performance Unit (APU) (1985) *A Review of Monitoring in Mathematics,* HMSO, London
Association of Teachers of Mathematics (1993) *Talking Maths, Talking Languages,* ATM, Derby
Bell, A W, Costello, J and Kuchemann, D (1983) *Research on Teaching and Learning,* NFER/Nelson, Windsor
Bishop, A J (1988) *Mathematical Enculturation: A cultural perspective on mathematics education,* Kluwer, Dordrecht
Brown, M (1999a) One mathematics for all?, in *Rethinking the Mathematics Curriculum,* ed C Hoyles *et al,* Falmer Press, London
Brown, M (1999b) Swings of the pendulum, in *Issues in Teaching Numeracy in Primary Schools,* ed I Thompson, Open University Press, Buckingham
Carraher, T N and Schliemann, A D (1988) Culture, arithmetic and mathematical models, in *Cultural Dynamics,* **1,** pp 180–94
Central Advisory Council for Education (1967) *Children and their Primary Schools* (Plowden Report), HMSO, London
Clayton, M (1999) Industrial applied mathematics is changing as technology advances: what skills does mathematics education need to provide?, in *Rethinking the Mathematics Curriculum,* ed C Hoyles *et al,* Falmer Press, London

County of Durham Education Committee (1976) *The Use of Electronic Calculators in Secondary Schools*, Darlington Teachers' Centre

D'Ambrosio, U (1984) Ethnomathematics and its place in the history and pedagogy of mathematics, *For the Learning of Mathematics,* **5** (1)

Dean, P (1982) *Teaching and Learning Mathematics*, Woburn Press, London

Department of Education and Science (DES) (1960) *Secondary School Examinations Other Than the GCE* (Beloe Report), HMSO, London

DES (1963) *Half Our Future* (Newsom Report), HMSO, London

DES (1972) *Teacher Education and Training* (James Report), HMSO, London

DES (1982) *Mathematics Counts* (Cockcroft Report), HMSO, London

Department for Education and Employment (DfEE) (1999) *The National Numeracy Strategy: Framework for teaching mathematics from reception to year 6*, DfEE, London

Dowling, P (1991) A touch of class: ability, social class and intertext in SMP 11–16, in *Teaching and Learning School Mathematics*, ed D Pimm and E Love, Hodder and Stoughton, London

Gibbons, R (1975) An account of the School Mathematics Individualised Learning Experiment, *Mathematics in School*, **4** (6)

Harris, S, Keys, W, and Fernandes, C (1997) *Third International Mathematics and Science Study*, NFER, London

Howson, G (1982) *A History of Mathematics Education in England*, Cambridge University Press, Cambridge

Hoyles, C and Healy, L (1999a) Students' views of proof, *Mathematics in School*, **28** (3)

Hoyles, C and Healy, L (1999b) Can they prove it?, *Mathematics in School*, **28** (4)

Hoyles, C, Noss, R and Pozzi, S (1999) Mathematizing in Practice, in *Rethinking the Mathematics Curriculum*, ed C Hoyles *et al*, Falmer Press, London

Joffe, L and Foxman, D (1986) Attitudes and sex differences: some APU findings, in *Girls into Maths Can Go*, ed L Burton (to accompany the OU/ILEA course PM 645), Holt, Rhinehart and Winston, London

Kitchen, A (1999) The changing profile of entrants to mathematics at A level and to mathematical subjects in higher education, *British Educational Research Journal*, **25** (1)

Lerman, S (1983) Problem-solving or knowledge-centred: the influence of philosophy on mathematics teaching, *International Journal of Mathematical Education in Science and Technology*, **14** (1)

Lew, H (1999) New goals and directions for mathematics education in Korea, in *Rethinking the Mathematics Curriculum*, ed C Hoyles *et al*, Falmer Press, London

London Mathematical Society, Institute of Mathematics and its Applications, and Royal Statistical Society (1995) *Tackling the Mathematics Problem*, London Mathematical Society, London

Mathematical Association (MA) (1955) *The Teaching of Mathematics in Primary Schools*, Bell, London

MA (1959) *Mathematics in Secondary Modern Schools*, Bell, London

MA/Association of Teachers in Training Colleges and Departments of Education (1963) *The Supply and Training of Teachers of Mathematics*, Bell, London

Morgan, C (1998) *Writing Mathematically: The discourse of investigation*, Falmer, London

National Curriculum Council (NCC) (1989) *Mathematics: Non-statutory guidance*, NCC, York

Nunes, T (1992) Ethnomathematics and everyday cognition, in *Handbook of Research in Mathematics Teaching and Learning*, ed D A Grouws, Macmillan, New York

Polya, G (1957) *How to Solve It*, Doubleday, New York

Qualifications and Curriculum Authority (QCA) (1999) *The National Curriculum*, QCA, London

Reynolds, D and Muijs, D (1999) Numeracy matters: contemporary policy matters in the teaching of mathematics, in *Issues in Teaching Numeracy in Primary Schools*, ed I Thompson, Open University Press, Buckingham

Royal Society (1997) *Teaching and Learning Algebra pre-19*, Report of a Royal Society/ Joint Mathematical Council Working Group, Royal Society, London

Ruthven, K (1999) Reconstructing professional judgement in mathematics education, in *Rethinking the Mathematics Curriculum,* ed C Hoyles *et al*, Falmer Press, London

Schoenfeld, A H (1985) *Mathematical Problem-Solving*, Academic Press, New York

Shuard, H *et al* (1991) *Calculators, Children and Mathematics*, Simon and Schuster, London

Sutherland, R (2000) Disjunctions between school and university: the case of mathematics, in *The Maths We Need Now: New demands, deficits and remedies*, ed C Tikly and A Wolf, Institute of Education, University of London, London

Thwaites, B (1972) *SMP: The first ten years*, Cambridge University Press, Cambridge

Tikly, C, Noss, R and Goldstein, H (2000) Pupils and policy: what is the target?, *Forum*, **42** (1)

TTA (1998) Annexe A of DfEE circular April 1998, 4k (xiii)

University of London Examinations and Assessment Council (ULEAC) (1992) *Graded Assessment in Mathematics: A teacher assessment scheme for the National Curriculum*, Nelson, London

Walden, R and Walkerdine, V (1985) *Girls and Mathematics: From primary to secondary schooling*, Paper 8, Institute of Education, University of London, London

Walsh, A (1991) The calculator as a tool for learning, in *Teaching and Learning School Mathematics*, ed D Pimm and E Love, Hodder & Stoughton, London

Woodhouse, G and Goldstein, H (1996) The statistical analysis of institution-based data, in *Assessment: Problems, developments and statistical issues*, ed H Goldstein and T Lewis, John Wiley and Sons, Chichester

Woodrow, D (1996) Cultural inclinations towards studying mathematics and sciences, *New Community*, **22** (1)

Wolf, A (2000) Mathematics for some? Or mathematics for all? Curious UK practices in international context, in *The Maths We Need Now: New demands, deficits and remedies*, ed C Tikly and A Wolf, Institute of Education, University of London, London

Wolf, A and Steadman, H (1998) Basic competence in mathematics: Swedish and English 16 year olds, *Comparative Education*, **34** (3)

Chapter 3

Science teaching in an era of change
Sheila Turner and Tony Turner

Introduction

Science teachers in England and Wales entered 2000 with a new science National Curriculum (NC) (DfEE/QCA, 1999) and the prospect of renewing their schemes of work for the following September. Thus the 21st century continued in much the same way as the last decade of the old century.

This chapter looks broadly at events in science education across the last century but in more detail at changes that have occurred during the past two decades. We consider mainly the period of compulsory schooling. This period ushered in a real attempt to provide 'science for all' for pupils from 5 to 16. What has been the effect of these and many other changes on the teaching and learning of science and have they affected teachers' and pupils' enjoyment and understanding of science?

Part 1 The present position: where we have come from

Much has been achieved in the science education of young people in the 20th century. The position of science in the school curriculum has moved from one of relative weakness, where science was offered to a select few at the dawn of the era, to one that occupies prime position alongside mathematics and English in the education of all boys and girls from 5 to 16 years at the end of the century. At the same time the structure of schooling has changed out of all recognition.

Before 1900 science did not feature strongly in the curriculum of the grammar and independent (public) schools, but played 'second fiddle' to the classics. Science was not taught consistently in all schools largely because of the relatively low status of science and the lack of suitably qualified teachers. In elementary schools there was guidance for science in the programmes for different standards but the realization was patchy. Several enlightened scientists influenced the teaching of science in elementary and grammar schools, notably T H Huxley and Armstrong. Science was seen as a way of exercising the hands, eyes and senses and explaining how things worked. By the turn of the century 'object lessons' were one preferred teaching approach and heavily reliant on books (Jenkins, 1979: 38). A practical, hands-on approach to teaching science (called 'heurism' at that time) was developed by Armstrong in the late 19th century in order to motivate and apply common-sense approaches to learning science (Van Praagh, 1973). Although briefly successful it did not survive into the early 20th century but reappeared in the 1960s. Reasons for its demise may include the cost of equipment, space needed for laboratories, an unpopularity of a hands–on approach in the independent schools and the particular view of science that heurism portrayed (Jenkins, 1979: 41).

The founding of two professional associations of science teachers was of great importance (see Figure 3.1). In 1884 women science teachers in (largely) girls' independent schools formed the Association of Science Teachers (AST) and 1901 saw the appearance of the Association of Public School Science Masters (APSSM). The AST grew in numbers and influence and in 1922 became the Association of Women Science Teachers (AWST) offering a wider and more flexible membership. The AWST always had a smaller membership than the APSSM, partly because of the smaller number of women scientists but also because of the prevailing attitude of society towards the employment of married women. Amalgamation of the two associations was discussed in 1922; however, at this time a science education appropriate to girls was deemed important and so, for a further 40 years, science teachers enjoyed two separate professional associations. In 1963, the two associations became the Association for Science Education (ASE), which is now the largest subject association in the UK (Layton, 1984). The current membership is 24,000 and includes primary, secondary and tertiary phase teachers.

At their beginnings, the APSSM and AWST addressed the perceived different needs of boys and girls as well as common issues familiar to science teachers today such as the role of practical work in science, the provision of technical support in school and the relation of mathematics teaching to science teaching (Nightingale, in Ingle and Jennings, 1981: 17). A significant

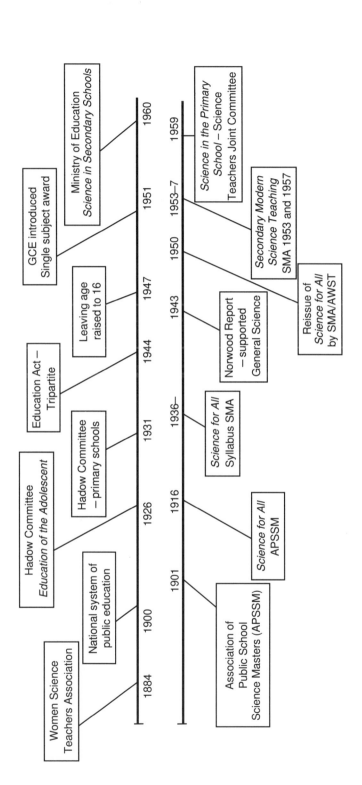

Figure 3.1 *Some events in education and science education 1884–1960*

development for the science education of independent and grammar school boys and girls was the introduction of a general science curriculum as a means of humanizing and broadening their education (APSSM, 1916). The general science movement developed in the inter-war years and both associations worked together on developing a general science course for secondary schools. This syllabus eventually attracted considerable support from many teachers and scientists of the day (SMA, 1936, 1938) although the syllabus needed modifying to meet 'the normal interests of the average girl' (Jenkins 1979: 85). At that time the AWST/APSSM rejected specialist science teaching of the sciences in the context of general education (Ingle and Jennings, 1981: 17); the tension between the specialist approach and the generalist approach was a recurrent theme throughout the last century.

General science remained popular in the immediate post-Second World War period (Jenkins 1979: 88). A leading figure throughout its growth was Joseph Lauwerys, tutor in science teaching methods at the Institute of Education, University of London (Lauwerys, 1937), also a prime supporter of biology in the school curriculum (Lauwerys, 1934). However, science teachers and others concerned with science education identified weaknesses in the general science approach, in particular the lack of an organizing curriculum principle and the difficulty of one teacher teaching the whole syllabus. Detractors pointed also to its lack of wider academic status and the absence of a professional rationale for its working methods; general science has no counterpart in the scientific world as does, for example, physics. Even as late as 1959 a joint policy statement (Science Teachers Joint Sub-Committee, 1959) recommended a 'science for all' course containing elements of biology, physics and chemistry together with geology and astronomy. This position reflected earlier statements by the AWST/SMA (1953, 1957, 1961). By the end of the 1950s the general science movement was in decline and was largely abandoned in grammar and independent schools in favour of teaching the separate sciences, under pressure from the growing national demand for scientists. There had been a massive growth in the number of pupils, both girls and boys, studying science in the sixth forms (post-16) of grammar and independent schools. The preparation of such pupils at GCE O level led rapidly, and some said naturally, to the abandonment of general science (Connell and James, 1958: 285). General science remained in the secondary modern (SM) schools, the successors to the senior elementary schools (called senior schools).

Most developments described above applied only to the small minority of able pupils. Up until the immediate post-war period, pupils in state (senior) schools who did not gain entrance to a grammar or independent school frequently received a fragmented science education. The science education on offer was limited (Ingle and Jennings, 1981: 18). In girls' schools, botany was favoured and in elementary schools, some nature study was a preferred approach to science. Biology later came to replace botany in the inter-war years. Science teaching in senior schools was limited due, in part, to the school-leaving age remaining at 14 until 1947. During the 1950s the work of teachers in SM schools, where the majority of pupils were educated, did not receive the same attention as that of their grammar school counterparts. SM schools were often underfunded, lacked resources and qualified science teachers and had no recognized qualification towards which pupils could work. One of the few accounts of that work to be published (AWST/SMA 1953, 1957) later influenced science curriculum reform for the comprehensive school (Misselbrook, 1969).

In elementary schools, science teaching revolved around nature study and observation lessons, the provision of which was in the hands of teachers who were either ill prepared for such responsibility or had other priorities. Advice included 'cultivating small gardens' and the 'study of mechanical toys' (Board of Education, 1937: 90). Many schools up to 1945 were dominated by preparing pupils for the entrance examinations to fee-paying selective schools. For some pupils, free entry to selective schools was possible through a scholarship awarded by competitive examination. One description of the state of primary education in the first half of the 20th century makes no mention of the place of science teaching, apart from references to descriptions of animals and their location (Loundes, 1954: 46–63). It was not until 1963 that the ASE began to interest itself in 'primary science', and not until 1982 that the needs of primary teachers teaching science were addressed by the ASE (Layton, 1984: 117).

The 1960s saw a flood of changes that altered the face of science teaching (see Figure 3.2). These changes were largely the result of social policy and government initiatives but were also affected by the competitive space exploration in the USA and USSR. The tripartite system of schooling arising from the 1944 Act consolidated separate systems of schooling for pupils and made secondary education more widely available. Pupils unable to gain a grammar school place went to SM schools and left school at 15 without any qualifications, except for a minority of pupils who sat GCE from their SM school or took lower-level examinations outside the GCE system.

In the late 1950s and early 1960s, a section of the SMA/AWST (soon the ASE) led the development of new science courses for grammar and independent schools at both GCE O level and A level. Initially supported by the Nuffield Foundation (NF), radical new approaches to the teaching and assessment of science were developed focusing on understanding and first-hand experiences by pupils instead of rote learning of facts and principles,

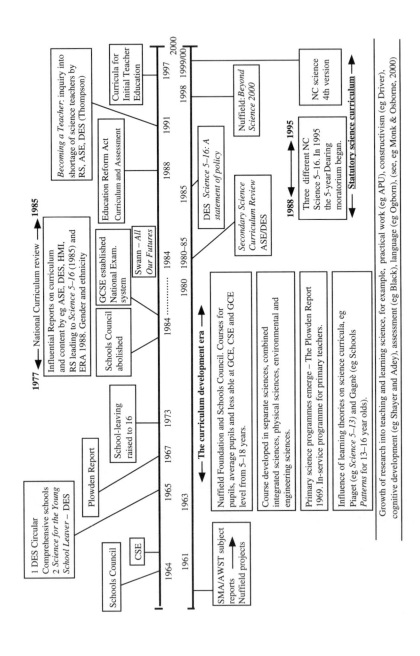

Figure 3.2 *Some events in education and science education 1960–2000*

building in some ways on Armstrong's heuristic approach. The intention was to move science teaching into the 20th century, to present science as an experimental activity and to motivate pupils to be scientists. The approach adopted was novel both in treatment of content and management of curriculum change. The development model adopted was the centre-to-periphery model using an expert team to develop ideas for dissemination. The decision by the NF first to make changes for the able minority at GCE O level was probably more a reflection of the background and composition of the team of science teachers they assembled than a considered response by the associations to the needs of most pupils (Booth, 1975; Waring, 1979). This decision is perhaps surprising when contemporary policy statements from both associations and the government supported the development of a general science course for secondary pupils (AWST/SMA 1961; MoE 1960).

In the mid-1960s the newly formed Schools Council began to develop new curricula for both primary and secondary schools. By contrast with the Nuffield model of curriculum development, the Schools Council encouraged local developments, with greater emphasis on a periphery-to-centre approach to change. The revolution in approaches to primary school science teaching led to some ambitious and innovative curriculum resources (eg Schools Council, 1972), which stretched the science backgrounds of many primary school teachers despite in-service support. Nevertheless primary science beyond nature study was here to stay.

As the Nuffield Foundation Science Teaching Projects (NSTP) for both primary and secondary schools got under way in the early 1960s, including later substantial Advanced level programmes, radical changes to secondary schooling altered the context in which these curricula had been planned. New legislation created comprehensive schools and signalled the abandonment of the tripartite system (DES, 1965). In 1964 the first examination system for pupils of average attainment was introduced, the Certificate of Secondary Education (CSE), although not until 1973 were pupils required to stay in school until they were 16. The CSE encouraged school-based science curriculum development under Mode 3 regulations, which continued until the advent of GCSE (a Mode 3 examination was one set and marked by teachers with external moderation by an examination board). In curriculum terms, different approaches to teaching science were needed than those envisaged by the SMA/AWST (1957, 1961). The work of science teachers in secondary modern schools, which took a broad approach to science teaching, was being recognized. In the new comprehensive schools these courses were renamed 'combined' or 'integrated' science, many of which were designed for the 'average' pupil. A variety of new integrated science courses for 11–14- and 14–16-year-olds emerged, each with a different focus and aimed at different audiences. Broad science for the younger age group allowed a wider variety of choice of subjects for pupils at 14 but teachers were then faced with the difficult choice of guiding pupils towards either GCE or CSE.

One of the first of these courses was Nuffield Combined Science (NCS, 1970) for the 11–14-year-olds. The NCS course was a selection from the resources of separate science O level courses. It was used mainly as a resource in comprehensive schools up until the early 1980s. Research later showed it was too difficult for many pupils (Shayer, 1978).

NCS had strong competition from the Scottish Integrated Science (SIS). Written in the early 60s, this programme eventually implemented successfully the Scottish national policy on science teaching (Scottish Education Department, 1969). Both NCS and SIS gave rise to local adaptations to meet the needs of specific groups of pupils. The uptake of most NSTP curriculum materials in this age group never achieved the success of SIS. Most independent and grammar schools in the 1970s continued to teach the sciences separately.

In the mid-1960s, the NSTP had embarked on a radical programme of science curriculum development for the pupils in the 13–16 age group, the impetus for which was *Science for the Young School Leaver* (Schools Council, 1965). Called Secondary Science (Misselbrook, 1969), it comprised a set of teacher resources around eight themes instead of a ready-made teaching and examination package. The themes reflected in part the GCE O level separate science resources but the content was placed in a real-life context instead of an academic context. Science teachers were expected to construct a course from the resources, selecting sections from each theme to suit local needs, interests and teacher expertise. Later, a text was supplied to assist teachers construct a Mode 3 CSE examination. The Secondary Science resources placed great trust and confidence in the professionalism of teachers. Despite the high quality of resources, a survey at the time suggested that less than 10 per cent of teachers said they were 'fully' doing this course. Many teachers were not ready to take on this onerous task but the challenge encouraged some teachers to do their own thinking instead of following prescription.

Another integrated science approach to challenge the domination of the separate sciences was the Schools Council Integrated Science Project (SCISP). Called Patterns (from its learning theory base), the course integrated not only aspects of the O level science courses but included social and technological issues in the science curriculum. Learning theory (Gagnè, 1965) was used as the basis for ordering activities and structuring pupil learning. SCISP introduced the notion of a double award at GCE because it used twice the curriculum time of one subject. Some of the course (20 per cent) was assessed by teachers. Its novelty and breadth of vision challenged conventional wisdom of what constituted school science. These features attracted enthusiasts but worried some employers. University admissions staff were uncertain about its equivalence to O level, which also may have contributed to its low uptake. Some commentators at the time regarded SCISP as one of the most integrated science courses of its type in the world (Ingle and Jennings, 1981: 41).

The period 1960–1980 was one of continuous curriculum development across a wide spectrum of school science. Integrated science courses became popular in many comprehensive schools because they allowed pupils to maintain a balanced curriculum, without the separate sciences taking up too much time in the timetable. However, most remaining grammar and independent schools retained the single sciences. General science went out of favour in the 1950s but returned as 'integrated science' in the 1970s in comprehensive schools. The tension between 'education in science' for the intending specialist and 'education through science' for the non-specialist re-emerged in the context of 'science for all' for most pupils aged 5 to 16.

The wide range of choice of science courses was both a strength and a weakness of science education. A severe problem was that pupils had to choose subjects for GCE at age 13. One attempt to simplify the range of science courses was Nuffield Science 13–16 (1981), which combined Patterns and Secondary Science. The age range of this project reflected the emergence of middle schools and anticipated the common examination system (GCSE).

The examination system had a powerful influence on the way the sciences were taught. The single subject system (the GCE) was introduced in 1951 to replace School Certificate (a group examination) and also gave opportunities for pupils in SM schools to enter GCE. For science teaching this meant choices between mainly biology, chemistry and physics. However, freedom of choice caused some pupils to have an unbalanced science curriculum. The introduction of CSE in 1964 widened opportunities for pupils of average performance through locally developed examinations. The common examination system (GCSE), set up in 1984, was run by national examination boards but retained the single subject system. It was finally the introduction of the National Curriculum that made 'broad science' a compulsory subject examined on a national basis and required teachers to address the needs of all pupils.

The late 1970s saw the beginning of a period of review, discussion and debate about the effects of new science curricula, legislation and pupil needs set in the context of a wider debate about the nature of the school curriculum. Computers for schools were on the horizon. Inspections of schools

by HMI had revealed alarming disparities in curriculum access and performance of pupils in secondary schools (DES, 1979). Many secondary pupils
studied only one science after age 13 and some pupils dropped science
altogether. Inspections identified the sketchy provision of science teaching
as a major weakness in primary schools (DES, 1978). Dated expectations
existed in society and schools about the educational opportunities for girls
(HMI, 1980) and emerging concerns about the performance of many pupils
of working class and minority ethnic origins (DES, 1984a).

In 1979 the ASE produced a visionary consultation document (ASE, 1979)
on the future of the science curriculum. Regrettably, despite serious debate
in professional organizations and university departments of education the
document had little impact on most science teachers, perhaps because the
proposals were too far ahead of current practice. The consultation document
evolved two years later into a more conservative policy document (ASE,
1981), but which developed the theme of 'science for all', adopted by *Science
5–16* (DES, 1985). With government support, the ASE then embarked on
an ambitious programme of grass roots curriculum development through
which practising teachers explored curriculum issues raised by national
discussion and illustrated their responses by means of innovative classroom
teaching material (*Secondary Science Curriculum Review*, Michell, 1987). This
development not only raised the morale and profile of both teachers and
the Association but prepared teachers for *Science 5–16* and the science
National Curriculum.

In the early 1980s, significant proposals concerning school science education were made by a working group of scientists (Royal Society, 1982),
which supported the emerging consensus about the importance of a common
'science for all' curriculum. The professional organizations such as the Institute
of Biology, the Institute of Physics and the Royal Society of Chemistry
broadly supported this view.

This consensus was expressed through the government policy paper *Science
5–16* (DES, 1985). This paper proposed a balanced approach to science
education, emphasizing breadth of study for all pupils throughout the period
of compulsory education but with courses differentiated by ability. Regrettably, issues concerning the social and technological implications of science,
a growing feature of science courses in the curriculum development era,
were minimized and further reduced through assessment. This bias towards
'pure science' remains today as a historical legacy.

Science 5–16 was a landmark in education in England and Wales as the
first policy document about a subject and its content and for the first time
gave entitlement to a science education for all pupils throughout the period
of compulsory schooling. It bridged the primary–secondary divide and

promoted continuity of experience for pupils. After a two-year 'quiet period', due to the imminent 1987 general election, events moved rapidly for science education. A government-invited committee dominated by professional science educators, together with a few teachers and industrialists, was asked to draft a science curriculum based on the policy document. In six months a consultation document was produced and after another six months proposals for the science curriculum were finalized. The consultation period was short and some criticized the limited changes made to the original proposal. The curriculum document was to prove an ambitious proposal (DES/WO, 1988).

The curriculum that emerged initially gained the support of most science teachers and other science educators and included earth sciences, space science and environmental issues alongside the traditional sciences. A significant feature was the importance attached to investigations by pupils. The content was not arranged in traditional ways of separate sciences but was described in a set of 22 elements (attainment targets) reflecting both the breadth of subject matter identified for science and the need to meet the assessment structure of the NC in England and Wales: see below. The programme included aspects of the social and technological dimensions of science and a novel feature was one attainment target addressing the nature of science. Most radical, perhaps, was the inclusion of 'communication' as a distinct skill to be assessed. Issues of equity were recognized through a consideration of access and differentiation. The content of the science NC was used to develop national criteria for the school-leaving certificate, the GCSE, by providing guidance to examination boards. In meeting all these requirements there was a price to pay and this was in length and complexity; also science may have suffered from being the first curriculum subject to be developed for the NC.

In parallel with the development of subject curricula for the NC an assessment structure was devised by a dedicated Task Group on Assessment and Testing (TGAT) (DES, 1988). The TGAT started work at approximately the same time as the science subject group – mid-1987 – and there was some limited overlap in the group membership. The science group developed their proposals, as least for a while, in ignorance of the final assessment framework within which the science curriculum must operate. The TGAT model of assessment addressed both formative and summative assessment but emphasized the primacy of formative methods in supporting learning and teaching in the classroom as the key to raising standards, by contrast to summative assessment for comparative purposes.

The TGAT proposed a system of 10 developmental levels, representing descriptions of stages in knowledge and understanding (but not attitudes) through which a pupil would move during compulsory education. Each curriculum subject would devise ways to describe pupil progression through these 10 levels in terms of its own subject knowledge and understanding. By placing pupils on a level on the basis of their performance, teachers could recognize achievement in pupil learning, monitor progress and focus new learning. The level statements also provided a means of communicating progress to pupils, to parents and others with a legitimate interest. The first science NC contained 17 attainment targets (ATs) to be assessed (reduced from an original 22!) for each of which 10 development levels were described. Working to the TGAT framework produced a detailed, lengthy curriculum statement for science, the complexity of which contained the seeds of its own destruction. The 'grand design' of the science curriculum (Jennings, 1992: 8) foundered on the issue of assessment by demanding the impossible of science teachers in secondary school; and many teachers in primary schools lacked expertise in science.

The first NC science was taught in schools in September 1989 to Years 1 and 7, just four years after the generic science policy document had been published. Even as the science curriculum was introduced into the schools it became clear that the combination of new and old subject matter structured in new ways, together with the daunting assessment demands referred to above, would not work. Simplification was necessary and within two years a second science NC replaced the first model, containing now just four ATs (DES/WO, 1991).

The third version of the science NC (DES/WO, 1995) was implemented in 1995 after the Dearing interventions. Of equal importance at that time was the promise by government that no further change would occur for five years and this moratorium gave a breathing space for reflection by the science education community.

The haste with which policy was translated into curriculum was breath-taking, more revolution than evolution. The pace was driven, we suggest, by a political agenda, which demanded results on the time-scale of a five-year cycle of national elections rather than the longer period usually necessary for curriculum development. The price paid for haste was an ill-thought-out package of reform, which teachers of science could not handle without greater preparation, directed in-service training and a longer run-in period than that provided. As a model of curriculum development the introduction of the science NC left much to be desired. It was launched nation-wide into schools as though a finished product. There was no proposal for limited trials or any stated desire by government to move forward slowly on a basis of feedback and analysis. The process has not worked and the evidence for that must surely lie in the need for four different science national curricula in 12 years. Each change has presented a steady erosion of the vision of the first working party and a gradual reversion towards a traditional curriculum model of biology, physics and chemistry. However, the emphasis on practical work by pupils, including investigations, has been retained and improved.

In parallel with subject changes has been the distortion of the original TGAT proposals to the point where naïve summative assessment through external testing dominates the assessment process, a position predicted by observers at the time, eg Jennings, 1992: 29–31, and recently criticized by government inspectors (OFSTED, 2000: 107). It is worth noting at this point that despite commissioning research into the development of practical activities (Standard Assessment Tasks – SATs) to assess skills and processes in science at the end of KS1 (5–7-year-olds) and KS3 (11–14-year-olds), the government abandoned this work after completion of two years of expensive, intensive work (CATS, 1992). The main factor in rejecting this work was the manageability of SATs and their high cost in money and teacher time; short, written tests marked externally were adopted in preference to longer, practical investigations given by the teacher. Science teachers have borne the burden of this simplistic approach to the management of curriculum change and many have paid the price in stress and lowered morale. Despite the difficulties there are gains, including an established national programme of study in science for pupils from 5 to 16. Most science departments now have schemes of work and teachers have retained responsibility for assessing practical work, which contributes 25 per cent of the marks towards the total assessment.

It remains to be seen how 'Science 2000' will fare (DfEE/QCA, 1999). The fourth version of the NC has broadened the way in which practical work is interpreted, an important step forward, but has retained and consolidated the separation of the sciences. It is interesting to note that key skills have returned, lost after the proposals for science in 1988. In common with other subjects in the NC, science will need to provide opportunities for promoting thinking skills, enterprise and entrepreneurial skills, work-related learning and education for sustainable development. The touchstone of real progress will be how the assessment system responds to these desirable educational goals and supports their implementation rather than inhibiting them.

Part 2 Science teaching in a changing world

The previous section considered the changes that had taken place in the teaching of science during the 20th century, placing the changes in a social and political context. As we enter a new century it is worth considering where we are and how science education may develop in the coming era. Given the rate of scientific change and technological innovation and the increasing globalization of world economies, the pace and extent of change may well be greater than those we have witnessed in the past five decades. The rapid growth of information retrieval and processing is forcing us to reappraise the meaning of education. Within those contexts specific issues arise for science teaching that need to be resolved including those related to, for example:

- the purpose of science in the curriculum, including practical work;
- the nature of science;
- assessment of pupils in science;
- science teacher education;
- research in science education.

It is perhaps by addressing issues such as these that science education will be able to progress in ways that are supportive of change and enable pupils to become informed and questioning citizens, able to make sense of the natural and technological worlds and exercise choice.

The purpose of science in the curriculum

Until the 1988 Education Act, the science curriculum sought to meet the needs of pupils through a variety of curricula for different groups of pupils. These groupings were most often based on pupil performance and the higher performing pupils were expected to study more academically focused courses. Those pupils who were not academically minded were given more vocationally based courses or even did no science at all.

The introduction of the NC science has resulted in all pupils having an entitlement to science. However, it is the academic science curriculum that has been imposed on all pupils. Whether taught through science or through a combination of biology, chemistry and physics all courses are more suited to those pupils intending to study science at A level and beyond. In our view there is at present no science curriculum designed specifically for the non-specialist, but which gives a broad grounding in science and has the general acceptance of employers. The KS4 single science award has a low take-up and in any case is a selection from the double award syllabus.

This curriculum situation can be traced back to the development era of the early 1960s. The decision by the ASE/AWST, realized through the Nuffield Science Teaching Project, to identify the GCE O level science curriculum with the separate scientific disciplines was taken in order to prepare some pupils for advanced study in science. This focus deflected the emerging impetus for a general science course, advocated by both science teacher associations, and frustrated the development of a science course for the 'average' pupil. There was also the difficulty science teachers faced when teaching outside their specialist area. This decision affected profoundly the development of many other science courses because subsequently the Nuffield GCE O level materials became the mine from which resources were quarried to shape new course materials for the average pupil.

The strengths of the Nuffield GCE O level resources included an injection of new approaches to the teaching and learning of science with an emphasis on process and hands-on experience. New equipment was introduced into schools, often developed by teachers. Above all, the projects raised teacher awareness of the need to review and identify new purposes for science education. With hindsight there were major weakness in these projects that have had long-lasting effects on the evolution of the science curriculum. The first of these weaknesses was the omission of social and ethical issues from the resource materials although there was some attention in the background material to the industrial aspects of science and to practical application of scientific ideas. Secondly, these courses were assessed mainly through pupils' knowledge and understanding of science and laid greater stress on the fundamentals of science than on science in context. The third important aspect was that the development of the courses occurred mostly in isolation from one another and from the mathematics course. There was no sense of shared purpose or common goals, much less of working within a framework of a whole-school curriculum policy.

The consensus surrounding *Science 5–16* (DES/WO, 1988) and the first science National Curriculum (DES, 1989) has been eroded. This erosion is due mainly to the assessment pressures and to demand by some for curricula of high academic status needed for university entrance. Thus a key issue for science education is to identify a purpose for the school science curriculum that addresses the needs of most pupils. It is quite inadequate to use the needs of a small minority of pupils to generate the goals for the majority.

There is no link or justification made between choice of content and purposes in the science curriculum, an issue identified recently in an influential report on science education (Millar and Osborne, 1998). This lack of justification for the content makes it difficult to evaluate success, except in terms of GCSE and GCE A level grades. Significant contributions have been made in recent years in identifying ways to justify the place of science in the curriculum but they have yet to be translated into practice; examples include Millar, 1996; Ogborn, 1986; Ogborn and Macaskill, 1996 and Power, 1990.

The nature of science

The history of science has been one of increasing change and complexity. The list of discoveries in science continues to grow at an exponential rate. How best can teachers of science meet the challenges of such change and the growing demands to consider the social and ethical issues surrounding new developments, for example in biomedical and technological research? How can science teachers give pupils a glimpse of the excitement and importance of 'frontier science'?

Science 2000 (DfEE/QCA, 1999) remains very content-focused despite both the rhetoric of its introduction and the prominence given to scientific enquiry. Much of the content would have been familiar to pupils in schools 50 years ago and in one sense little has changed. There is little emphasis given to the history or nature of science, the role and importance of science in everyday life, or decision making and the assessment of risk. This lack of emphasis does not mean that science teachers are precluded from teaching such topics but unless topics are assessed they may receive less coverage by teachers. The attainment targets are very content-focused and do not appear to address the spirit of the curriculum. It remains to be seen whether those curriculum features identified in the sections called 'Breadth of Study' at the end of each key stage are to be assessed. The science curriculum in England – and elsewhere – is driven by summative assessment and it appears that only those features of the curriculum that can be reliably assessed are tested.

The development of one science curriculum for all means that the purposes of the curriculum are substantially the same for all pupils. Whereas not every pupil will achieve all that is hoped for, one would expect the core to be addressed by most. The introduction of the science NC has attempted to move science teaching to this new position. In doing so it has assumed that acquiring the knowledge of some key facts and principles of the three main sciences will enable the pupil to function in the adult world of further education, industry and commerce, and at the personal level. This seems a tall order unless, accompanying that expectation, additional knowledge is built in to the science curriculum. This other knowledge is about 'capability', such as:

- **study skills**, to enable the pupil to develop into a confident, enquiring, autonomous learner; and as part of this:
- **information retrieval skills**, to help learners to use books, journals, libraries, databases and the Internet purposively;
- **interpersonal skills**, including the ability to talk to others, including contemporaries, in order to further one's own understanding and share ideas;

- **technological skills** – how to use materials, tools and equipment confidently to assist with problem solving, and at the same time to engender confidence in dealing with domestic technology.

Knowledge, facts and principles can be taught through personal enquiry, by pupils designing, carrying out and evaluating their own investigations. In this way pupils can get a feel for how evidence is gained and evaluated. At the same time, capability can be enhanced. The most recent science NC (DfEE/QCA, 1999) promises to develop aspects of capability through the promotion of the key skills but they read as an 'add-on', rather than an integral part of the curriculum. In the Nuffield O level projects pupils were encouraged to act as 'scientists for a day'; investigations were used to generate evidence from which pupils were asked to draw their own conclusions. By judicious choice of activities, pupils needed both knowledge and capability to complete the task successfully. Nuffield investigations have been criticized for lack of real purpose because the answer was known to the teachers; pupils were learning what the teacher wanted them to learn and they often knew this. Investigations such as these were closed and not genuinely open-ended as occurs in real science. Nevertheless, practical activity and enquiry was motivating and allowed pupils to see phenomena and how they were interpreted, and to develop understanding.

Other curriculum projects in the 1970s and 1980s adopted different approaches. Secondary Science (Misselbrook, 1969) sought relevance to pupils' daily lives and attempted to provide them with scientific knowledge and skills and useful personal knowledge and understanding. By contrast, Patterns (Hall, 1973) used 'pattern seeking' and 'pattern using' as a foundation for problem solving, reflecting an important dimension of science.

The 1995 science NC has been squeezed from several directions, limiting the capacity of teachers to relate real science to school science. From one direction has come pressure to focus on the science needed to equip pupils to study A level, a pressure the GCSE began to resist. The second pressure comes from the national assessment structure, which favours teachers who emphasize content and recall at the expense of process and understanding. Another pressure is the GCSE examination, which limits teacher-assessed coursework to 25 per cent of the total marks, which has dampened the initiative of some teachers. Assessment feeds the league tables to which schools and their staff are very sensitive.

These pressures affect the way science is taught and distort the view of science that pupils take from school. Learning science in school under the NC is to expect pupils to recall a large amount of science, much of which they have not been able to adequately digest and understand; some pupils are bored and many teachers unhappy under this constraint (Donnelly, 2000: 33; Millar and Osborne, 1998).

Assessment

This section is short not for lack of importance but because some issues were addressed above. The National Curriculum was a national system defining both content and its assessment. We have described in Part 1 the assessment structure proposed by TGAT (DES, 1988). All subjects were to be assessed through Standard Assessment Tasks at ages 7, 11 and 14 but now only English, mathematics and science are tested. This situation places science under pressure because the results are used to make judgements about a school and to compare schools, locally and nationally.

Prior to the introduction of the National Curriculum, extensive research had been carried out on pupils' responses to practical work. Several summary reports were published in 1989 reviewing the findings in relation to pupils in both primary and secondary phases, eg DES, 1989. This research laid the basis for the assessment of practical work in the science NC. Teachers have retained the role of assessing pupils' capability of carrying out practical work at GCSE, such work contributing 25 per cent of the total marks.

We have said that the science curriculum is heavily influenced by the assessment process. Pupils are externally assessed in science at ages 11, 14 and 16, which can constrain teaching, by causing teachers to focus unduly on the content of the tests. It is important, clearly, to monitor standards of pupils at 11 and 14 across the country but we query current practice that requires all pupils in an age cohort to be tested in science. A lighter touch in the testing procedure would enable teachers to widen the scope of their teaching.

Assessment through written tests at 11 and 14 limits the ability of pupils to show what they can do. More attention needs to be given to teacher assessment of both theoretical and practical work. The introduction of practical tests at age 11 and 14 would enhance the quality of information collected about national standards. Sampling the work of pupils in practical activities using nationally generated tests would achieve that goal, much as the SAT pilot tests were intended to do (CATS, 1992).

The original TGAT model emphasized both formative and summative assessment. Much greater emphasis was placed on the summative aspect of assessment in the early stages of the NC. More recently, there has been a recognition of the need to return to the TGAT proposals and seek ways to improve teaching and learning through better use of formative assessment (Black and Wiliam, 1998). A recent OFSTED report has identified formative assessment as an area of weakness in science teaching (OFSTED, 2000: 107).

Science teacher education

The past century witnessed significant changes in teacher education, both in initial teacher education and in the provision of in-service education. These changes, mostly affecting state education, include:

- A move from two-year certificate courses for elementary/primary and secondary modern teachers together with graduates who could teach without any professional qualification, to an all-graduate teaching profession, all of whom are trained. Most teachers today are trained on the '3+1' model, a three-year degree course followed by a one-year postgraduate certificate in education (PGCE).
- The recognition of the importance of continuing professional development (CPD), particularly school in-service education.
- The recognition that CPD requires teachers to take responsibility for their own development in a supportive school framework. This approach to CDP, the reflective practitioner model, starts with the PGCE course.
- The provision for science teachers to update their subject knowledge through professional organizations. Departments of education in institutions of higher education (IHE) play an important role in this respect.

Since January 1970 no one could take up a teaching post in a state primary school unless qualified; and the same conditions applied after January 1974 in state secondary schools. Independent schools are not required to employ professional teachers although many do so. The shortage of science teachers had been a serious hindrance to raising standards for most of the post-war period, in both state and independent schools (Jenkins, 1979: 236–44). Science teacher supply has been a serious problem (Thompson, 1991) and remains so. In 1998 the number of science graduates recruited to secondary ITE courses was 2,288, about 25 per cent below the target of 3,050. In 1999, 2,362 graduates were recruited against a reduced target of 2,390 (TTA, personal communication, March 2000).

Initial teacher education programmes for those preparing to teach in elementary/primary and secondary schools have traditionally been different. Primary school teachers are generalists whereas secondary teachers are subject specialists, but the science NC requires all teachers of science to know some biology, chemistry, physics, earth science and astronomy.

The primary phase

Prior to the emergence of the four-year BEd courses in the late 1960s the majority of primary teachers took certificate in education courses; it was rare for primary teachers to take a specialist degree followed by a one-year PGCE course. During the 1990s the PGCE became a more common route for those preparing to teach in primary schools in England and Wales. One reason for this shift reflected the need to respond quickly to increasing demands for primary teachers and occurred at a time of more central intervention in the curriculum for both ITE and schools. The inclusion of science in *all* ITE courses, to meet the demands of the science curriculum for 5- to 11-year-olds, was of particular importance. The recent introduction of national auditing of student teachers' knowledge and understanding of science is a further pressure, especially for those students with limited exposure to science at school. One outcome has been to increase further the demanding nature of primary PGCE courses.

The review of primary schools (DES, 1978) allied to reports by the Assessment of Performance Unit (APU) on the extent and type of science teaching taught in primary schools (Harlen, Black and Johnson, 1981) led to increasing demands for science in-service (INSET) courses for primary teachers, most of whom were not science specialists and had taught little, if any, science. Such INSET was vital if the assessment demands of the NC were to be implemented satisfactorily in the 1990s, especially as initially the SAT assessments for seven-year-olds included science. The logistics and cost of implementing science INSET for all primary schools was such that INSET focused on the training of co-ordinators for science, with local authority advisers and IHEs working in partnership with schools. The cascade model of INSET with co-ordinators working with colleagues in schools is not ideal but was probably a sensible compromise. It is perhaps significant that the original DES-funded 35-day programmes for co-ordinators of science in the early 1980s, funded by the Department of Education and Science (DES), were rapidly replaced by shorter courses to enable the DES and local education authorities (LEAs) to meet the needs of other specialists in primary schools.

The secondary phase

Most intending secondary science teachers today follow a similar PGCE course. Until 1984, teacher education was diverse with each IHE constructing its own programme and providing a different balance of experiences for its students.

Teacher education in the immediate post-Second World War period was dominated by the disciplines of education. It was considered important for intending teachers to study the history, philosophy and psychology of education (and later sociology). For the aspiring secondary school teachers at that time this emphasis on the disciplines of education did little, it has been argued, to help them teach pupils, divorced as it often was from the day-to-day events of the classroom. This approach to ITE was rooted in the academic traditions of university education departments.

In the 1970s most IHEs began to recruit student teachers for both comprehensive and selective schools and this situation triggered a fundamental change in outlook in this sector of teacher education. The focus became more classroom-based and pupil-centred. The disciplines of education were used to illuminate the teaching situations or to help devise management or teaching strategies. This important development anticipated the partnership model of ITE, in due course advocated by central government. (Partnership involves schools working with an IHE to provide an initial teacher education course. Each school takes in student teachers and provides for them teaching and other experiences. Designated teachers in the school, together with the IHE tutor, decide whether the student teacher has reached the required teaching standard.)

The partnership model altered the way in which IHE staff worked both with students and with teachers. Concurrent with moves in the 1980s to reform the school curriculum, the teacher education curriculum in IHE and colleges became the responsibility of a government quango, the Council for the Accreditation of Teacher Education (DES, 1984b) and removed the autonomy of the IHE to direct the content, direction and pace of teacher education. The effects of the 1988 Education Reform Act led to a tightly structured curriculum for teacher education and specific standards that science teachers must achieve to gain Qualified Teacher Status (QTS) (DfEE, 1998: 116). These standards are identified separately for teachers of the primary and secondary phases.

The increased time in secondary schools has been of great benefit to student teachers in developing classroom skills but breadth of teacher education has been sacrificed. Science teachers are expected to teach all the sciences at KS3 (sometimes to KS4); there is little time for graduates to expand their science knowledge beyond their specialist degree subject. Much science is learnt on the job but is limited to that needed for lesson preparation. Student teachers are expected to audit their subject knowledge but comment on the lack of opportunity to respond to the audit. There is also concern for students who, while meeting requirements for the standards, are not helped to progress further.

The shift in PGCE towards a school-focused course has left little time to enrich the student's background through educational theory or the products of research. Science education has a rich research tradition, which is scarcely tapped (Monk and Osborne, 2000). Another casualty of the new PGCE is often fieldwork, although some schools invite their student teachers to join school field trips. The wider educational issues, for example equal opportunities policies and schooling, especially racism, may be left to schools to raise with student teachers. The potential contribution of science teachers to this issue is significant (Thorp, Deshpande and Edwards, 1994).

The present arrangements have upset the balance between theory and practice. Secondary science teachers are in danger of becoming technicians, capable of delivering the National Curriculum but short on understanding of the wider context of science education. The problem is one of perspective; the focus on initial teacher *training* is a narrower perspective than that of initial teacher *education*.

The shortage of science teachers returned in the 1990s. In the 1980s more applicants came forward and this was coincident with a drop in the pupil population. The supply of physics teachers has always been a problem but is now desperate; the recent financial training inducements to all science teachers may be only a temporary solution. The combined effect of the academic, professional and financial hurdles placed before intending science teachers may turn some away. These hurdles include:

- passing the GCSE in mathematics and English before entry;
- passing an examination in literacy and numeracy at the end of the PGCE course;
- reaching the standards required for QTS through school experience, practical science teaching and academic coursework in science and educational issues;
- completing the induction year successfully by meeting additional standards in order to have QTS confirmed.

In addition, many student teachers experienced financial hardship during the one-year PGCE course, but the recent proposed changes in funding for student teachers from September 2000 should reduce financial barriers to training.

Research in science education

Science education has a rich background in research. Research studies cover a wide field and we select below three issues to illustrate the importance of research to pedagogy.

The first example concerns research into the nature, extent and understanding of practical work, which has featured strongly in the research literature over many years (Klainin, 1988; Hofstein, 1988). Practical work has always been carried out although not on the scale seen in schools in England and Wales since the Nuffield projects in the 1960s. Practical work has a powerful influence on pupils' perceptions of science and many pupils today regard science lessons as synonymous with 'doing experiments'.

One concern in science education is the overemphasis on practical work. One consequence is a loss of purpose, when 'doing' replaces 'thinking'. Some pupils reject the more difficult 'before' and 'after' mental activity that accompanies meaningful investigations and this aspect of science teaching remains weak.

The purpose of practical work and its assessment has been a central issue in science education for many years (Woolnough and Allsop, 1985), recently through studies by the APU, which contributed to the development of assessed practical work in the science NC. The introduction of the science NC has increased the research interest in practical work at both primary and secondary levels (Millar *et al*, 1994; Harlen, 1992). This interest is reflected in the range of articles that has appeared recently in the journal of the Association for Science Education, the *School Science Review*. These articles reflect both research and good practice in schools.

The new model of the science NC (DfEE/QCA, 1999) has improved the flexibility of the attainment target concerned with experimental work (scientific enquiry), by including whole investigations as part of a broader purpose for practical work (Watson, Goldsworthy and Wood-Robinson, 1999). There remains a persistent question of what practical work is supposed to achieve for pupils in the compulsory period of schooling. The question is worth asking because so many pupils fail to grasp the purpose of what they are doing. This is not only a teaching problem but also an economic one. Much time and money are invested in practical activities and the returns in knowledge and understanding of science are not obvious. The Nuffield model of 'being a scientist for a day' has emotional appeal but the reality is that a 'day' is one or two periods on a timetable. Can the present type of science curriculum be taught properly in the current crowded timetable of secondary schools *and* acknowledge the proper role of experiment in understanding science?

A second example concerns Piaget's studies into the growth of logical thinking. Piaget used physical science contexts to study how young people explained phenomena and described how their explanations changed with age. Piaget proposed a stage theory of cognitive development, which, in recent decades, has driven much research in science education. Stage theory has been used to guide curriculum development, such as Science 5–13 in the UK (Schools Council, 1972) and to direct pedagogy (Schools Council, 1977). Piaget's work stressed the importance of personal experience in learning and contributed to the growth of child-centred learning.

A major study begun in the 1970s provided a description of primary and secondary pupils' grasp of science in terms of Piaget's stages of development (Adey and Shayer, 1981). The findings revealed differences in cognitive skills used by an able minority and the larger pool of 'average' pupils. These national studies provided a means of describing pupils' development in learning school science and suggested an instrument with which to analyse the cognitive demand of science curriculum material (Shayer, 1978); cf Nuffield Combined Science described earlier.

Stage theory, together with the ideas of Vygotsky and Feuerstein, has been used to promote improved learning in pupils. This research may have far-reaching consequences for science teaching (Adey and Shayer, 1994). The 'Cognitive Acceleration in Science' Project (CASE) has shown that pupils could be taught 'thinking skills' that would allow them to engage with curriculum material hitherto thought beyond them. By promoting thinking and providing contexts in which self-confidence can blossom, pupils demonstrated improved cognitive skills. An equally exciting outcome is that this effect appears to be long lasting and influences pupil performance in other curriculum subjects. Teaching thinking is now part of the remit of all NC subjects to teach key skills.

Stage theory has attracted much discussion and has stimulated wider research in science education and beyond. It is not so much the results of Piagetian studies that are in dispute as is their interpretation. Piaget's claim that the stages of development are biologically controlled has been questioned, particularly the implication that development is dependent on age and physical maturation. Other researchers have focused on the importance of experiential learning and some have argued that it is the prior experiences of pupils that are important determinants in learning. Pupils from educationally and culturally poor backgrounds can be disadvantaged in school unless steps are taken to address those deficiencies, which is one of the CASE objectives.

The final example concerns children's explanations of scientific phenomena. The importance of prior knowledge, of both facts and explanations, has been central to much research since the 1980s, both in the UK and overseas (Driver et al, 1994). This work has focused on children's explanations of the natural world and revealed how explanations generated from out-of-school experiences interact with taught science. An important outcome has been the wider realization that pupils are not empty vessels and, arising from their out-of-school experiences, have functionally adequate explanations for many phenomena. These explanations, or alternative constructs, may be in conflict with accepted science and can be resistant to teaching, that is, alternative explanations may persist after leaving school.

These findings suggest that science teaching has not created powerful enough conflicts between scientific explanations and common-sense ones; many pupils are not persuaded that a scientific explanation of events is better than their own. This reminds us that teaching is not telling but so much more. Recent reports of school inspections (OFSTED, 2000) say that pupils do not progress in science as expected in their first three years in secondary school, that repetition of KS2 work creates problems of motivation, and the report suggests that an inadequate account is taken by teachers of pupils' prior experiences and the successful work of primary teachers.

This work on children's alternative constructs has moved on to consider the communication between teacher and pupil. By being aware of children's own conceptions of events, teachers are more ready to listen to what children say and be sensitive to their views. In recent years the focus has switched to a study of the ways in which pupils explain things – their reasoning – and to a study of the dialogue between pupil and teacher. In the second example classroom interactions have been analysed to reveal the ways that teachers explain ideas. This work has shown how teachers use different strategies to help pupils understand scientific ideas. Teachers use, for example, demonstrations, spoken language and body language in different ways to transform scientific knowledge into effective pedagogy (Ogborn *et al*, 1996).

Concluding remarks

A major task for the future is to identify the knowledge, skills and attitudes we value in science and identify those that can contribute to general education. This set of knowledge, skills and attitudes can be used to help identify purposes for our science teaching. Once established the content and its assessment can follow. This course of action may lead us to reassess the purposes of A level; but is it necessary to teach academic science to 11-year-olds in order that they may study science at university at 19 years of age?

Turning to teacher education, the standards set for Qualified Teacher Status are specified at too detailed a level and many skills are unlikely to be achieved in a one-year course. More importantly, some skills are too subtle to be simply achieved, or not achieved, and so 'reaching standards' may represent an unhelpful way of discussing teacher progress.

The shift from a discipline-based approach to teacher education to a problem-solving approach does not eliminate the educational disciplines from teacher education but situates them differently. The current model of teacher education tends to marginalize the educational disciplines by placing practice above theory. This policy may deny many student teachers the benefits of research and scholarship of science education (some of which we have cited above) and limit the quality of their teaching.

Partnership with schools has been a significant gain enabling science tutors and teachers to clarify their roles and work together, although there is some way to go. However, schools are not required to provide places for student teachers or enter into initial teacher education programmes. Consequently partnership arrangements are difficult to maintain at the levels required to meet student needs. Schools and IHE need to be staffed and funded in recognition of their new roles.

The challenges of the new century to both primary and secondary phases of schooling include seeking answers to questions such as these:

- What type of science is appropriate for young children and those in adolescence?
- How can we best harness the natural curiosity of pupils to enable them to engage in scientific dialogue and maintain that interest throughout the compulsory years of schooling?
- What scientific knowledge and skills do teachers require to teach young children?
- How can we enhance teachers' knowledge and skills and encourage positive attitudes to science through both initial teacher education and in-service teacher education?
- In what ways can research in science education be used to encourage teachers to make links between theory and practice and to promote reflection on that practice?
- Can we maintain a healthy research agenda in science education and persuade others of its importance?

These questions are not new. They have been asked before but they now relate to all pupils and their teachers. Communication today is faster and more flexible; information access, retrieval and storage are available now in a manner hitherto unimagined and this situation may necessitate a rethink of what knowledge, skills and attitudes we ought to develop in young people. We need to empower young people to ask questions about science and to feel it is legitimate to exercise their curiosity in this way. Research has provided a better knowledge base and theoretical underpinning on which to plan pedagogy. How can science teaching contribute to an improved vision of education in these new and changing conditions?

Acknowledgement

We are most grateful to our colleague Dr Jenny Frost for reading and commenting on this chapter.

Abbreviations used

APSSM	Association of Public School Science Masters (later SMA)
APU	Assessment of Performance Unit
ASE	Association for Science Education (see SMA/AWST)
AST	Association of Science Teachers, later AWST
AWST	Association of Women Science Teachers (later incorporated in ASE)
BAAS	British Association for the Advancement of Science
CSE	Certificate of Secondary Education
DES	Department of Education and Science (later DfEE)
DfEE	Department for Education and Employment
GCE	General Certificate of Education
GCSE	General Certificate of Secondary Education
HMI	Her Majesty's Inspectorate
IHE	Institutions of higher education
ILEA	Inner London Education Authority
INSET	In-service teacher education
LEA	Local education authority
MoE	Ministry of Education (later DES)
NF	Nuffield Foundation
NSTP	Nuffield Science Teaching Project
PGCE	Postgraduate Certificate in Education
QTS	Qualified Teacher Status
RS	Royal Society
SAT	Standard Assessment Tasks
SC	Schools Council
SCISP	Schools Council Integrated Science Project
SMA	Science Masters' Association (later incorporated in ASE)
TGAT	Task Group on Assessment and Testing
TTA	Teacher Training Agency
WO	Welsh Office

References

Adey, P and Shayer, M (1981) *Towards a Science of Science Teaching*, Heinemann, London

Adey, P and Shayer, M (1994) *Really Raising Standards: Cognitive intervention and academic achievement*, Routledge, London

Assessment of Performance Unit (APU) (1985) *Science at Age 15*, Report 1, Department of Education and Science (DES), London

Association for Science Education (ASE) (1979) *Alternatives for Science Education*, ASE, Hatfield

ASE (1981) *Education through Science*, ASE, Hatfield

Association of Public School Science Masters (APSSM) (1916) *The Aims of Science Teaching in General Education and 'Science for All'* (see also *School Science Review*, **2** (6), pp 203–04)

Association of Women Science Teachers and Science Masters Association (AWST/ SMA) (1953) *Secondary Modern Science Teaching*, Part 1, John Murray, London

AWST/SMA (1957) *Secondary Modern Science Teaching*, Part 2, John Murray, London

AWST/SMA (1961) *Science and Education: A policy statement*, John Murray, London

Black, P and Wiliam, D (1998) *Inside the Black Box: Raising standards through classroom assessment*, School of Education, King's College, London

Board of Education (1937) *Handbook of Suggestions for Teachers* (reprinted 1947), HMSO, London

Booth, N (1975) The impact of science teaching projects on secondary education, *Education in Science*, **63** (June), pp 27–30

Central Advisory Council for Education, England (1963) *Half Our Future* (The Newsom Report), HMSO, London (addressed the needs of the majority of pupils in schools)

Connell, L and James, W S (1958) General science today, *School Science Review*, **39**, p 138

Consortium for Assessment and Testing in Schools (CATS) (1992) *CATS Science at Key Stage 3: Pilot 1991*, report and appendices, unpublished

Department for Education and Employment (DfEE) (1998) *Teaching: High status, high standards*, DfEE, London

Department of Education and Science (DES) (1967) *Children and their Primary Schools* (The Plowden Report), HMSO, London

DfEE and Qualifications and Curriculum Authority (QCA) (1999) *The National Curriculum for England: Science, Key Stages 1–4*, DfEE, London

Department of Education and Science (DES) (1965) *Circular 10/65: The organisation of secondary schools*, HMSO, London (comprehensive reorganization)

DES (1978) *Primary Education in England: A survey by HMI*, HMSO, London

DES (1979) *Aspects of Secondary Education: A survey by HMI*, HMSO, London

DES (1984a) *All Our Futures* (The Swann Report), HMSO, London

DES (1984b) *Criteria for the Accreditation of Courses of Initial Teacher Education*, DES, London (realized through CATE, the Council for the Accreditation of Teacher Education)

DES (1985) *Science 5–16: A statement of policy*, HMSO, London

DES (1988) *National Curriculum: Task group on assessment and testing*, a report, HMSO, London

DES (1989) *National Assessment: Science at age 13, a review of APU findings 1980–84*, HMSO, London

DES and the Welsh Office (WO) (1988) *Science for Ages 5–16: Proposals of the Secretary of State for Education and Science and the Secretary of State for Wales*, HMSO, London

DES and the Welsh Office (WO) (1989) *Science in the National Curriculum*, HMSO, London

DES/WO (1991) *Science for Ages Five to Sixteen*, HMSO, London

DES/WO (1995) *Science in the National Curriculum*, HMSO, London

Donnelly, J F (2000) Secondary science teaching under the National Curriculum, *School Science Review*, **81** (296), pp 27–35

Driver, R *et al* (eds) (1994) *Making Sense of Secondary Science*, Routledge for the Open University, London

Gagnè, R M (1965) *The Conditions of Learning*, Holt, Rinehart and Winston, New York

Hall, W (1973) *Schools Council Integrated Science Project, Teachers' Handbook* (known as *Patterns* and *SCISP*), Longman, Harlow

Harlen, W (1992) In defence of AT1: scientific investigations, *Primary Science Review*, **21**, Association for Science Education, Hatfield

Harlen, W, Black, P and Johnson, S (1981) *Science in Schools, Age 11*, report 1, HMSO, London (report on the 1980 survey of science performance of pupils aged 11 in primary and middle schools)

Her Majesty's Inspectorate (HMI) (1980) Girls and science, *HMI Series: Matters for Discussion*, 13, HMSO, London

Hofstein, A (1988) Practical work and science education 2, in *Development and Dilemma in Science Education*, ed P Fensham, The Falmer Press, London

Ingle, R and Jennings, A (1981) Science in schools: which way now?, *Studies in Education*, 8, Institute of Education, University of London, London

Jenkins, E (1979) *From Armstrong to Nuffield*, John Murray, London

Jennings, A (1992) National Curriculum science: so near and yet so far, *The London File*, Institute of Education, University of London, London

Klainin, S (1988) Practical work and science education 1, in *Development and Dilemma in Science Education*, ed P Fensham, The Falmer Press, London

Lauwerys, J A (1934) *Education and Biology*, a pamphlet, Institute of Education, University of London, London

Lauwerys, J A (1937) General science, *School Science Review*, **18** (12), p 471

Layton, D (1984) *Interpreters of Science: A history of the Association for Science Education*, John Murray, London

Loundes, G A N (1954) *The British Educational System*, Hutchinson University Library, London

McGuiness, C (1999) From thinking skills to thinking classrooms: a review and evaluation of approaches for developing pupils' thinking, *Research Report No 115*, DfEE, HMSO, Norwich

Michell, M (1987) *Secondary Science Curriculum Review: Better science – curriculum guide 1, key proposals*, Heinemann, London

Millar, R (1996) Towards a science for public understanding, *School Science Review*, **77** (280), pp 7–18

Millar, R and Osborne, J (1998) *Beyond Science 2000: A report with ten recommendations*, King's College School of Education, London

Millar, R *et al* (1994) Investigation in the school science laboratory: conceptual and procedural knowledge and their influence on performance, *Research Papers in Education*, **9** (2), pp 207–48

Ministry of Education (MoE) (1960) *Science in Secondary Schools*, HMSO, London

Misselbrook, H (organizer) (1969) *Nuffield Secondary Science*, The Longman Group, London (comprises eight themes, teachers' guide, apparatus guide, text 'examining at CSE' and some pupil booklets)

Monk, M and Osborne, J (2000) *Good Practice in Science Teaching: What research has to say*, Open University Press, Buckingham

Newsom Report: see Central Advisory Council for Education, England, 1963

Nuffield Combined Science (NCS) (1970) *Teachers' Guides 1–3*, Longman, London

Nuffield Science 13–16 (1981) *Teachers' Handbook*, Longman Resources Unit, Harlow

OFSTED (2000) *Annual Report of Her Majesty's Chief Inspector of Schools, 1998/99*, HMSO, London

Ogborn, J (1986) Science and the rationality system, in *School Curriculum Planning*, ed D Lawton, Hodder & Stoughton, London

Ogborn, J and Macaskill, C (1996) Science and technology, *School Science Review*, **77** (281), pp 55–61

Ogborn, J *et al* (1996) *Explaining Science in the Classroom*, The Open University Press, Buckingham

Patterns: see Hall, W (1973)

Power, C (1990) Policy issues in science education: an international perspective, in *Policy Issues and School Science Education*, ed E Jenkins, Centre for Studies in Science and Mathematics Education, Leeds University, Leeds

Royal Society (1982) *Science Education 11–18 in England and Wales*, Royal Society, London

Schools Council (1965) *Science for the Young School Leaver*, Schools Council, London

Schools Council (1972) *Science 5–13: With objectives in mind*, MacDonald Educational, London

Schools Council (1977) *Progress in Learning Science Project*: Match and mismatch; Raising questions; Leader's guide; Fitting learning experiences in science to development for 5 to 13 year olds, Schools Council, London

Science 5–16: see DES, 1985

Science Masters Association (SMA) (1936) *The Teaching of General Science*, Part 1, John Murray, London

SMA (1938) *The Teaching of General Science*, Part 2, John Murray, London

Science Teachers Joint Sub-Committee (representing the Association of Teachers in Training Colleges and Lecturers in Departments of Education, the AWST, the

SMA and the London Association of Science Teachers) (1959) *Science in the Primary School,* John Murray, London

Scottish Education Department (1969) Science for general education, *Curriculum Paper,* 7, HMSO

Shayer, M (1978) Nuffield Combined Science: do the pupils understand it?, *School Science Review,* **211** (December), pp 210–23

Thompson, G (1991) *Only a Teacher? An inquiry into science teacher provision,* report of a joint working party of the ASE, BAAS and RS, Association for Science Education, Hatfield

Thorp, S, Deshpande, P and Edwards, C (1994) *Race, Equality and Science Teaching: A handbook for teachers and educators,* Association for Science Education, Hatfield

Van Praagh, G (ed) (1973) *H.E. Armstrong and Science Education,* John Murray, London

Waring, M (1979) Background to Nuffield Science, *History of Education,* **8** (3), pp 223–37

Watson, R, Goldsworthy, A and Wood-Robinson, V (1999) What is not fair with investigations?, *School Science Review,* **80** (292), pp 101–06

Woolnough, B and Allsop, T (1985) *Practical Work in Science,* Cambridge University Press, Cambridge

Chapter 4

What should history be?

Alaric Dickinson

Introduction

> Perhaps the hardest battle I fought on the national curriculum was about
> history. Though not an historian myself, I had a very clear – and I had naïvely
> imagined uncontroversial – idea of what history was. History is an account of
> what happened in the past. Learning history, therefore, requires knowledge of
> events… I was, therefore, very concerned when in December 1988 I received
> [Secretary of State] Ken Baker's written proposals for the teaching of history
> and the composition of the History Working Group on the curriculum…
> His initial names included the author of the definitive work on the 'New
> History' which, with its emphasis on concepts rather than chronology and
> empathy rather than facts, was at the root of so much that was going wrong.
> Ken saw my point and made some changes. But that was only the beginning
> of the argument.
>
> (Thatcher, 1993: 595–96)

This extract from Prime Minister Margaret Thatcher's memoirs provides
evidence of a high level of political interference in the curriculum, and the
depth of controversy in the late 20th century about the nature of school
history and what history should contribute to the education of young people.

In the 20th century three traditions of history teaching hugely influenced
what happened in classrooms. In the first half of the century there was
widespread acceptance and support for what, in the words of Sylvester (1996:
9), might be called 'a great tradition'. The main features of this approach
were fixed by 1900, promulgated in a series of Board of Education publications and widely accepted throughout the first half of the 20th century. By
the 1960s, however, confidence in this approach was waning. In the 1970s

and 1980s a new philosophy and approach, loosely termed 'new history', achieved ever-increasing support among teachers. The 'new history' emphasized thinking as well as memory and learning something of the nature of historical enquiry as well as acquiring factual knowledge. However, this 'new history' was based on a contested redefinition of school history and had different meanings for different groups. After the passage of the 1988 Education Reform Act authorizing the introduction of a national curriculum in England, Wales and Northern Ireland, heated debates ensued about what should be included in National Curriculum history.

Is National Curriculum history, first taught in schools in 1991 and revised in 1995 and 1999 (DES, 1995; DfEE/QCA, 1999), likely to achieve the longevity of the 'great tradition' or the popularity with teachers of 'new history'? To what extent has there been continuity as well as change in curriculum development in history? Who and what influenced these developments substantially? What are the main ongoing challenges, and what further developments seem most appropriate? This chapter endeavours to offer answers to these questions. It begins by considering the main characteristics of the three traditions. The second section provides evidence of non-governmental contributions to curriculum development in history, past and present. Finally, ongoing challenges and appropriate ways forward for school history are considered in a section concerned with the future of history in schools.

Changing traditions in history teaching

'A great tradition'

For two-thirds of the 20th century a particular philosophy and approach dominated history teaching in England, and to some extent Wales, Northern Ireland and Scotland. The ideas underpinning that tradition were evident in a series of Board of Education publications. For example, *Suggestions for the Consideration of Teachers and Others Concerned in the Work of Public Elementary Schools* contained clear pronouncements on history teaching, such as the following: 'A further and most important reason for teaching history is that it is, to a certain extent, a record of the influence for good or for evil exercised by great personalities. No one would dispute that our scholars should have examples put before them, whether for imitation or the reverse, of the great men and women that have lived in the past' (Board of Education, 1905: 61).

Evidence of the durability of this reason for teaching history can be found in the decision of so many teachers to include a study of 20th-century dictators in courses for GCSE and A level. It can be argued that it is also evident in Prime Minister Blair's recent announcement of an annual Holocaust Memorial Day in which he said, 'I hope it will be a day when we reflect and remember and give our commitment and pledge that the terrible and evil deeds done in our world should never be repeated.' This and other recent proposals to mark the inhumanity of humans to humans in the 20th century make the Board of Education's 1905 suggestions seem very poignant. They also provide evidence of some continuity in ideas about history in education.

Other key assumptions underpinning 'great tradition' history were that pupils should learn something about their nationality, become aware of their rights and duties and how they had arisen, and achieve an accurate framework of events and outstanding people. Methodology, syllabus content and assessment were also clear cut. In the words of Sylvester:

> The history teacher's role was didactively active; it was to give pupils the facts of historical knowledge and to ensure, through repeated short tests, that they had learned them. The pupil's role was passive; history was a 'received subject'. The body of knowledge to be taught was also clearly defined. It was mainly political history with some social and economic aspects, and it was mainly British history, with some European, from Julius Caesar to 1914.

> (Sylvester, 1996: 9)

Eventually this approach was widely criticized, including the complaint that too little emphasis was placed on making history interesting. Ironically the Board's *Report on the Teaching of History* criticized 'the dry and excessive drill in dates and names... which distinguished the history methods of our grandparents' and told teachers, 'it is necessary to recognise that there is no conflict between this accurate framework of events and the right desire to make history a living, social and interesting thing' (Board of Education, 1923: 13). However, by the beginning of the second half of the 20th century 'great tradition' history was under attack on this and other points.

'New history'

In the 1960s and 1970s there was growing concern about what was seen as excessive emphasis on factual learning and insufficient attention to making history intelligible and interesting to pupils. By the late 1970s and early 1980s history teaching in England was being influenced increasingly by a new philosophy and approach. The most important driving force for change was the feeling that school history should require thinking as well as memory.

This, and Bruner's challenge that teachers should teach understanding of the basic ideas and structure of a subject (Bruner, 1960: Chapter 2), led teachers to look for ways in which history could be given a more rigorous structure, something that might provide a basis for progression in children's understanding of history, as opposed to the aggregation of historical facts or the memorizing of accounts. Shemilt (1980), in a seminal publication arising from the Schools Council History 13–16 Project, argued that pupils cannot be said to 'know' anything until they have grasped something of the nature of historical enquiry, and that understanding the present requires not only knowledge of the past but also a grasp of the fundamental concepts of history (Shemilt, 1980: 6). Adolescents, Shemilt urged, should learn something of the logic of history and the meaning of such concepts as evidence, empathetic reconstruction, causation, change and continuity.

The project's justification for history as a secondary school subject varied in important respects from that of the 'great tradition'. It emphasized the value of history as a means of acquiring and developing cognitive skills, a source of leisure interest and a vehicle for analysing the contemporary world and pupils' place within it. It also emphasized the value of history as an avenue to self-knowledge and awareness of what it means to be human through the study of the lives and beliefs of people very different from oneself, and 'as a means for developing understanding of the forces underlying social change and evolution' (Shemilt, 1980: 2).

The value of school history in providing pupils with lessons they should learn was emphasized in both 'great tradition' and 'new' history, but the lessons were very different. The former stressed that history provided pupils with examples of past behaviour to be imitated or avoided. The lessons that Shemilt (1980: 3) thought adolescents needed to learn included the following: while society can always be changed, there are limits to what it can be changed into; the way people see and judge things is conditioned by the society within which they live; and the social world is the outcome of the unintended as well as the intended consequences of action.

Two further significant differences in the two traditions were that the 'new history' advocated pupil participation in learning in all parts of the history syllabus and argued the case for replacing the traditional, chronological syllabus with a course structure that was discontinuous and encouraged a wide variety of options. The History 13–16 syllabus for CSE and O level, for example, consisted of an introductory course on history as a 'form of knowledge' plus four independent sections (fieldwork on a selected topic; an enquiry in depth; a modern world study; and a study in development). The most far-reaching changes in this 'new' history, however, were those concerned with developing children's understanding of history as a discipline.

The philosophy and other details of the History 13–16 Project were increasingly applied by teachers to their work with pupils of other ages. Some of these teachers pressed the changes too far, treating substantive content as a mere vehicle for developing concepts and skills. Critics of 'new history' expressed particular concern about this and about encouraging pupils to 'empathize with their forebears' and what they saw as an abandonment of chronology in the discontinuous course structure of History 13–16 and other 'new history' syllabuses. When the Education Reform Act of 1988 required the creation of a national curriculum, teachers waited to see how much of the thinking of the 'new history' would be enshrined in the new curriculum.

National Curriculum history

The interim and final reports of the History Working Group and the comments and proposals of the prime minister and the secretary of state for education showed the influence of different sets of ideas about school history. The prime minister strongly criticized the *Interim Report of the History Working Group* (DES, 1989): 'I was appalled. It put the emphasis on interpretation and enquiry as against content and knowledge. There was insufficient weight given to British history. There was not enough emphasis on history as chronological study... In particular, I wanted to see a clearly set out chronological framework for the whole history curriculum' (Thatcher, 1993: 596).

The secretary of state echoed the prime minister's concerns, calling for more emphasis upon chronology, British history, historical knowledge and its assessment. In their *Final Report*, the History Working Group stressed that their overall objective had been to design a course of history for pupils from the ages of 5 to 16 that gave *equal* weight to knowledge, understanding and skills (DES, 1990: Section 2.10).

The secretary of state's requirements, published in *History in the National Curriculum: England* (DES, 1991), set out the basic content for school history, but left teachers to turn the statutory programmes of study into schemes of work for classroom teaching. Another important feature was the attempt to achieve a balance regarding the importance of achieving detailed factual knowledge and developing pupils' understanding of history as a discipline. This was evident in, for example, the three specified attainment targets: knowledge and understanding of history, interpretations of history, and the use of historical sources. These attainment targets were couched in terms of second-order understandings, not in terms of content, but the introduction to each of them stressed the need for pupils to demonstrate their knowledge of the historical content in the programmes of study in achieving each level of attainment. Similarly each study unit was required to provide opportunities for the development of knowledge, understanding and skills necessary for each of the attainment targets.

The fact that each of the attainment targets (three in 1991, a single one incorporating the previous three from 1995 onwards) was broken down into sets of statements of attainment, or levels, meant an emphasis on progression in learning. Furthermore, the wording of the statements meant that attainment was to be assessed in terms of key elements of the discipline, not simply aggregation of knowledge. This was made more overt in the 1995 version where the key elements were listed for each key stage under five headings: chronology, range and depth of historical knowledge and understanding, interpretations of history, historical enquiry, and organization and communication. In the 1999 version (to be implemented from September 2000 onwards) the five headings were retained and used in listing what pupils should be taught, though the term 'key elements' was not used.

This use of sets of statements of attainment, summarized as levels, reflected the changes in history teaching during the previous 15 years, and the even more rapid developments in assessing history since the mid-1980s. For many years examinations had rewarded discrete items of content, and allowed only one or two marks out of 20 for historical understanding (see Figure 4.1). These examinations had been replaced by an assessment system in which candidates had to demonstrate their historical understanding and in so doing show an appropriate knowledge of content (see Figure 4.2). Experience would tell to what extent National Curriculum history would lead to the achievement of a better balance of factual detail and understanding in public examinations as well as school history.

Future developments would also tell how influential several other requirements would prove to be. One of these was the seemingly very demanding requirement that pupils in Key Stage 3, in their study of local, British, European and world history, should be taught about history from a variety of perspectives including political, religious, social, cultural, aesthetic, economic, technological and scientific (DfEE/QCA, 1999: Key Stage 3, Section 6). Another potentially influential requirement was that pupils in each key stage should be given opportunities to apply and develop ICT capability in all subjects and also to develop knowledge, understanding and skills related to several cross-curricular themes – including citizenship.

Whether National Curriculum history will achieve the longevity of the 'great tradition' and popularity with teachers of 'new history' will depend on many factors, including its ability to adapt successfully to challenges, new ideas and opportunities. Politicians, government agencies and examining boards will continue to exercise considerable influence on what is done in classrooms, but the potential contribution of other groups to curriculum

---

Instructions on marking

Ticks

Examiners must always make clear the point where a mark is awarded within an answer. Thus in each answer a tick should be placed accurately and boldly in the body of the answer at the point where a mark is awarded. One tick should normally be regarded as the awarding of one mark; where this is not so, the discrepancy should be explained. Team leaders cannot accept marking where there is no clear relationship between the number of ticks, the sub-totals and the final mark for an answer.

Structured questions (essay answers)

1 or 2 marks may be allowed for a suitable introduction or conclusion. The same 1 or 2 (not a further 1 or 2) may be used for suitable material outside the date limits or for suitable supplementary material appropriately introduced, or as a bonus to an answer that shows signs of really good historical under-standing. Examiners are urged not to search for the possibility of awarding such mark(s).

Figure 4.1   *Extracts from the history marking scheme, GCE Ordinary level, June 1977, University of London General Certificate of Education*

development and raising standards also needs to be realized and utilized. From the good practice and aspirations of history teachers will come examples of successful teaching and learning that can help and inspire others. From writers and publishers, researchers, subject associations and other providers can come support in ideas and resources to enable further achievements in curriculum development and raising standards. The next section sketches how contributions from sources other than politicians and government agencies have influenced developments in history teaching hitherto.

Non-governmental influences on development

Non-governmental as well as governmental influences stimulated and helped shape developments in history teaching throughout the 20th century. Many more individuals than it is possible to name here – historians, researchers, teacher trainers, producers of resources and, above all, teachers – influenced principles underpinning school history, syllabus revision, and advances in methodology, resources and assessment. Keatinge (1910; Keatinge and Frazer,

---

Question

When people like those shown in Source G¹ were not cured, they often followed the King around, being touched over and over again. Why did people living in the Middle Ages still believe in cures like this, even if they did not work?

Mark scheme

Level 1

Explanation from the outside. Reference to concrete historical factors. Believed in supernatural cures because lived in a religious age. **(1–3 marks)**

Level 2

Explanation from the inside. Everyday empathy, because genuine attempt to show royal touch could have seemed reasonable to people at the time, but reconstruction remains locked in twentieth-century world view. No attempt to recreate an alien form of life, or way of thinking, ie 'people desperate and had nothing to lose, because no alternative recourse'. **(4–6 marks)**

Level 3

Explanation from the outside – historical empathy. Attempt to show how belief in royal touch was reasonable to the medieval mind. Genuine attempt to shed twentieth-century preconceptions and to recreate alien world view. Disease the reward of sin; cure signals forgiveness; forgiveness must be merited; following king around may be thought of as a penance. **(7–10 marks)**

¹Source G was a picture from a 13th-century manuscript showing Edward the Confessor touching for 'scrofula'. Scrofula was probably a tuberculosis-type infection; it showed itself in multiple ulcers and swellings. This was the third of four questions based upon three sources (two written, one picture), which together counted for 40 marks..

Figure 4.2 *Mark scheme for a question from the Southern Examining Group GCSE specimen paper, 1988*

1920) advocated the use of sources in teaching history and won some support for his ideas more than half a century before the use of sources became common practice in classrooms in the United Kingdom. Happold (1928) indicated ways in which pupils might become active learners rather than passive participants of history more than 40 years before this approach became a tenet of 'new history'. Syllabus construction was influenced in the 1930s and later by Walker (1935), who argued for the inclusion of local history, and Jeffreys (1939) who advocated the 'line of development' principle of selection. Jeffreys, a lecturer at the University of London Institute of Education, believed that pupils should travel down the ages looking at a particular aspect of life at a time, for example agriculture, transport, writing and medicine. The principles underlying Jeffrey's suggestions were made clear in his advocacy. 'The value of the study', he wrote, 'consists in the cultivation of a "historical sense" rather than in the acquisition of a body of factual knowledge', and 'The subject-matter must be intelligible and interesting to the pupil' (Jeffreys, 1939: 8, 33).

Marjorie Reeves, creator of the *Then and There* series in the 1950s (see Reeves, 1954), and Carpenter (1964) of the Cambridge Institute of Education also supported the need for pupils to achieve understanding as well as knowledge. They, however, stressed the importance of in-depth studies of eras or 'patches' of history. Local history continued to have strong advocates, including Douch (1967), and world history featured in more and more syllabuses in the 1960s (DES, 1967; Henderson, 1968). Examining boards supported developments in world history with new GCE syllabuses that attracted a quickly rising candidature. Evidence of the long-lasting influence of some principles and practices advocated by Keatinge, Jeffreys, Reeves and others was to be found in the structure and syllabus content of the History 13–16 course, *vide* the five segments of the course – 'What is History?', 'History Around Us', a study in development, an enquiry in depth and a modern world study.

In the 1950s and 1960s various historians were involved in developments in the study of history that were to prove influential on history in schools as well as on professional historians. Throughout the period 1900–39 most British history was produced by non-professional historians for a non-professional audience. In the post-war period, seminal works by professional historians included Elton's *The Tudor Revolution in Government* (1953), Hill's *The Century of Revolution 1603–1714* (1961), Briggs's *Victorian People* (1954), Thompson's *The Making of the English Working Class* (1963), and Stone's *The Crisis of the Aristocracy 1558–1641* (1965). These and other scholars retold the story of Britain's past. In the words of Cannadine:

> This account stressed that Britain's past was unique only in being first rather than in being totally unusual: it began modern state building in the sixteenth century, it instigated the first modern, bourgeois revolution in the seventeenth, it generated the first instance of modern economic growth in the eighteenth, and it became the first modern urban society in the nineteenth. The extraordinary pioneer had become the prototypical exemplar.

> (Cannadine, 1987)

With hindsight this period was seen as a golden age of British history and British historians. Their interpretation was coherent; their books proved appealing to a wide audience and inspired many teachers and A level students. The ferment of new ideas and approaches also encouraged developments in economic, urban, social and family history, a considerable increase in the number of university-employed practitioners, and a massive proliferation of PhD-inspired scholarship. These developments and the work of the History Workshop with its attention to 'history from below', particularly to working-class, local and women's history, advanced understanding significantly. However, it also led to many historians becoming more concerned about scholarly techniques and the increasingly introverted debates of separate subspecialisms than the needs of a wider audience. Very significantly for school history, the challenge to the traditional supremacy of political history brought into question the central and agreed themes that had long provided structural coherence to courses.

Mary Price's article 'History in danger' (1968) was published at a time when confidence in a long-established approach to school history was also being affected by educational changes. Interest in Piaget's work led to new concerns about the limitations of pupils' thinking and the implications for history teaching and history's place in the curriculum. The Plowden Report suggested that primary schoolchildren should study 'topics such as exploration which link history and geography' (Central Advisory Council for Education, 1967: 226). At the secondary level too there was discussion of the advantages or otherwise of studying history as a single subject or within an interrelated or integrated humanities scheme, and also of the relative importance of studying different aspects of history. In 'History in danger', Price reviewed the educational changes of the 1960s and concluded that history was losing out as a subject in its own right with the growth of social studies, civics and integrated humanities courses.

Price's article was condemned by some as unrealistically pessimistic, but it showed how a brief article could prove very influential. Her suggestion that there should be a periodical that would act as a forum for ideas and experiment led to the publication of *Teaching History*, a periodical published twice a year (later quarterly) by The Historical Association. The first edition was published in May 1969 and *Teaching History* has continued to provide an influential forum of the kind envisaged by Price. Her article may also indirectly have influenced the funding of a major curriculum development project. In 'History in danger', Price noted that the Schools Council did not seem interested in sponsoring a history project; in 1972 it awarded a grant of £126,000 for such a proposal. The proposal was for a project that would 'help teachers to reconsider the place of history within the changing curriculum' and 'provide stimulus, support and materials to help them revitalize their own practice in general and more particularly help them to encourage more pupil participation in their study of history' (Schools Council History 13–16 Project, 1976: 8).

The History 13–16 Project benefited in its formative years very considerably from the directorship of Sylvester (1972–75), Boddington (1975–77) and then Shemilt. They stressed that the project was a way of helping teachers to help themselves. Furthermore, they focused the project on examining current good practice together with considering the nature of history and its place in secondary schools, the design of a syllabus framework that showed the uses that history could have in the education of adolescents, and setting up experimental O level and CSE examinations for pupils aged 16. In addition they ensured that both the practical details and the philosophy of the project were disseminated widely and effectively. It was also of benefit to the project that the central team could draw upon much good practice and experimentation, including attempts to relate history teaching to the objectives examined by Coltham and Fines (1971) and resources that provided opportunities for pupils to work with documents in the classroom. The first archive teaching unit emanating from the University of Newcastle Department of Education under the editorship of Tyson, published in 1968 on the theme of coals from Newcastle, set a standard that other producers sought to emulate. Also influential was the decision by the Schools History Project (SHP), after Schools Council funding had ceased, to support teachers through a network providing information bulletins, publications and conferences.

Less direct was the impact of ideas stimulated in the 1960s by Carr's *What is History?* (1961), Elton's *The Practice of History* (1967), and later by Tosh's *The Pursuit of History* (1991) and the polemical postmodern discussions of history by Jenkins (1991, 1995). Carr's book raised important questions about the discipline of history and led to more systematic thinking than hitherto about the implications of the nature of history for teaching and learning in schools. Elton's disagreements with Carr and his emphatic views on the discipline of history achieved a considerable reaction. Some teachers found Kitson Clark's *The Critical Historian* (1967) more helpful, particularly his excellent discussion of the relation between history and evidence.

The views of historians influenced the thinking of many entrants to the teaching profession, as also did those of Burston, whose *Principles of History Teaching* (1963) was the first systematic attempt to relate certain features of history as a specific kind of enquiry to the teaching and learning of history in schools. Burston emphasized that history teachers need a clear conception of their discipline since at every level, from the choice of teaching method to the construction of a syllabus, problems arise from the nature of historical thinking itself. Burston, whose approach was more important than the particular views he advocated, influenced many who studied and worked under him at the University of London Institute of Education. This influence was particularly evident in two edited collections of articles, Burston and Thompson's *Studies in the Nature and Teaching of History* (1967) and Dickinson and Lee's *History Teaching and Historical Understanding* (1978).

In the 1970s and 1980s the writings of Rogers, Shemilt and Lee proved particularly influential in the search for ways in which history could be given a more rigorous structure than hitherto and for something that might provide a sound basis for progression in pupils' understanding of history. Rogers (1979) sought to apply Bruner's ideas about learning and instruction to the teaching and learning of history. A rigorous thinker, he accepted Bruner's psychology but not his views on history. Rogers regarded history as an autonomous discipline, offered suggestions for a spiral curriculum for history, and subjected the 'new' history to constructive, critical scrutiny:

> In what sense, if any, can pupils become 'mini-historians' and at what age or ability level? What does this mean – in what activities would the children have to engage to fulfil this programme? Why is it desirable? Is it? That these and other questions remain unresolved is due (it is suggested) to the failure to provide an adequate answer to the fundamental epistemological question – namely, 'What is historical knowledge?'. It is only in terms of an answer to this question (if at all) that the concept 'New' History can be clarified.
>
> (Rogers, 1979: Introduction)

Rogers sought to answer the question 'What is historical knowledge?' in terms of the conceptual, propositional ('know that') and procedural ('know how') characteristics of history. His ideas influenced many teachers and teacher trainers, and also researchers who were reacting against the Piagetian framework of investigation into pupils' thinking (particularly Booth, 1983, 1987) and moving to the investigation of pupils' understanding of second-order concepts such as evidence, cause and empathy, which appeared to offer a way of picking out what was different about history (Lee, 1978; Shemilt, 1980, 1987; Dickinson and Lee, 1984; and Ashby and Lee, 1987). Meanwhile the research and writings of West (1981) and Joan Blyth (1982) aided developments in primary schools, and the influence of John Slater was evident in *History in the Secondary and Primary Years* (DES, 1985). Clear and perceptive, it achieved its aims of stimulating reflection on the role of history in the curriculum and offering guidelines for improving practice.

The advent of the National Curriculum meant that a relatively decentralized system was replaced by common programmes of study and common assessment targets. Phillips (1998) has provided a full and illuminating account of the making and impact of National Curriculum history, examining the politics of what became known as 'the great history debate' and claiming that the debates about the aims and purpose of history are closely connected with future visions of Britishness. The changes introduced by the National Curriculum were also partly a reflection of new teaching approaches and developments in assessment, and partly a consequence of psychological research on children's understanding. It was clearly especially important for the National Curriculum assessment arrangements to have some understanding of pupils' ideas – it is difficult to justify a particular set of levels of attainment without some understanding of how pupils' ideas develop. In history it was possible to draw upon considerable assessment experience in devising and applying criterion-referenced grades. It was also possible to draw upon some research on pupils' thinking, for example that of Hilary Cooper (1991, 1992) and the work continued by the CHATA project (Lee, Dickinson and Ashby, 1996), an investigation of children's concepts of history and teaching approaches in Key Stages 2 and 3.

A decade after the introduction of the National Curriculum the extent of the centralization of curriculum decision-making in England remains unclear. However, there is much evidence that individuals can still make a significant contribution to the development of history teaching through their teaching, workshops, publications, and through their role in the SHP or the Historical Association. This has been shown by, among others, Culpin, Lomas, Walsh and Christine Counsell. It is also clear that history teaching is facing various challenges at the start of the 21st century. What are the main challenges, and what should be done to strengthen history as a school subject?

Ongoing challenges and ways forward

History in the primary years

Perhaps the greatest ongoing challenge is to maintain the advances achieved in the 1990s. The 1991 National Curriculum requirements for history were particularly demanding on primary schools where there was little tradition of teaching history as a separate subject. However, the 1994–98 review of primary schools in England by inspectors from the Office for Standards in Education reported that history was prospering in primary schools and that there had been a steady improvement in standards achieved by pupils in both key stages (OFSTED, 1999: Section 12.7). These gains were put in jeopardy by the requirement that primary schools allocate more time to teaching literacy (from September 1998) and numeracy (from September 1999), and the lifting of the statutory requirement for schools to follow the programmes of study for history and the other foundation subjects. These decisions by the secretary of state meant that time available for history was likely to be reduced by schools. This raised the question 'Should history remain part of the primary school curriculum?' and if it should, then the further question, 'What form should it take?'.

There are strong reasons why history should continue to be part of the curriculum. The first is that there is still a statutory requirement on schools to provide a broad and balanced curriculum. Another reason stems from the fact that pupils frequently encounter images, accounts or references to the past through TV programmes, books and conversations. Surely, therefore, they should also gain knowledge and understanding of the past and learn something of the methodology of historical enquiry *through the curriculum*. A further reason is that there is now a substantial body of research findings as well as evidence from inspection reports and teachers' observations regarding pupils' achievements. Research studies show that pupils in the primary years can progress considerably in their understanding and analysis of source material (Cooper, 1991; Lee, Ashby and Dickinson, 1995), and can consider alternative viewpoints and suggest reasons for behaviour (Knight, 1988; Lee, Dickinson and Ashby, 1997). The CHATA project found some Year 3 children distinguishing clearly between reasons for actions and causes of outcomes, and evidence also of considerable progress in pupils' ideas about accounts between Years 3 and 6. Whereas in Year 3 three-quarters of the pupils tested treated accounts as 'stories', two and a half years later the majority were stressing that it was essential that history stories be true. OFSTED reports also provide evidence of what young pupils and perceptive teaching can achieve, *vide* the following account of teaching that developed an understanding in Year 2 pupils that interpretations of the past differ and that this can arise because of the limitations of the available evidence:

In a Year 2 class, pupils listened to the story of the wooden horse of Troy, and then quickly drew their own version of what the horse looked like. The teacher used the different versions to show that there are many possible interpretations of what the horse looked like. Pupils discussed why this was the case, establishing that it was impossible to be precise for lack of evidence. In turn, this was related to work already done on the difference between 'facts' and 'myths', including an appreciation that in telling a story people may exaggerate the truth.

(OFSTED, 1999: Section 12.7)

How can time for such teaching and learning be achieved given the 'literacy hour' and other initiatives, and should history be taught as a separate subject or via a topic approach? Suggestions have been forthcoming from official and unofficial sources that the 'literacy hour' offers an opportunity to explore a range of different historical texts including diaries, biographies and myths (DfEE, 1998; Nichol, 1998). On the other hand, the pressure to link subjects together and to study topics, as advocated in the 1960s, seems inappropriate. Given all that has been achieved in recent years through teaching history as a separate subject, a much sounder policy is surely to consolidate the achievements identified by OFSTED inspectors and follow their advice regarding improving standards. According to their 1994–98 review, history teaching should give more attention to interpretations of history and historical enquiry, and in many schools planning for progression and continuity could be improved through using key elements to determine learning objectives and through further use of the level descriptors. They also suggest asking the following questions in reviewing progress:

- Does the planning do justice to the areas of study or study unit?
- In deciding on the objectives for lessons, is there sufficient focus on progression in the key elements?
- Are resources well chosen to support historical objectives?
- Are good ideas and dynamic practice in history teaching being shared?
- Is assessment being used to inform pupils of strengths and weaknesses, and move them forward?
- Are opportunities for mutual support of history and literacy being recognized and exploited? (OFSTED, 1999: Section 12.7)

The many instances of good practice in history at Key Stages 1 and 2, only some of which reach a wider audience through conferences, workshops, books and *Primary History*, show how much teachers have to offer one another. Further sharing of ideas and practice would help to raise standards and strengthen the case for teaching history in the primary years.

History in the secondary years

The OFSTED report at the turn of the century on history in the secondary years noted continued improvement in pupils' progress, with two of the main strengths being pupils' working knowledge of the subject and their grasp of the skills of enquiry (2000: Section 112). OFSTED also reported that some pupils showed a lack of critical skills in use of evidence. These skills are, of course, particularly important for history and for pupils in the information-rich world of today. Lee and Ashby have drawn attention to a related issue, suggesting that some 'source-work' questions on GCSE papers 'show signs of returning to the comprehension exercises of the past, rather than rewarding students who have a concept of evidence' (1999: 13).

Two further weaknesses were identified in the OFSTED report (2000: Section 112). One was limited overview knowledge and understanding needed to establish a sound context and to enable pupils to make relevant connections; the other was that many pupils have little opportunity to understand, evaluate and compare interpretations. Postmodernists' views of history as merely the sum total of individual experiences and memories, all equally valid, may be influential here. Postmodernists also reject any notion of a 'grand narrative', an overarching theme. In the classroom, however, more use of good narrative accounts and some reference to current historical debate might stimulate interest and convince more pupils that history, far from being past its sell-by date, is alive and can offer intellectual excitement.

One of the main gains of the last decade or so has been the advance in understanding about progression in pupils' ideas in history and the implications of this for teaching and learning. However, Counsell (2000: Chapter 5) has sounded a warning that history teachers and researchers now need to analyse much more carefully the relationship between what have traditionally been called 'content' and 'skills'. Elsewhere, Lee and Ashby have suggested that history in the curriculum would benefit from further attempts to distinguish 'skills' and 'understanding', and also further attention to the goals of history (1999: 15). The best examples of conceptual analysis from the 1970s, for example Rogers (1979) and Lee (1978), are worth revisiting in this pursuit of a new clarity about concepts, which are at the heart of National Curriculum history.

Further challenges, particularly at the secondary level, arise from the requirement that pupils should develop knowledge, skills and understanding of several cross-curricular themes, including citizenship. Regarding citizenship and history, Davies (2000: Chapter 11) argues for raising the status of work on education for citizenship and finding a meaningful structure in which citizenship can be taught and learnt. This would mean, he claims, 'that citizenship would go from being an aim targeted by history teachers to a process in which investigations could take place to establish what it means to be a citizen' (2000: 145). Lee and Ashby offer a more sanguine message, pointing to the danger of history drifting into a situation where it is blurred with citizenship and loses its importance and place in schools (1999: 13).

Concerns expressed by university tutors include that many new entrants lack a sense of the sweep of human development, regard anything before the Victorians as not important, and cannot express themselves clearly and cogently (see, for example, Rubinstein, 2000). It will take at least 14 years for pupils who have proceeded through National Curriculum, GCSE and A level history courses to reach university, though some of the 1999–2000 intake may have completed Key Stage 3 history. There is potential, through reference to the various study units, for building a sense of the sweep of human development and enabling pupils to see themselves in perspective.

Secondary school history could also benefit from further efforts by examining boards to provide examinations that are not too burdensome, achieve a good balance between essay and source-work questions, and do all that is possible to ensure that justice is done in the marking of each candidate's work. Rechecking candidates' scripts where they are 'at risk' of achieving a final grade one or more grades below that predicted seems appropriate in a subject where marking is particularly subjective. Computer-assisted technology now enables grade award meetings to have detailed information on the performance of each examiner as well as individual candidates, their school peers, and the past and present mean grades and grade distribution in each subject for that and every school. Implementation of the best possible set of checks to catch any injustices prior to the release of grades would increase fairness and could raise confidence in the system; it might also encourage more pupils to choose history as one of their A level options.

History and ICT

An ongoing challenge to teachers in all schools is how best to deal with the general requirement that pupils should be given opportunities to apply and develop their ICT (information and communications technology) capability through their learning in all subjects. Use of ICT with pupils with special educational needs has shown its value in enabling access to the programmes of study and assisting pupils to demonstrate achievements. Walsh (1998) has demonstrated the power of word processing to aid pupils' thinking and writing in history. In another study Counsell has analysed the ways in which two departments used and evaluated a particular set of published history–IT materials (BECTA/HA, 1999). Her study provides evidence of effective learning in history through ICT as well as guidance on how to make such learning happen. These studies are illuminating and helpful, suggesting ways to satisfy ICT requirements through work that enhances history learning. However, we should, above all, bear in mind that the greatest benefit for pupils from school history comes from the historical knowledge, understanding and skills that they acquire. Acquiring higher sets of ideas to handle historical tasks enables solutions to problems that lower sets create or leave unresolved. For instance, in testing claims linked to a set of sources pupils use more powerful ideas when they move from appeal to the authority of 'experts' (including museums and libraries) to considering the plausibility and corroboration of information (whether it was intrinsically likely or whether most other information supported it). Further steps forward are to check the credentials of the reporter, and to raise methodological questions about the status of the sources as evidence – a step that the CHATA project team found taken by some (few) pupils in Years 7 and 9.

Ideas about evidence and testing claims are of particular importance in the information-rich world in which young people now study and live. Hands-on experience of information-handling skills can be developed and practised in many contexts. In history, however, tasks can be set that enable pupils to bring into play distinctions between information, evidence, facts and interpretations as well as widening the range of data used in learning about these distinctions and in testing claims. It is also through history that pupils can gain awareness of possible effects of developments in information technology. In attributing significance to past events, history makes comparisons with the present and raises questions about the future. This means that history is in an important position to aid consideration of the implications of technology for pupils, both now and in their future life and work.

The burgeoning use of ICT in homes and elsewhere has brought about new pressures on teachers, but also new opportunities to demonstrate the importance of understanding and skills learnt through history. This is particularly true with regard to the use of Web sites. In history pupils can be encouraged to view them as interpretations, not simply as sources of information, and evaluate them, including analysis of their origins and purpose. Haydn (2000: 106–10) provides a useful summary of Internet and other ICT applications that appear to have particular potential for enhancing learning in history as well as enabling pupils to apply and develop their IT capability. One such set of resources is the materials produced by the *History Using IT* initiative for improving pupils' writing in history using word processing and enabling pupils to look for patterns in the past using databases and spreadsheets (NCET/HA, 1997, 1998). Underlying the work of this initiative were the assumptions that the concerns of history education are paramount and that software should be usable 'off the shelf' but also easily adapted and developed by individual teachers for use in their own schemes of work. Nevertheless, use of ICT requires considerable time for planning. If standards in the use of ICT are to be raised then history teachers need time for exploring applications and planning their use. They will also need training that goes beyond that currently available under the New Opportunities Fund (NOF), focusing on pedagogical implications and evaluation of the impact on learning of the use of ICT in history teaching.

Teacher training

What more can be done to raise standards in and via teacher training? The introduction of a national curriculum for initial teacher training (ITT) in the 1990s signalled a policy move towards school-based and standards-based courses. An HMI perspective on courses in history in England (Baker, Cohn and McLaughlin, 2000: Chapter 15) has reported that they are mostly of good or very good quality and well above the all-subjects secondary average. Less happily they report that entrants have an almost bewildering array of first degrees and that shortcomings in subject knowledge have been especially revealed in the teaching of ancient, medieval and early modern periods. Regarding these shortcomings, they report, 'There was a tendency to fall back on stereotypes – in teaching about medieval people and society, for example, or explanations about the nature of the religious conflicts in England in the sixteenth and seventeenth centuries' (Baker, Cohn and McLaughlin, 2000: 197). These are serious weaknesses and place a further burden on the providers of ITT courses already stuffed full of requirements and expectations.

The aspect of their practice in which trainees were reported to be least confident, practised and proficient was in the assessment, recording and reporting of pupils' progress. HMI also reported that school history departments increasingly have detailed schemes of work that leave trainees little planning to do, and that:

> Those trainees who adapted and modified departmental practice in the keeping of records found the whole process of record keeping much more useful, informative, interesting and beneficial in shaping and informing their planning and teaching than did those who simply adopted, and conformed to, the practice that prevailed.
>
> (Baker, Cohn and McLaughlin, 2000: 200)

This raises the issue of the appropriate balance between opportunities to innovate and requirements that must be met, both in initial teacher training and in the history curriculum.

Also needing further attention according to HMI are: the tendency for trainees to 'plateau', to achieve an acceptable level of proficiency at which they remain for the rest of their practice; trainees' difficulty in practice in planning for and achieving progress through their teaching; problems in gauging the levels at which students were working on National Curriculum GCSE and A level courses; and wide variations in opportunities to gain confidence in the use of ICT for teaching purposes (Baker, Cohn and McLaughlin, 2000: 198–200). These wide variations, which occurred despite many trainees being personally skilled in the use of ICT, could be reduced by ending the anomaly that funding for each trainee does not necessarily find its way to the department in which trainees are based. Where appropriate, departments could then use the funding to buy the non-contact time, resources and training needed to improve use of ICT in departments and in trainees' training.

The issue of what should be expected of initial, induction and in-service training is especially important in an era of rapid change. Initial training forms professional habits; it cannot produce the full professional. Progressive improvement of practice requires further advice, experience and reflection. If practice is to be more than a series of random responses to external stimuli then it must enshrine patterns of action. These in turn carry assumptions about history and about pupils. Hence, in an important sense, any coherent practice manifests adherence to theory. Training should help teachers to make their theoretical assumptions explicit, encourage them to see how far they are justified in terms of both logical coherence and empirical evidence, and help them to build positive alternatives and improvements. To achieve all this teachers need reflection enriched by more than experience, and time for that reflection.

Research, international developments and raising standards

In what ways can awareness of research and curriculum developments in other countries contribute to raising standards in our history classrooms? The problems evident in the 1950s and 1960s from applying a Piagetian framework to history bear witness to the need for caution in applying research methods and findings across contexts. On the other hand, it is important to find out, for example, what notions of evidence and explanation pupils bring to the history classroom. If teaching history meant helping children to see how assertions in history are related to evidence, it is important to find out what notions of evidence children bring to history lessons. If they are to be helped to give better historical explanations, teachers need to know how their ideas about explanation are likely to develop. Teaching is likely to be less than maximally effective if it attempts to change ideas that pupils do not in fact hold.

Research is time-consuming and costly, but ITT partnerships offer opportunities to share expertise and involve personnel (tutors, mentors and students) in small-scale investigations of aspects of teaching and learning in history (see Husbands and Pendry, 2000). At the national level, government has shown increased awareness of the need and opportunities to improve teaching and learning by promoting evidence-based policy and practice. Furthermore, there is acceptance on the part of researchers as well as government of the need for partnership with users and practitioners at all stages in research investigations. This will be the case with all the projects in the ESRC's Teaching and Learning Research Programme, launched in November 1999. Information on this programme is available on the programme's Web site at: www.ex.ac.uk/esrc-tlrp.

Swinnerton and Jenkins (1999) have compiled a review of empirical research in secondary school history teaching in England and Wales from 1960 to 1998. A valuable summary of the development and position of research into the psychology of learning and teaching from a US perspective has been provided by Wineburg (1996). Further accounts of research in history education undertaken in France, Italy, Spain and especially the United States can be found in three collections, Voss and Carretero (1998), Carretero and Voss (1994) and Leinhardt, Beck and Stainton (1994). These publications give a good picture of the way in which research has been developing in Europe and North America. Articles likely to be of particular interest include Young and Leinhardt (1998) on the role of analogy in the teaching and learning of history, Wineburg and Fournier (1994) on contextualized thinking in history, and Dominguez and Pozo (1998) on promoting the learning of causal explanation in history.

Conclusion

This chapter has sketched the main characteristics of three traditions of history teaching and the contribution of various individuals and networks to curriculum development in history. It has also considered some ongoing challenges to history teachers. It seems from this study that teachers and teacher trainers have a long and admirable tradition of contributing effectively to curriculum development. It also seems that the next phase in the development of National Curriculum history needs to be evolutionary, not revolutionary.

The final report of the History Working Group said that if history was to make its important and particular contribution to the school curriculum then courses should be challenging, relevant, and combine planned programming with rigour and intellectual excitement (DES, 1990: Chapters 1 and 2). In the first decade of the National Curriculum there has been much prescription, with the Teacher Training Agency in particular making extensive use of 'must do'. It seems appropriate now to begin to move from a culture of prescription and blaming to one of partnership and genuine consultation. Further strengthening of what is done in classrooms depends in the end on the commitment, ability and relevant knowledge of teachers. A move to genuine consultation seems appropriate given teachers' expertise and achievements. Most important of all, it is the policy most likely to lead to what the History Working Group advised, courses that are well planned, stimulate the imagination of teachers and pupils alike, and ensure that history makes its particular contribution to the school curriculum.

References

Ashby, R and Lee, P (1987) Children's concepts of empathy and understanding in history, in *The History Curriculum for Teachers*, ed C Portal, pp 62–88, Falmer, Lewes

Baker, C, Cohn, T and McLaughlin, M (2000) Issues in the training of history teachers, in *Issues in History Teaching*, ed J Arthur and R Phillips, pp 191–219, Routledge, London and New York

Blyth, J E (1982) *History in Primary Schools: A practical approach for teachers of 5 to 11 year-old children*, McGraw-Hill, Maidenhead

Board of Education (1905) *Suggestions for the Consideration of Teachers and Others Concerned in the Work of Public Elementary Schools*, HMSO, London

Board of Education (1923) *Report on the Teaching of History*, Pamphlet 37, HMSO, London

Booth, M (1983) Skills, concepts and attitudes: the development of adolescent children's historical thinking, *History and Theory*, **22**, pp 101–17

Booth, M (1987) Ages and concepts: a critique of the Piagetian approach to history teaching, in *The History Curriculum for Teachers*, ed C Portal, pp 22–38, Falmer, Lewes

Briggs, Asa (1954) *Victorian People: Some reassessments of people, institutions, ideas and events, 1851–67*, Odhams, London

British Educational Communications and Technology Agency (BECTA)/The Historical Association (HA) (1999) *Defining Effectiveness in History Using IT: Approaches to successful practice*, BECTA, Coventry

Bruner, J S (1960) *The Process of Education*, Vintage Books, New York

Burston, W H (1963) *Principles of History Teaching*, Methuen, London

Burston, W H and Thompson, D (1967) *Studies in the Nature and Teaching of History*, Routledge, London

Cannadine, D (1987) British history: past, present – and future, *Past and Present*, **116** (6), pp 169–91

Carpenter, P (1964) *History Teaching: The era approach*, Cambridge University Press, Cambridge

Carr, E H (1961) *What is History?*, Macmillan, London

Carretero, M and Voss, J (1994) *Cognitive and Instructional Processes in History and the Social Sciences*, Lawrence Erlbaum, Hillside, NJ and Hove, UK

Central Advisory Council for Education (1967) *Children and Their Primary Schools* (The Plowden Report), HMSO, London

Coltham, J B and Fines, J (1971) *Educational Objectives for the Study of History: A suggested framework*, Teaching of History Series, **35**, The Historical Association, London

Cooper, H (1991) Young children's thinking in history, unpublished doctoral thesis, Institute of Education, University of London, London

Cooper, H (1992) *The Teaching of History*, David Fulton, London

Counsell, C (2000) Historical knowledge and historical skills: a distracting dichotomy, in *Issues in History Teaching*, ed J Arthur and R Phillips, pp 54–71, Routledge, London and New York

Davies, I (2000) Citizenship in the teaching and learning of history, in *Issues in History Teaching*, ed J Arthur and R Phillips, pp 137–47, Routledge, London and New York

Department of Education and Science (DES) (1967) *Towards World History*, Pamphlet 52, HMSO, London

DES (1985) *History in the Primary and Secondary Years: An HMI view*, HMSO, London

DES (1989) *National Curriculum History Working Group: Interim report*, HMSO, London

DES (1990) *National Curriculum History Working Group: Final report*, HMSO, London

DES (1991) *History in the National Curriculum (England)*, HMSO, London

DES (1995) *History in the National Curriculum*, HMSO, London

Department for Education and Employment (DfEE) (1998) *Teachers Meeting the Challenge of Change*, HMSO, London

DfEE/QCA (1999) *The National Curriculum for England: History*, HMSO, London

Dickinson, A and Lee, P (1978) *History Teaching and Historical Understanding*, Heinemann, London

Dickinson, A and Lee, P (1984) Making sense of history, in *Learning History*, ed A Dickinson and P Lee, pp 117–53, Heinemann, London

Dominguez, J and Pozo, J (1998) Promoting the learning of causal explanations in history through different teaching strategies, in *Learning and Reasoning in History*, ed J Voss and M Carretero, pp 344–59, Woburn Press, London

Douch, R (1967) *Local History and the Teacher*, Routledge, London

Elton, G R (1953) *The Tudor Revolution in Government: Administrative changes in the reign of Henry VIII*, Cambridge University Press, Cambridge

Elton, G R (1967) *The Practice of History*, Sydney University Press, Sydney

Happold, F C (1928) *The Approach to History*, Christophers

Haydn, T (2000) Information and communications technology in the history classroom, in *Issues in History Teaching*, ed J Arthur and R Phillips, pp 98–112, Routledge, London and New York

Henderson, J L (1968) *Education for World Understanding*, Pergamon

Hill, Christopher (1961) *The Century of Revolution 1603–1714*, Nelson, Edinburgh

Husbands, C and Pendry, A (2000) Thinking and feeling: pupils' preconceptions about the past and historical understanding, in *Issues in History Teaching*, ed J Arthur and R Phillips, pp 125–34, Routledge, London and New York

Jeffreys, M V C (1939) *History in Schools: The study of development*, Pitman, London

Jenkins, K (1991) *Rethinking History*, Routledge, London and New York

Jenkins, K (1995) *On 'What is History?': From Carr and Elton to Rorty and White*, Routledge, London and New York

Keatinge, M W (1910) *Studies in the Teaching of History*, Black

Keatinge, M W and Frazer, N L (1920) *A History of England for Schools with Documents, Problems and Exercises*, 2nd edn, Black

Kitson Clark, G (1967) *The Critical Historian*, Heinemann, London

Knight, P (1988) Children's understanding of people in the past, unpublished doctoral thesis, University of Lancaster, Lancaster

Lee, P (1978) Explanation and understanding in history, in *History Teaching and Historical Understanding*, ed A Dickinson and P Lee, pp 72–93, Heinemann, London

Lee, P and Ashby, R (1999) How long before we need the US Cavalry?, *Teaching History*, **97**, pp 13–15, The Historical Association, London

Lee, P, Ashby, R and Dickinson, A (1995) Progression in children's ideas about history, in *Progression in Learning*, ed M Hughes, Multilingual Matters, Clevedon

Lee, P, Dickinson, A and Ashby, R (1996) 'There were no facts in those days': children's ideas about historical explanation, in *Teaching and Learning in Changing Times*, ed M Hughes, pp 169–92, Blackwell, Oxford and Cambridge, Massachusetts

Lee, P, Dickinson, A and Ashby, R (1997) 'Just another emperor': understanding action in the past, *International Journal of Educational Research*, **27** (3), pp 233–44, Pergamon, Exeter

Leinhardt, G, Beck, I L and Stainton, C (1994) *Teaching and Learning in History*, Lawrence Erlbaum, Hillside, NJ and Hove, UK

National Council for Educational Technology/The Historical Association (NCET/HA) (1997) *Improving Students' Writing in History Using Word Processing*, NCET, Coventry

NCET/HA (1998) *Searching for Patterns in the Past Using Databases and Spreadsheets*, NCET, Coventry

Nichol, J (1998) Nuffield Primary History: the Literacy through History Project and the literacy hour, *Primary History*, **20**, pp 14–17

Office for Standards in Education (OFSTED) (1999) *Primary Education: A review of primary schools in England, 1994–1998*, The Stationery Office, London

OFSTED (2000) *The Annual Report of Her Majesty's Chief Inspector of Schools*, The Stationery Office, London

Phillips, R (1998) *History Teaching, Nationhood and the State: A study in educational politics*, Cassell, London

Price, M (1968) History in danger, *History*, **53**, pp 342–47

Reeves, M (1954) *Then and There: The medieval village*, Longman, Harlow

Rogers, P (1979) *The New History: Theory into practice*, Teaching of History Series, **44**, The Historical Association, London

Rubinstein, W (2000) Has history gone past its sell-by date?, *Daily Telegraph*, 1 March 2000, London

Schools Council History 13–16 Project (1976) *A New Look at History*, Holmes McDougall, Edinburgh

Shemilt, D (1980) *History 13–16 Evaluation Study*, Holmes McDougall, Edinburgh

Shemilt, D (1987) Adolescent ideas about evidence and methodology in history, in *The History Curriculum for Teachers*, ed C Portal, pp 39–61, Falmer, Lewes

Stone, L (1965) *The Crisis of the Aristocracy 1558–1641*, Oxford University Press, Oxford

Swinnerton, B and Jenkins, I (1999) *Secondary School History Teaching in England and Wales: A review of empirical research 1960–98*, University of Leeds, Leeds

Sylvester, D (1996) Change and continuity in history teaching 1900–93, in *Teaching History*, ed H Bourdillon, pp 9–23, Routledge/The Open University, London and New York

Thatcher, M (1993) *The Downing Street Years*, HarperCollins, London

Thompson, E P (1963) *The Making of the English Working Class*, Gollancz, London

Tosh, J (1991) *The Pursuit of History: Aims, methods and new directions in the study of modern history*, 2nd edn, Longman, Harlow and New York

Voss, J and Carretero, M (1998) *Learning and Reasoning in History*, International Review of History Education, vol 2, Woburn Press, London

Walker, E C (1935) *History Teaching for Today*, Nisbet

Walsh, B (1998) Why Gerry likes history now: the power of the word-processor, *Teaching History*, **93**, The Historical Association, London

West, J (1981) *History 7–13*, Dudley Metropolitan Borough

Wineburg, S S (1996) The psychology of learning and teaching history, in *Handbook of Educational Psychology*, eds R C Calfee and D C Berliner, pp 423–37, Macmillan, New York

Wineburg, S S and Fournier, J (1994) Contextualized thinking in history, in *Cognitive and Instructional Processes in History and the Social Sciences*, ed M Carretero and J Voss, pp 285–308, Lawrence Erlbaum, Hillside, NJ and Hove, UK

Young, K M and Leinhardt, G (1998) Wildflowers, sheep and democracy: the role of analogy in the teaching and learning of history, in *Learning and Reasoning in History*, ed J Voss and M Carretero, pp 154–96, Woburn Press, London

Chapter 5

Geography: Changes and challenges

Ashley Kent

The story of geography's development as a popular subject in English schools is both fascinating and complex. This author's view is that it is both worth while and useful to have some historical perspective on contemporary challenges. This chapter attempts a personal overview of the evolution of geography education and this inevitably is influenced by the writer's long-standing involvement with the Institute of Education as both student and member of staff. The Institute throughout the 20th century has had a number of geography staff intimately involved with the subject's evolution. For instance, in order of appointment, Fairgrieve (1912), Scarfe (1935), Long (1946), Honeybone (1948), Roberson (1951) and Graves (1963) all have parts in the subject's history as indeed have more recent colleagues. This chapter will touch upon their contributions where appropriate.

A number of publications have discussed the history of geographical education but probably the most succinct and accessible are the four articles by Boardman and McPartland (1993a, 1993b, 1993c, 1993d) in successive issues of *Teaching Geography*, to mark the centenary of the Geographical Association (GA). Marsden too has written about the history of geography education in various places, for instance 1995, 1996 and 1997. The most recent and substantial work is that of Walford (2000) and unsurprisingly Balchin's history of the Geographical Association (1993) is a story closely intertwined with the subject's evolution.

Curriculum development

During most of this century regional geography has been the dominant paradigm in school curricula. A key influence was Herbertson, former Director of the School of Geography, Oxford University, whose seminal paper in 1905 divided the world into major natural regions. 'It is probable that his influence on what was taught in British schools was enormous and has since been unsurpassed' (Graves, 1975: 28). This was not only because he used modified natural regions in his successful series of school textbooks (written with his wife), but because the concept was used in textbooks written by schoolteachers. For instance Brooks, Pickles and Stembridge produced textbook series covering continent by continent. Indeed the prolific textbook writer Dudley Stamp acknowledged his debt to Herbertson and the natural region concept in 1957. A good illustration of the longevity of the regional framework underpinning syllabuses was the success of Preece and Wood's *The Foundations of Geography* (1938), which was still in print 50 years later having sold more than 2 million copies.

'The dominance of the regional framework in syllabus design continued during the post-war years', according to Boardman and McPartland (1993b: 65). As recently as 1960 the Ministry of Education lauded the regional framework, which it claimed lay at the 'very heart of geography' (1960: 38). The main criticism of this approach was its lack of intellectual challenge and that it tended 'to degenerate into the repetitive learning of factual information' (Boardman and McPartland, 1993a: 5). Some argued that the sample studies approach was introduced as a counter to the disadvantages of the regional approach. The argument went that such a detailed study of any geographical unit such as a farm, village, valley or factory required the knowledge and understanding of ideas and concepts that could be generalized and 'was grounded in the lives and occupations of real people in real places, giving it the sanctity of authenticity' (Boardman and McPartland, 1993b: 65). The 'study' element of sample study implied data description, analysis and evaluation. So successful was this approach that its popularity ranged from Fairgrieve and Young's *Real Geography*, the first of six books to be published in 1939, to the *Study Geography* series of five books by Bell and Dybeck (1967).

Over the years, books written for geography teachers have been influential on practice and have reflected the content and pedagogies of their times. Of particular early moment was James Fairgrieve's *Geography in School*, first published in 1926 and running to a fourth edition in 1937. He had left William Ellis School in 1912 to become a lecturer in the London Day Training College (later to become the University of London Institute of

Education). The book presented his views on geography as developed over 20 years at the Institute and contains the well-known remark that 'The function of geography is to train future citizens to imagine accurately the condition of the great world stage and so help them to think sanely about political and social problems in the world around' (Fairgrieve, 1926: 18). *Geography in School* remained the 'bible' on geographical education for several decades and a flavour of his thoughts is included in Figure 5.1.

Geography is at once one of the most important of school subjects and one of the most difficult to teach.

There is a claim from geography for a place in the curriculum, not because it pays, but because we cannot have an education worth the name without geography.

Geography enables man to place himself on the world and to know where he stands with regard to his fellows, so that he will neither exaggerate nor diminish his own importance; it enables us to understand other people, to some extent, by comparison with ourselves. By a study of geography we are enabled to understand facts without a knowledge of which it would be impossible to do our duty as citizens of this very confusing and contradictory world.

There is not one single thing which stands so much in the way of social and international advance as a lack of knowledge of geography. The function of geography in school is to train future citizens to imagine accurately the conditions of the great world stage, and so help them to think sanely about political and social problems in the world around.

Figure 5.1 *Extracts from* Geography in Schools
Source: Fairgrieve, 1926

His influence on geography teachers through teacher educators at the Institute continues through the generations. So Scarfe was a student of Fairgrieve, Honeybone a student of Scarfe and Graves a student of Honeybone, each respectively head of geography at the largest university school of education. Incidentally Long and Roberson were students of Scarfe! Perhaps it is no accident that generations of Institute (and wider) students (including this author) can recall one of his maxims that one should teach:

- from the known to the unknown;
- from the simple to the complex;
- from the indefinite to the definite (an unexpected reversal here);
- from the particular to the general.

Perhaps the zenith of Fairgrieve's approach and the regional framework underpinning curricula came with the publication of Long and Roberson's *Teaching Geography* in 1966 in which the authors significantly remarked, 'we have nailed our flag to the regional mast, and those who would not place the main emphasis on regional geography in school must justify themselves with some other viable philosophy' (1966: 24).

Already the 'new geography' of higher education in the USA and the UK with its emphasis on theoretical models, conceptual frameworks and quantitative techniques was influencing a new generation of teachers unhappy with the idiographic regional approach. Seminal publications of the time were *Frontiers in Geographical Teaching* (Chorley and Haggett, 1965); *Locational Analysis in Human Geography* (Haggett, 1965); and *Models in Geography* (Chorley and Haggett, 1967). Their messages were new, challenging and difficult. 'The books... contained ideas of baffling abstruseness and exciting novelty in about equal parts' (Walford, 1989: 310). Bringing this new 'content' into schools was no easy task and a key role was played by the Geographical Association Models and Quantitative Techniques Committee set up in 1967 and the special edition of *Geography* (January, 1969) focusing on such developments. Everson and FitzGerald, two young London teachers (and subsequently HMIs), had a considerable influence especially through the first A level textbook on the new geography, *Settlement Patterns* (1969).

Arguably within 10 years a paradigm shift had occurred in terms of changed syllabuses and textbooks in the direction of the 'new geography'. Examples of key textbooks of the time were the *Oxford Geography Project* (Rolfe *et al*, 1974) and the work of Cole and Beynon (1968), Briggs (1972), Dinkele, Cotterell and Thorn (1976) and Bradford and Kent (1977).

Already by the 1960s there had developed in higher education (HE) a backlash against the positivistic, spatial science paradigm. Behavioural geography, welfare geography, radical geography, humanistic geography, postmodern geography and new cultural geography have all had their adherents but there is, in this author's view, no longer the relatively coherent 'feel' for approaches at HE level that if nothing else the positivistic geographers gave. Johnston's concluding comment in *Geography and Geographers* (1979) that 'human geography will continue branching towards anarchy' (p 189) some could argue has some present-day validity.

The content of school curricula, it has been argued, remains more directly linked to the 'new geography' of the 1960s than some of the latest HE developments. This author would argue that is generally true for recent GCSE and A level cores and syllabuses as well as the three versions of the National Curriculum.

The evolution of ways of teaching and learning geography through the century can be traced via a number of important publications aimed at the geography teacher. Fairgrieve's *Geography in Schools* (1926), and the UNESCO *Handbook of Suggestions on the Teaching of Geography*, edited by Scarfe (1951), and its successors in 1965, edited by Brouillette, and in 1982, edited by Graves, were significant contributions. Probably most influential in the 1960s were the *Handbook for Geography Teachers* (Long, 1964) and *Teaching Geography* (Long and Roberson, 1966). These probably represented the last of a particular approach to the content and pedagogy of geography. The 1970s saw an explosion of new books reflecting both the 'new geography' and newer pedagogic approaches. These included Walford (1973), DES (1972, 1978), Graves (1975), Hall (1976), Boden (1976), Marsden (1976) and Graves (1979). At the same time began an influential series of GA handbooks for the geography teacher. The first was *Geography in Secondary Education* (Graves, 1971), followed by Graves (1980), Boardman (1986) and Bailey and Fox (1996). As important was the publication of the *Geographical Teacher* in 1901 by the GA, to become *Geography* in 1927, much regretted by Fairgrieve who feared the dominance of the university world in the affairs of the GA, and in 1975 the first issue of *Teaching Geography*, edited by Patrick Bailey. This professional journal actively sought articles written by practitioners sharing successful classroom experiences and that tradition has been maintained by the GA in its ever widening range of publications geared to supporting teachers. Particular strategies have been well considered by GA publications, for instance enquiry learning (Roberts, 1998); simulations (Walford, 1996); fieldwork approaches (Job, Day and Smyth, 1999); information technology (King, 2000); critical thinking (Leat and McAleavy, 1998); and values education (Reid, 1996).

The 1990s have seen another mini boom in publications aimed at the geography teacher's reflective practice. These include Walford (1999), Battersby (1995), Hacking (1992), Kent, Lambert and Slater (1996), Naish (1992), Slater (1993), Tilbury and Williams (1997), Lambert and Balderstone (2000) and Kent (2000).

A microcosm of changing teaching strategies in geography education is represented by fieldwork developments. In chronological order three distinctive models of fieldwork emerged:

1. field teaching/field excursion;
2. hypothesis testing;
3. framework fieldwork.

Field teaching, sometimes pejoratively called 'Cook's tour' fieldwork, has a long and established tradition. Associated with Wooldridge (1955), the objective of such field teaching was 'to develop an eye for country – i.e. to build up the power, to read a piece of country'. It is to do with a knowledge-able, skilled and often charismatic field teacher, leading a group of students to an area with which he or she is intimately associated. Field notebooks, mini lectures, field sketching and question-and-answer sessions are typical teaching strategies used. Its strengths as an approach include a direct (through the soles of one's feet!) experience of a new environment and having it interpreted in a holistic fashion by an expert. On the downside this can become a tedious and passive exercise.

The hypothesis testing tradition emerged in schools in the 1960s and 70s and is still arguably an entrenched and accepted approach. It reflected the quantitative, spatial-scientific nature of Anglo-American geography of the time. Particularly influential on schools were the writings of Everson (1969, 1973) and Chapallaz et al (1970). Its strengths included a focusing of activity around a testable hypothesis and the rigour of statistical techniques used. On the other hand too much emphasis can be given to data collection focused round highly specific and sometimes socially and environmentally irrelevant statements.

Another approach to emerge has been that of 'framework fieldwork', a term first coined by Hart in 1983 and formalized in the Geography 16–19 project teachers' handbook (Naish, Rawling and Hart, 1987). It is to do with fieldwork being 'framed' around a specific people-environment question, issue or problem. Its strengths are that the fieldwork centres on questions and issues of social and environmental concern and appropriate techniques of data collection are utilized where and when appropriate. However, this does not allow for a holistic look at and appreciation of environments nor does it allow specific studies of physical and/or human environments (and related processes) for their own sakes. Other approaches to fieldwork have been of a more sensory nature as proposed by Van Matre (1979) and colleagues, a part of the earth education movement in the USA. Hawkins (1987) echoes some of these suggestions.

Discussions of the evolution of fieldwork strategies are found in Kent (1996), Kent and Foskett (2000) and Job (1999). Job especially challenges fieldworkers to engage the senses of students and to consider fieldwork exercises incorporating the dimension of sustainability.

This author's argument is that overall pedagogic developments in geography education have been similar to those in fieldwork. Each has gone through the regional/descriptive-didactic, spatial-scientific, issues-oriented approaches with the beginnings of an appearance of more critical value-laden geographies.

Slater's work in values education while based at the Institute illustrates the engagement of this institution in current movements and debates (for example Slater, 1992, 1994a, 1996).

Following new curricula and related pedagogies there have been equally momentous changes in assessment strategies and styles. The establishment of the 'Assessment Matters' section in *Teaching Geography* reflects the import-ance of such developments. Another colleague in the Institute, David Lambert, has been particularly active and influential in this field (for example 1996 and 2000). Key influences on assessment have been the beginning of GCSE courses incorporating coursework and project work, often fieldwork-based; the influence on assessment schemes of the three Schools Council Geography projects; and the impact of the National Curriculum (as it has evolved in its three forms) on formative assessment and in particular identifying the levels that pupils have attained. For instance, the impact of the Geography 16–19 Project, funded for nine years from 1976 to 1985 and based at the University of London Institute of Education, had its greatest direct impact on the related A level syllabus run by the (then) University of London Examinations Board. At its peak in the mid-1990s, it generated an annual candidature of over 12,000 students. Arguably most innovative has been its decision-making paper first set in 1982.

Geography has always been well supported by a bewildering array of curriculum resources including textbooks, curriculum packs, audio-visuals and ICT resources. The latest *Geography Teachers' Handbook* has a whole section devoted to resources and their use and for many years now the annual GA conference has exhibited an extraordinary array of resources. Recently there has been rapid uptake by geography teachers of information technology. Unusually well financed by governments, there has been an energetic involvement of some geographers in this innovation and an ongoing commit-ment from the GA. For instance, it published a landmark book in 1980 by Shepherd, Cooper and Walker, who stated that it was their view 'that the computer can make a uniquely varied contribution to the teaching of geography. It can motivate in difficult areas of the curriculum, it can emancipate from the tedium of repetitious manual operations, and it can illuminate concepts and principles in a variety of ways.' The computer page in *Teaching Geography* first appeared in 1983 and its value has been most recently demonstrated by the compilation by King (2000) of a range of articles from what is firmly established as the publication's information and communications technology section. The fascinating story of these ICT developments has been told in various places, for example Kent (1982, 1992) and Freeman (1997). More troubling is the slow pace of uptake of even the most seductive elements of ICT such as multimedia equipment, e-mail and the Internet. Research into the process of uneven take-up includes those by Watson (1997, 2000) and Kent (1997a). Unlike other aspects of curriculum development in geography education, central funding has been available for the new technologies. Several curriculum projects have been based at the Institute of Education and in order have been: Learning Geography with Computers Project (1986–88); Project HIT – Humanities and Information Technology Project (1988–93); Remote Sensing in the Geography National Curriculum Project (1992–5); and Eurogame Project (1998–2000).

As discussed earlier, textbooks tend to reflect the pedagogic and content 'era' of their appearance and in England we have been fortunate to benefit from a wide range of publications though from a declining number of publishers. Some, however, including HMI, have expressed disquiet at the recent Waugh phenomenon whereby a number of textbooks produced by the same author have dominated the market. 'Many schools relied on a limited, and sometimes limiting, single textbook series' (OFSTED, 1995). A welcome resurgence of research interest into the ways textbooks are written, purchased and used has occurred recently, for example Kent (1998), Walford (1989), Wright (1996), Marsden (1988), Lidstone (1992) and Graves (forthcoming).

The three major geography projects also produced curriculum resources but it was the Geography for the Young School Leaver (GYSL) Project that published in 1974/5 three theme-based packs. The boxes consisted of pupils' resource sheets, filmstrips, overhead transparencies, audiotapes and teachers' guides. The 'man, land and leisure', 'cities and people' and 'people, place and work' packs were, it was claimed, in over 200 schools within five years, a remarkable achievement. The Geography 14–18 Project did produce curriculum resources, as did the Geography 16–19 Project but they, unlike GYSL, were not fully blown materials production exercises.

Audio-visual aids and now their modern guise of videos, TVs, multimedia machines, slide projectors, data projectors and digital cameras have rightly been a key concern and resource for geography teachers from the earliest days. Some of the earliest audio-visual equipment was used by Fairgrieve in his own designed geography room at William Ellis School; Price used lantern slides at Ruabon Grammar School (Price, 1929); and later there was a use of film as described by Fairgrieve (1932). Interest in the visual image was maintained later at the Institute by Long who reported on her research into use of photographs in geography classrooms in her presidential address to the GA in 1970. Most powerful and recent has been the emergence of televisual resources (Durbin, 1996), that is, television programmes, whether live broadcasts, recorded or bought on video. As ever such resources, as is true of all teaching resources, need careful monitoring for ideological underpinnings and likely biases.

Research matters

Although strictly curriculum research and development projects, the three main geography projects (GYSL, and 14–18 from 1970 to 1975 and Geography 16–19 from 1976 to 1986) were under much more pressure to 'develop' than 'research'. Their lasting memorial lies in the changes they brought about in assessment styles; new geographies they proposed, ie the content including a social and environmental concern geography; engagement of large numbers of pilot school teachers; and various forms of enquiry learning. Although examination candidature for the GYSL and 14–18 courses was limited, their indirect impact on geography education was considerable, not unlike the earlier American High School Geography Project, which though it sold minimal numbers of 'curriculum packs' had considerable indirect impacts. Geography 16–19, based at the Institute with its original team of Naish, Kent and Rawling, had more success in attracting large numbers of candidates to its A level course. Under the leadership of Naish it benefited from the supportive role of Graves, then chair of the geography committee at the Schools Council and head of geography at the Institute. The teachers' handbooks produced by the 14–18 Project (Tolley and Reynolds, 1997) and the 16–19 Project (Naish, Rawling and Hart, 1987) built on earlier curriculum process concepts and literature and had considerable indirect influence on geography teachers. Boardman's work (1988) evaluates the impact of the GYSL Project, and other pieces of research have evaluated the 16–19 Project (eg Stephens, 1988) and 14–18 Project (Lane, 1980).

Monitoring the geography education research work undertaken has become a much more challenging and large-scale task as research activity has grown over the years. Consequently the first bibliography of British sources (Lukehurst and Graves, 1972) describes 1,402 items in 78 pages between 1870 and 1970. The most recent equivalent (Foskett and Marsden, 1998) extends over 27 years between 1970 and 1997, contains 5,708 items and is a 209-page publication. As Graves remarked in its foreword:

...in 1970 there were probably no more than four general books in print on geographical education that had been published in the UK. Today there are far more. Further, there has been an explosion in the number of articles in specialized journals, and in the number of university theses, dissertations and short monographs in this field. This is a reflection of the increasing number of university tutors specializing in this area and of teachers who have pursued a higher degree and explored educational problems in geography.

(Foskett and Marsden, 1998: v)

Started in 1968 by Graves, the Institute of Education MA programme has generated a great deal of MA dissertation research, not to mention academic reflection and professional development (Graves *et al*, 1989) and is arguably the greatest concentration of specialist MA dissertations anywhere in the world. The benefits of undertaking such a course explains why to an extent similar programmes and modules have been developed at the University of Southampton and most recently at the University of Waikato in New Zealand and at the recently established Centre for Geographic Education at Southwest Texas State University. Slater (1999) describes the nature of such higher education and implies its worth. 'The concept of geography education develops from the conversations which arise from teachers teaching geography, thinking about teaching geography, having time to be aware of the many contexts in which they and it are embedded, investigating their teaching and researching and re-searching their beliefs and practices' (p 299).

At the same time the study of and research into the field of geography education has generated an increasing number of MPhil/PhD theses. So, for instance, since 1966 at the Institute of Education 37 theses have been successfully presented.

Publications sharing research findings and debating methodologies and the like have experienced a mini boom in the last few years. Examples include: *Understanding Geographical and Environmental Education: The role of research* (Williams, 1996); a series of monographs, *Reporting Research in Geography Education*, (Slater, 1994b); and a *Research Forum* series (Kent, 1998). Also there have been a number of research-oriented chapters in a number of recent books or journals, for instance Roberts (2000); Gerber and Williams (2000); Williams (1999); and Marsden (1996). Perhaps more interesting is the direction geography education research might take in the future. Marsden (1996) lists his 'possible agenda':

- ideologies of geographical education;
- the nature of geographical knowledge;
- geography's interface with:
  - other National Curriculum subjects; and
  - cross-curricular areas;
- connecting geography at the frontiers with geography in school;
- systematic historical studies of aspects of geographical education;

- applications of relevant research in other curriculum areas;
- systematic comparative research in aspects of geographical education (Marsden, 1996: 21).

In his chapter Marsden argues for a 'return to the values and rigours of fundamental research' (1996: 15). Indeed Williams (1998) argues that the culture of research in geographical education is only at the 'incipient stage', given his model. Gerber and Williams (2000) argue for 'greater networking amongst geographical educators around the world thus promoting a global geographical education community of scholars'.

Most significantly, in Britain today the government and others are asking how research evidence can inform and has informed practice. Worryingly this author could not think straight away of examples of pieces of research that had directly influenced practice yet feels that most completed research could influence practice. On reflection, however, the thesis of Biddle, 'An investigation into the use of curriculum theory in the formation of a systems model for the construction and evaluation of secondary school curricula in England and Wales' (1974), influenced the Geography 16–19 Project; Graves's book on curriculum planning in 1979; and curriculum developments in Australia (Biddle, 1976). More recently the research carried out by the Thinking Through Geography Team led by David Leat at the University of Newcastle has led to a publication (Leat, 1998) that is actively changing classroom pedagogies (see Bright and Leat, 2000). Roberts (2000) has helpfully considered the role of research in supporting teaching and learning.

Subject associations

Since the meeting held at Christ Church, Oxford in 1893 when a resolution was approved to form an association 'for the improvement of the status and teaching of geography', the Geographical Association (GA) so founded has been the leading national subject-teaching organization for geographers. With the aim of 'furthering the study and teaching of geography', it has become an organization with nearly 11,000 members and 60 local branches in England, Wales and Northern Ireland. As recorded in Balchin (1993) the GA over the years has represented the subject, provided support for teachers, and encouraged and published curriculum and subject innovations.

It has successfully undertaken a particularly important role in the era leading up to and including the National Curriculum by making the case for geography in a number of quarters, particularly the political. For instance in the early 1980s it became clear that there would be a national curriculum and Sir Keith Joseph indicated that any subject wishing to be included would have to justify itself. The GA invited Sir Keith to a gathering of its members at King's College, London on 19 June 1985. His address was well received in spite of a highly sceptical audience and he concluded with a request to geographers and the GA to answer seven questions. A first and initial response was sent to Sir Keith in August 1986 and a fuller response published in 1987, both edited by Bailey and Binns. A small delegation of GA officers met with the subsequent secretary of state, Kenneth Baker, in June 1987 by which time he had read the more considered response. These proactive overtures to secretaries of state probably secured geography's position in the upcoming National Curriculum. Such GA involvement with political actors has continued since the early 1980s with positive effects. A recent example of this is the GA's position statement (1999a), which is clearly of value to the community of geographers, as well as a useful political statement.

The GA's trio of publications, *Primary Geography*, *Teaching Geography* and *Geography*, support the work of geographers at all levels as do the burgeoning publications list of the Association. In the latest catalogue (1999/2000), for instance, there are categories on: curriculum planning and delivery; fieldwork; information technology; international studies; mentoring; photo resources; place studies; professional development; promoting geography; quiz books; research; and statistics and data.

The GA offers a number of other services to its members including activities at the 60 local branches, a worldwise quiz system, a quarterly newsletter and its three-day annual conference with its major publishers' exhibition, lectures, seminars and workshops. Given the ongoing challenge to the subject of maintaining its place in the curriculum and its popularity with students, some of its recent initiatives have been particularly opportune. Geography Action Week was first launched as an annual event in November 1996. Based on the USA's Geography Awareness Week, it gave schools the chance to give the subject a high profile and show its educational value and interest. In 1996 the week focused round the Land–Use UK Survey; in 1998 round Geography Through the Window; and in 2000 round Coastline 2000 (Spooner and Morron, 2000). This initiative has certainly generated a host of original and creative activities upon which schools have engaged (Walford, 1997). The Land–Use UK Survey of 1996 (Walford, 1999) and the Coastline 2000 survey have rightly given considerable publicity to the involvement of thousands of students in worthwhile survey activities and follow on from the proud traditions of the first and second Land Utilisation surveys directed by Stamp and Coleman respectively.

Membership of the GA has traditionally been from across the constituencies of geography with an ongoing majority from secondary schools.

However, in spite of Fairgrieve's fear in the 1920s of the dominance of the university world in the affairs of the Association, the worry nowadays is that it is the exception to the rule when a university academic is a member. However, the Institute's staff has played a full role in the affairs of the GA as council members (for example Naish); conference officers (Honeybone and Hilton); publications officers (Lambert); and presidents (Fairgrieve, Graves, Long and Kent).

The Royal Geographical Society (now with the Institute of British Geographers) has also played a key role in geography education in England through its various education committees, conferences and publications. Its latest director and secretary, Dr Rita Gardener, is particularly aware of the needs of geography education and has helped set up a number of initiatives, several of which are in partnership with the Geographical Association. Examples of geography education activities include: careers conferences and publications; update conferences for sixth formers with lectures from university geographers; help with expeditions and fieldwork advice particularly with expeditions abroad; a variety of prizes for schools and students; and production of resources based on research expeditions for schools such as Wahiba Sand Sea Slide Set and the Maraca Pack. Because of its strong political connections the RGS–IBG has been especially successful in campaigning for geography and consulting with government and related organizations.

Teacher education

Tutors in university schools of education with responsibility for initial teacher training in geography have over the years tended to plough a lonely furrow in their respective institutions. That was until 1964, when Norman Graves, recently arrived as head of geography at the Institute of Education (from the University of Liverpool), set up the first national-level tutors' meeting so that colleagues could share experiences and expertise. That meeting has now become an annual weekend conference, each year held in a different location. Now arguably one of the best attended and established of the tutors' groups, in recent years the agenda has reflected the twofold concerns of the age: firstly, the standards for the award of QTS as defined by law, how these can be 'delivered' and the related OFSTED inspection process; and secondly, sharing of research findings. The latter has always been an element of such annual meetings but this now assumes rather greater import with university academics subject to the four-yearly research assessment exercise (RAE).

In-service education and training (INSET) or, as it is now known, continuing professional development has had a patchy history. There have always been one-off lectures by academics at local GA meetings and the same local GA branches laid on popular workshop conferences at the time of the 'new geography' in the 1960s and 1970s. But most progressive and supportive INSET until the 1980s was under the auspices of the education authorities until the Thatcher government diverted funding away from them. This put greater pressure on individual schools or groups of schools to provide INSET opportunities for geography staff. It also did the same for the national, regional and local levels of the GA. Similarly institutions of higher education increased the number of short, one-day or half-day courses for teachers in their catchment areas. A particular yet important offshoot of that was the establishment in 1968 of an MA course at the Institute of Education, which was a genuinely critical, reflective higher degree with clear practical benefits to geography teachers. That continues and in 2001 will also become a distance learning programme. Former graduates have become university lecturers, government inspectors, heads of departments, deputy heads and heads, authors and heads of sixth form.

Sadly, however, it is this writer's view that such reflection and professional development are not sufficiently widespread for most geography teachers. I believe professional development of teachers should be ongoing, well resourced and of a top priority. It is not! Teachers should be regularly offered the refreshment and renewal a sabbatical or teacher-fellowship brings. They are not! Well-resourced in-service education and training are fundamental to developing teacher expertise and boosting morale. Sadly, such developments happen all too rarely. The extreme difficulty faced by teachers wishing to undertake vital and ongoing professional development is damaging to both their health and that of the system. There is insufficient 'space' for teachers to allow them to develop professionally' (Kent, 1997b: 301). Perhaps recently announced National Standards for Subject Leaders (TTA, 1998) and their concomitant for geography (GA, 1999b) might provide a boost for a better-resourced continuing professional development.

International developments

Geography educators (particularly university staff) in Britain, partly through colonial legacies, have had strong research and academic links with other parts of the English-speaking world, especially North America, Australasia, parts of South and South-East Asia and parts of Africa. But it was the establishment of the Geography Education Commission of the International Geographical Union (IGU) in 1952 by Neville Scarfe that formalizes relationships between colleagues world-wide by the holding of major four-yearly commission conferences as well as a number of intervening regional conferences. So, for instance, the main commission meetings in the last few years have been in Brisbane (1988); Boulder (1992);The Hague (1996); and Kyongju (South Korea) (2000).

The chair of the Commission has played a key leadership role in the organization so Scarfe (1952–56) and Graves (1972–80) were influential as result. As a subset of the Commission (usually consisting of 10 commissioners), Graves established in the 1970s the British Sub Committee, which ran conferences and engaged in research activities.The chair's position was taken over by Naish in 1984 and by Kent in 1997. Recent conferences run by the British Sub Committee were those in 1997 on 'values in geography education' and in 1999 on 'geography and environmental education'. Publications of the group include, for example: teaching materials (Butt *et al*, 1998); bibliographies (Foskett and Marsden, 1998); conference proceedings (Kent, 2000) and research findings (Naish, 1990).

The history of the IGU Commission on Geography Education is told by Wise (1992), too late to relate the important achievement of the Commission under Haubrich's leadership (1988–96) of the publication (in 1992) of the *Journal of International Research in Geographical and Environmental Education* (IRGEE), edited by Gerber and Lidstone. British geography educators have written a good deal in their new academic journal. For instance, the Forum in Volume 8, Number 3, 1999 was co-ordinated by Marsden in which seven other British geographers report on 'Geographical education in England and Wales: the state of play at the end of the millennium'.

Probably the most significant achievement of the Commission was the publication of the *International Charter on Geographical Education*, first published in 1992 and later in 21 languages in 1994. It was published in the April 1995 issue of *Teaching Geography*. Its significance is that it offers a curriculum framework and justification for those colleagues around the world attempting to establish or at least strengthen geographical education in their system. In some senses it 'spread the word' about geography education in the way that the UNESCO source books did in 1965 (Brouillette) and 1982 (Graves).

Challenges for the subject

Relatively recently Bailey suggested that 'Geography has never before achieved such a high status in the British curriculum' (1991: 2) but it can be argued that since then its position is far from firmly secured and established. The subject needs to meet a number of challenges successfully, some of which have been identified in other places (for example Kent, 1997b; Marsden, 1997; and Carter, 1999). Some of these challenges include:

- maintaining its popularity in all levels of the system;
- making the case effectively for the value and study of geography;
- communicating more effectively the nature of modern geography, offsetting stereotypical and ill-informed images (Kent, 1999);
- improving communications between geographers (Kent and Smith, 1997);
- maintaining the fieldwork tradition;
- bringing curricula and school-based geographers up to date with the latest geographies at HE level;
- improving the quality of thinking in geography classrooms (see Leat, 1998);
- raising the quality and standards of KS3 geography since there are some suggestions from recent OFSTED inspections that geography does less than well (OFSTED, 1998);
- to ensure future curricula satisfy the needs of 5–19-year-olds (such as in the GeoVisions Project – Robinson, Carter and Sinclair, 1999);
- geography's contribution to a rethought 14–19 curriculum with a stress on numeracy, literacy, citizenship, sustainable development and personal, social and moral development;
- for geography courses to move beyond the strictures of National Curriculum geography (the observant reader will have noticed minimal reference to it in this chapter since the author feels it has almost obsessively been fully considered in other places);
- that future geography curricula learn the lessons from 100 years' experience of teaching the subject in schools – the lessons from history, some of which are outlined in Boardman and McPartland (1993a, b, c and d: 161) and indeed in this chapter.

It is to be hoped geography and geographers rise to these changes and challenges. They have so far.

References

Bailey, P (1991) *Securing the Place of Geography in the National Curriculum of English and Welsh Schools*, The Geographical Association, Sheffield
Bailey, P and Binns, T (eds) (1986) *A Case for Geography*, The Geographical Association, Sheffield
Bailey, P and Binns, T (eds) (1987) *A Case for Geography*, The Geographical Association, Sheffield
Bailey, P and Fox, P (1996) *Geography Teachers' Handbook*, The Geographical Association, Sheffield

Balchin, W G V (1993) *The Geographical Association, The First Hundred Years 1893–1993*, The Geographical Association, Sheffield

Battersby, J (1995) *Teaching Geography at Key Stage 3*, Chris Kington Publishing, Cambridge

Biddle, D (1974) An investigation into the use of curriculum theory in the formation of a systems model for the construction and evaluation of secondary school curricula in England and Wales, unpublished PhD thesis, Institute of Education, University of London, London

Biddle, D (1976) *Translating Curriculum Theory into Practice in Geographical Education: A systems approach*, Australian Geography Teachers Association, Victoria

Boardman, D (ed) (1986) *Handbook for Geography Teachers*, The Geographical Association, Sheffield

Boardman, D (ed) (1988) The impact of the Curriculum Project: geography for the young school leaver, *Educational Review*, Occasional Publications, 14, University of Birmingham, Birmingham

Boardman, D and McPartland, M (1993a) Building on the foundations: 1893–1945, *Teaching Geography*, **18** (1), pp 3–6

Boardman, D and McPartland, M (1993b) From regions to models: 1944–69, *Teaching Geography*, **18** (2), pp 65–69

Boardman, D and McPartland, M (1993c) Innovations and change: 1970–82, *Teaching Geography*, **18** (3), pp117–20

Boardman, D and McPartland, M (1993d) Towards centralisation: 1983–93, *Teaching Geography*, **18** (4), pp159–62

Boden, P (1976) *Developments in Geography Teaching*, Open Books, London

Bradford, M G and Kent, W A (1977) *Human Geography: Theories and their applications*, Oxford University Press, Oxford

Briggs, K (1972) *Introducing Transportation Networks*, University of London Press, London

Bright, N and Leat, D (2000) Towards a new professionalism, in *Reflective Practice in the Teaching of Geography*, ed W A Kent, Sage, London

Brouillette, B (1965) *Source Book for Geography Teaching,* Longman/UNESCO, Paris

Butt, G *et al* (1998) *Living and Working in Berlin*, The Geographical Association, Sheffield

Carter, R (1999) Connecting geography: an agenda for action, *Geography*, **84**, part 4, pp 289–97

Chapallaz, D P *et al* (1970) Hypothesis testing in field studies, *Teaching Geography*, **11**, The Geographical Association, Sheffield

Chorley, R J and Haggett, P (eds) (1965) *Frontiers in Geographical Teaching*, Methuen, London

Chorley, R J and Haggett, P (eds) (1967) *Models in Geography*, Methuen, London

Cole, J P and Beynon, N J (1968) *New Ways in Geography*, Basil Blackwell, Oxford

Department of Education and Science (DES) (1972) *New Thinking in School Geography Education*, Pamphlet 59, HMSO, London

Department of Education and Science (1998) *The Teaching of Ideas in Geography Matters for Discussion: Some suggestions for the middle and secondary years of education*, HMSO, London

Dinkele, G, Cotterell, S and Thorn, I (1976) *Harrap's Reformed Geography*, Harrap, London

Durbin, C (1996) Teaching geography with televisual resources, in *Geography Teachers' Handbook*, ed P Bailey and P Fox, The Geographical Association, Sheffield

Everson, J A (1969) Some aspects of teaching geography through fieldwork, *Geography*, **54** (1), pp 64–73

Everson, J A (1973) Fieldwork in school geography, in *New Directions in Geography Teaching*, ed R Walford, Longman, London

Everson, J A and FitzGerald, B P (1969) *Settlement Patterns*, Longman, London

Fairgrieve, J (1926) *Geography in School*, University of London Press, London

Fairgrieve, J (1932) The use of film in teaching, in *Geography*, **17**, pp 129–40

Fairgrieve, J and Young, E (1939) *Real Geography*, Philip, London

Foskett, N and Marsden, B (eds) (1998) *A Bibliography of Geographical Education 1970–1997*, The Geographical Association, Sheffield

Freeman, D (1997) Using information technology and new technologies in geography, in *Teaching and Learning Geography*, ed D Tilbury and M Williams, Routledge, London

Geographical Association (GA) (1999a) Geography in the curriculum: a position statement from the GA, *Geography*, **84**, part 2, April, pp 164–67

GA (1999b) *Leading Geography: National Standards for Geography Teachers in Secondary Schools*, The Geographical Association, Sheffield

Gerber, R and Williams, M (2000) Overview and international perspectives, in *Reflective Practice in the Teaching of Geography*, ed W A Kent, Sage, London

Graves, N J (1971) *Geography in Secondary Education*, The Geographical Association, Sheffield

Graves, N J (1975) *Geography in Education*, Heinemann Educational Books, London

Graves, N J (1979) *Curriculum Planning in Geography*, Heinemann, London

Graves, N J (1980) *Geographical Education in Secondary Schools*, The Geographical Association, Sheffield

Graves, N J (1982) *New UNESCO Source Book for Geography Teaching*, Longman/The UNESCO Press, Paris

Graves, N J (1995) *Geography in Education*, Heinemann Education Books, London

Graves, N J (forthcoming) *Two Hundred Years of Geography Textbooks*, publisher unknown

Graves, N et al (1989) *Research in Geography Education: MA dissertations 1968–1988*, Institute of Education, University of London, London

Hacking, E (1992) *Geography into Practice*, Longman, Harlow

Haggett, P (1965) *Locational Analysis in Human Geography*, St. Martin's Press, London

Hall, D (1976) *Geography and the Geography Teacher*, Allen and Unwin, London

Hart, C (1983) *Fieldwork the 16–19 Way*, Geography 16–19 Project Occasional Paper, Institute of Education, University of London, London

Hawkins, G (1987) From awareness to participation: new directions with the outdoor experience, *Geography*, **72** (3), pp 217–22

Herbertson, A J (1905) The major natural regions, in *Geographical Journal*, **25**

Job, D (1999) *New Directions in Geographical Fieldwork*, Cambridge University Press, Cambridge

Job, D, Day, C and Smyth, T (1999) *Beyond the Bikesheds: Fresh approaches to fieldwork in the school locality*, The Geographical Association, Sheffield

Johnston, R J (1979) *Geography and Geographers*, Arnold, London

Kent, W A (1982) The challenge of the microcomputer, in *Geography in Education Now*, ed N Graves *et al*, Bedford Way Papers, 13, Institute of Education, University of London, London

Kent, W A (1992) The new technology and geographical education, in *Geography and Education, National and International Perspectives*, ed M Naish, Institute of Education, University of London, London

Kent, W A (1996) A strategy for geography fieldwork, in *Innovation in Geographical Education*, ed Van der Schee *et al*, pp 167–77, International Geographical Union, Utrecht/Amsterdam

Kent, W A (1997a) Process and pattern of a curriculum innovation, unpublished PhD thesis, Institute of Education, University of London, London

Kent, W A (1997b) Challenging geography: a personal view, *Geography*, **82** (4)

Kent, W A (1998) *Research Forum 1: Textbooks*, International Geographical Union with the Institute of Education, University of London, London

Kent, W A (1999) Image and reality – how do others see us?, Guest editorial in *International Research in Geographical and Environmental Education*, **8** (2), pp 103–07

Kent, W A (ed) (2000) *Reflective Practice in the Teaching of Geography*, Sage, London

Kent, W A and Foskett, N (2000) Fieldwork in the school geography curriculum – pedagogical issues and development, in *Fieldwork in Geography: Reflections, Perspectives and Actions*, ed R Gerber and G K Chuan, Kluwer Academic Publishers, Dordrecht

Kent, W A and Jackson, S (eds) (2000) *Geography and Environmental Education: International perspectives*, International Geographical Union with the Institute of Education, University of London, London

Kent, W A, Lambert, D M and Slater, F A (eds) (1996) *Geography in Education: Viewpoints on teaching and learning*, Cambridge University Press, Cambridge

Kent, W A and Smith, M (1997) Links between geography in schools and higher education, in *Handbook of Post 16 Geography*, ed A Powell, The Geographical Association, Sheffield

King, S (ed) (2000) *High-Tech Geography ICT in Secondary Schools*, The Geographical Association, Sheffield

Lambert, D M (1996) Assessing pupils' attainment and supporting learning, in *Geography in Education: Viewpoints on teaching and learning*, ed W A Kent, D M Lambert and F A Slater, pp 260–89, Cambridge University Press, Cambridge

Lambert, D M (2000) Using assessment to support learning, in *Reflective Practice in the Teaching of Geography*, ed W A Kent, Sage, London

Lambert, D M and Balderstone, D (2000) *Learning to Teach Geography in the Secondary School*, Routledge, London

Lane, J A (1980) An evaluation of some aspects of the Kent Consortium 14–18 Geography Project, unpublished MA dissertation, Institute of Education, University of London, London

Leat, D (1998) *Thinking Through Geography*, Chris Kington Publishing, Cambridge

Leat, D and McAleavy, T (1998) Critical thinking in the humanities, *Teaching Geography*, **23** (3), July, pp 112–14

Lidstone, T (1992) In defence of textbooks, in *Geography and Education: National and international perspectives*, ed M Naish, pp 177–93, Institute of Education, University of London, London

Long, M (ed) (1964) *Handbook for Geography Teachers*, Methuen, London

Long, M and Roberson, B S (1966) *Teaching Geography*, Heinemann Educational Books, London

Lukehurst, C T and Graves, N J (1972) *Geography in Education: A bibliography of British sources 1870–1970*, The Geographical Association, Sheffield

Marsden, B (1996) Geography, in *A Guide to Educational Research*, ed P Gordon, The Woburn Press, London

Marsden, W E (1976) *Evaluating the Geography Curriculum*, Oliver and Boyd, London

Marsden, W E (1988) Continuity and change in geography textbooks: perspectives from the 1930s to the 1960s, *Geography*, **74** (4), pp 327–43

Marsden, W E (1995) *Geography 11–16: Rekindling good practice*, David Fulton, London

Marsden, W E (1996) The place of geography in the school curriculum: an historical overview, 1886–1976, in *Teaching and Learning Geography*, ed D Tilbury and M Williams, pp 7–14, Routledge, London

Marsden, W E (1997) On taking the geography out of geographical education: some historical pointers, *Geography*, **82** (3), pp 241–52

Ministry of Education (1960) *Geography and Education*, HMSO, London

Naish, M C (ed) (1990) *Experiences of Centralisation*, International Geographical Union with the Institute of Education, University of London, London

Naish, M C (ed) (1992) *Geography and Education: National and international perspectives*, Institute of Education, University of London, London

Naish, M C, Rawling, E and Hart, C (1987) *Geography 16–19: The contribution of a curriculum project to 16–19 education*, Longman, London

Office for Standards in Education (OFSTED) (1995) *Geography: A review of inspection findings, 1993/94*, HMSO, London

OFSTED (1998) *Secondary Education: A review of secondary schools in England, 1993–97*, HMSO, London

Preece, D M and Wood, H R B (1938) *The Foundations of Geography*, University Tutorial Press, London

Price, E S (1929) The lantern and the geography room, in *Geography*, **15**, pp 294–98

Reid, A (1996) Exploring values in sustainable development, *Teaching Geography*, **21** (4), pp 168–72

Roberts, M (1998) The nature of geographical enquiry at Key Stage 3, *Teaching Geography*, **23** (4), October

Roberts, M (2000) The role of research in supporting teaching and learning, in *Reflective Practice in the Teaching of Geography*, ed W A Kent, Sage, London

Robinson, R, Carter, C and Sinclair, S (1999) Wiser people – better world?, in *Teaching Geography*, **24** (1), January, pp 10–13

Rolfe, J *et al* (1974) *Oxford Geography Project*, Oxford University Press, Oxford

Rushby, J G, Bell, J and Dybeck, M W (1967) *Study Geography*, Longman, London

Scarfe, N V (1951) *A Handbook of Suggestions on the Teaching of Geography*, UNESCO, Paris

Shepherd, I D H, Cooper, Z A and Walker, D R F (1980) *Computer Assisted Learning*, CET with the Geographical Association, London

Slater, F A (1992) ...to travel with a different view, in *Geography and Education: National and international perspectives*, ed M Naish, pp 97–113, Institute of Education, University of London, London

Slater, F A (1993) *Learning Through Geography*, National Council for Geographic Education, Indiana

Slater, F A (1994a) Education through geography: knowledge, understanding, values and culture, *Geography*, **79** (2), pp 147–63

Slater, F A (ed) (1994b) *Reporting Research in Geography Education*, Monographs, 1, Institute of Education, University of London, London

Slater, F A (1996) Values: towards mapping their locations, in a geography education, in *Geography in Education: Viewpoints on teaching and learning,* ed W A Kent, D M Lambert and F A Slater, pp 200–30, Cambridge University Press, Cambridge

Slater, F A (1999) Notes on geography education at higher degree level in the United Kingdom, *International Research in Geographical and Environmental Education*, **8** (3), pp 295–99

Spooner, D and Morron, M (2000) Coastline 2000: a survey for the new millennium, *Geography*, **85**, part 1, January, pp 69–70

Stamp, L D (1957) Major natural regions: Herbertson after 50 years, *Geography*, **42**, pp 201–16

Stephens, P (1988) An enquiry into the extent to which the Geography 16–19 Project has fulfilled its objectives with regard to its enquiry approach to learning and its distinctive approach to geographical education, unpublished MA dissertation, Institute of Education, University of London, London

Teacher Training Agency (TTA) (1998) *National Standards for Subject Leaders*, TTA, London

Tilbury, D and Williams, M (eds) (1997) *Teaching and Learning Geography*, Routledge, London

Tolley, H and Reynolds, J B (1997) *Geography 14–18: A handbook for school-based curriculum development*, Macmillan Education, Basingstoke

Van Matre, S (1979) *Sunshine Earth – An Acclimatisation Program for Outdoor Learning*, American Camping Association

Walford, R (ed) (1973) *New Directions in Geography Teaching*, Longman, Harlow

Walford, R (1989) On the frontier with the new model army: geography publishing from the 1960s to the 1990s, *Geography*, **74** (4), pp 308–20

Walford, R (1991) *Viewpoints on Geography Teaching*, Longman, Harlow

Walford, R (1996) The simplicity of simulation, in *Geography Teachers' Handbook*, ed P Bailey and P Fox, The Geographical Association, Sheffield

Walford, R (ed) (1997) *Land Use – UK A Survey for the 21st Century*, The Geographical Association, Sheffield

Walford, R (1999) The 1996 Geographical Association Land-Use Survey: a 'geographical commitment', *International Research in Geographical and Environmental Education*, **8** (3), pp 291–94

Walford, R (2000) *Geography in British Schools 1850–2000: Making a world of difference*, Woburn Press, London

Watson, D (1997) Information technology in geography classes: the appearance and reality of change, unpublished PhD thesis, School of Education, King's College, University of London, London

Watson, D (2000) Issues raised by research into ICT and geography education, in *Research Forum 2: Information and communications technology*, ed W A Kent, International Geographical Union with Institute of Education, University of London, London

Williams, M (ed) (1996) *Understanding Geographical and Environmental Education: The role of research*, Cassell Education, London

Williams, M (1998) Review of research in geographical education, in *Research Forum 1: Textbooks*, ed W A Kent, pp 1–10, Institute of Education, University of London, London

Williams, M (1999) Research in geographical education, *International Research in Geographical and Environmental Education*, **8** (3), pp 301–04

Wise, M J (1992) International geography, the IGU Commission on Education, Chapter 15, in *Geography and Education: National and international perspectives*, ed M Naish, Institute of Education, University of London, London

Wooldridge, S W (1955) The status of geography and the role of fieldwork, *Geography*, **40**, pp 73–83

Wright, D (1996) Textbook research in geographical and environmental education, in *Understanding Geographical and Environmental Education*, ed M Williams, pp 172–82, Cassell, London

Chapter 6

Modern languages:
Searching for success

Alan Hornsey

Learning a foreign language in English secondary schools is adversely affected by two uncomfortable circumstances: the learners already speak the world's lingua franca and there is a popular belief that a language can be learnt 'without tears'. The former is demotivating; the latter is sustained by adverts promising that we can learn a new language in a matter of weeks and by the observation on visits abroad that quite ordinary people seem to have mastered English. Once the novelty has worn off, there is therefore dis-appointment on finding that language learning is demandingly complex and that there is a lot to learn given only four brief lessons a week with 30 pupils vying for practice opportunities, and little conviction that the effort leads to something that is needed. Painfully slow progress ensues with subject matter lagging well behind learners' maturity and interests and they are inclined to capitulate. In spite of the dedicated efforts of teachers well aware of the value of learning another language, the comprehensive school with an entry of some 150 pupils at age 11 is left with only a handful still persevering at sixth-form level when the experience could start to have meaningful rewards.

It is consequently not surprising that in the 50 years since the Second World War there has been a succession of attempts to overcome these difficulties by seizing on technical, social and linguistic innovations as welcome panaceas: twin-track audiotapes made language laboratories possible; slide projectors brought audio–visual courses; increased foreign travel inspired day trips to Boulogne and necessitated courses that claimed to be instantly 'communicative'; studies in general language development led to a belief in the value of an early start and the subsequent teaching of French in the primary school; television and video made possible the presentation of authentic situations. All brought undoubted gains but none was a panacea. Constant innovation and the initial excitement it generated simply glossed over the difficulties and the negative experiences.

The unchallenged acceptance of behaviourist views of learning in audio-visual and audio-lingual courses was an example of such glossing over. Constant repetition of fixed phrases led to boredom and, at best, the memorizing of a repertoire of material that was so overlearnt it actually blocked the ability to create appropriate language. Pupils were invited to repeat 'j'ai onze ans' so many times in their first year of French that the Assessment of Performance Unit (1985) found them still saying 'j'ai onze ans' two years later at age 13. Again the fixed phrase was a hindrance when they wanted to express hopes ('quand j'aurai vingt ans') or their past ('quand j'avais cinq ans') or even to refer to other people ('elle a vingt-cinq ans'). The words 'quel âge', whatever followed, simply triggered the fixed overlearnt response.

Examples such as the above give a sense of the context in which language teachers have been trained, advised and educated. Their work after 1945 has to be understood in terms of their being able to handle the tension between helping young people in the artificial setting of a classroom to learn something about language and to gain a modest skill in using it while at the same time seriously questioning the uncritical espousal of the latest attractive innovation.

From grammar-grind to sight and sound: 1945–1967

Before 1945 language teaching had been dominated by the written word embodied in books like *A French Course for Schools* (Collins, 1930) with its comprehensive grammar rules, occasional pictures, lists of vocabulary, unreal texts, translations and exercises of grammatical knowledge rather than potential language use. Such courses were popular, thorough and rigorous and they continued to be used with occasional child-friendly modifications during the post-war austerity years. The approach they fostered has come to be known as 'grammar-grind'. The top classes in the selective grammar schools – foreign languages were not generally taught in the secondary modern schools – coped reasonably well and the tradition might have survived unchanged had not tape recorders, slide projectors and language laboratories provided new possibilities and the promise of a 'language teaching revolution'. In publications like *A Guide to Modern Language Teaching Methods* (Dutton, 1965) and with the support of the newly formed Audio-Visual Language Association (AVLA), audio-visual courses were welcomed as both scientific and possessed of almost magical didactic properties. They were the new orthodoxy.

Thus in the 1950s and 1960s advisers and tutors found themselves having to provide a much needed critique of 'grammar-grind' while simultaneously helping students and teachers to avoid the pitfalls in the *son et lumière* of the new courses. In doing so they came under attack from both traditionalists and innovators. Nevertheless the Modern Languages Department at the Institute of Education in London – F M Hodgson, E C Bearman, M Gilbert, C V Russell and N Hill – did provide such a critique. They developed their characteristically eclectic 'oral approach', challenging trainees and teachers to stand back from the innovations and to engage in debating what were then the significant issues: the importance of meaning; the role of the spoken word; the written text and its pictorial equivalent or support; the place of grammar; translation and the use of the mother tongue.

Meaning

Meaning had to relate to reality while also being associated with providing ample evidence of both structure and syntax. In 'grammar-grind' it had been subservient to rules of grammar and bilingual world lists. Pupils would for example be asked to place indefinite articles in front of nouns as a test of knowledge of gender even if this meant producing expressions as unlikely to be meaningfully used as 'un courage'. The new audio-visual courses were often no better because, in a desperate attempt to dispense with help from English equivalents, they regularly assumed that meaning could be deduced unambiguously from a picture. They even tried to represent abstractions pictorially, or failed to recognize that many pictures have reversible meanings: is a person holding the handle of a door opening it or closing it? Further clues to the context were obviously needed. Students and teachers had to be encouraged to devise situations where language was used meaningfully with an emphasis on clarity and unambiguity. Both ingenuity and imagination were required. Practising negative sentences in French or German, for example, had previously been simply a matter of giving lists of positive statements and telling learners to 'turn them into the negative' by using 'ne... pas', 'nicht' or 'kein': 'je suis un garçon' became 'je ne suis pas un garçon'; 'nous sommes dans la salle de classe' became 'nous ne sommes pas dans la salle de classe'; 'j'apprends le français' became 'je n'apprends pas le français'.

Pupils did what they were asked even if the outcome required a rapid change of sex, a baffling sense of dislocation or even a satirical view of the activity itself. Time had to be spent in producing alternative exercises where negatives were used because the meaning required them. Negative statements became possible responses to defective pictures: a face without a nose ('il n'y a pas de nez') or a dog without a tail ('il n'a pas de queue'); or to simple definitions: a blind person ('er kann nicht sehen'), an orphan ('er hat keine Eltern') or to deficient sets: if a normal place setting in an imaginary restaurant is defined as having knife, fork, spoon, plate and glass, then use of a blackboard duster and the question 'c'est un couvert complet?' could elicit answers such as 'non, il n'y a pas de couteau' or 'non, il n'y a ni couteau ni fourchette'.

Devising such alternative materials, many of which might subsequently have to be rejected as too long-winded or impractical, required time and persistence. It also required a reliable command of the target language since students and teachers were being weaned from total dependence on a course book and had to create many of their materials from their own experience. Consequently PGCE students were often required to have, in addition to their degree, an entry qualification of the equivalent of an academic year's residence in the country whose language they proposed to teach – a require-ment frequently challenged by university language departments. Tutors and the profession as a whole, however, valued new entrants who knew the language as well as knowing about it and who had had a modest experience of living in the culture where the language is spoken.

The spoken word

The residence abroad was further justified by efforts to make school language teaching less dependent on the written word – a dependence apparently condoned by the public examinations of that time, which gave scant reward to oral skills, allotting them less than 10 per cent of the total mark for the subject. Students were encouraged to use their oral skills. This meant a great deal of oral question-and-answer to provide pupils with plenty of opportunity for speaking. It also meant organizing questions to highlight grammatical structure and grading and selecting materials to provide for meaningful progression. The great value of F M Hodgson's *Learning Modern Languages* (1955) and *Language Learning Material* (1961) was her attempt to define such work, to distinguish it from random conversation and to insist on responses that were plausible and language-like rather than just formulaic. Much of the classroom oral work before her books were published had been artificial, reminiscent of the memorized chanting of religious responses:

Teacher: Que faisait l'homme à la barbe noire qui était assis sous l'arbre?
Pupil: L'homme à la barbe noire qui était assis sous l'arbre lisait.

Teacher: L'homme à la barbe noire où était-il assis?

Pupil: L'homme à la barbe noire qui était assis sous l'arbre lisait; etc, etc.

She wanted pupils to answer 'where' questions with a place or 'who' questions with a person or name. Her questions were not tests of content but stimuli to use certain forms. They gave evidence that learners had genuinely understood the force of interrogative sentences and allowed the teacher to control the point where more complex responses could be required. Thus, if in a text about the actions of a number of people we learn that 'une vieille dame est entrée dans l'hôtel à trois heures', 'who', 'when' and 'where' questions will initially be satisfactorily answered with single word or short phrase responses as a preliminary to the more demanding requirements of more complex questions like 'Qu'est-ce qu'elle a fait, la vieille dame?' or 'Qu'est-ce qui s'est passé à trois heures?'

If a full-sentence answer is required to every question and a regurgitation of all the facts (possibly just read aloud from an original text), there is no proof that important question words have been understood and there can be no surprise if, after five years of such work, examination candidates still think that French 'où' means 'who' or that German 'wer' means 'where'. In addition the pace of lessons will have been slowed by all the full sentences, leaving many learners silent and deprived of opportunity for practice. Ultimately their impression will be that the language they are learning is only spoken in dauntingly long clauses, that pronouns are only a very rare phenomenon and that foreign really is worse.

Texts and pictures

Course book stories were not generally suitable for this way of teaching and it was essential to devise and edit plausible texts that would act as springboards for appropriate graded question-and-answer work. These would be short – often no more than 100 words – and would tell an easily remembered story with a clear sequence of events. They were a significant step towards reality after the quite artificial equivalents constructed by earlier course book writers to illustrate rules of grammar – texts in which milkmaids would groan ('gémir') at the lowing ('mugir') of the cows as they accomplished ('accomplir') their tasks, simply because all the verbs belonged to the group whose infinitives ended in -ir. Mrs Hodgson ran Friday evening seminars at the Institute of Education on a regular basis for French and German teachers in which everyday stories, fables, jokes and anecdotes were identified, modified and edited to serve the kind of oral work that would familiarize learners with the structures, patterns and lexis they needed and which provided pertinent examples enabling them to form hypotheses of how the language operated. These seminars met over a 12-year period (1958–1970) and had some 50 teachers as regular participants.

Another very useful springboard for effective question-and-answer work was afforded by the picture-story – either a narrative or description based on a single picture (What has this person just done? What is s/he about to do? What is s/he doing?) or a series of pictures. *Cours illustré de français* (Gilbert, 1967) was the most consistent and popular example of a course that had such a pictorial bias and was in many ways a precursor of the second generation of audio-visual courses. Gilbert commissioned pictures (drawn by a former PGCE student who understood what was needed) that led to talk in the foreign language about what they actually illustrated or unambiguously suggested.

Grammar

The excesses of the traditional course books had given grammar a bad name and a belief developed that plenty of oral work made grammatical explanation unnecessary. There was justifiable criticism of abstruse terminology – future perfect continuous passive, etc – and of rules distinguished by needless completeness and lists of exceptions. Pupils were spending too much time mastering forms like the parts of the verb 'acquérir' simply because they represented grammatical curiosities. Learners of German in English schools went on learning 'dieser' and 'jener' as equivalent to the contrasting 'this' and 'that' long after native speakers of German had ceased to use them in this way except in very formal circumstances.

Students at the Institute of Education, however, were advised to systematize the presentation of the language along structural lines since the time available for the foreign language in classrooms was too short for random presentation to be effective. Summaries of grammar learnt were not discouraged. Grammar divorced from meaning was generally avoided. Those favourites of the grammar-grind era, the so-called gap-filler exercises, were eschewed:

> Put au, à la, à l', aux in the gaps in the following sentences:
> Il est allé… cinema;
> Elle travaille… Banque; etc.

Such exercises were easily mastered by anyone good at algebra but they required no grasp of meaning and were operations that simply meant following instructions. Generations of pupils had diligently placed partitive articles (du, de la, de l' or des) in such gaps but had continued to the end of their French course to say or write 'il a mangé pain' (he ate bread) in any context of real French.

Translation

By the 1960s a growing body of teachers was looking for ways of curbing the use of word-for-word translation as the principal means of teaching and testing the language. Frequent translation practice reinforced the learners' tendency to render everything into English in order to confirm their understanding and consequently undermined their confidence in their ability to understand and use French directly. 'Il a mangé pain' (above) and thousands of other Anglicisms were the outcome. 'Depuis' is remembered as a stumbling-block by many who have done French at school but it is largely a difficulty created by making learners start from the English 'since', which leads them to use the wrong tense – 'he has been waiting since midday' is hardly the right cue to help the struggling learner to use the required present tense in French.

Such dangers were self-evident but at the same time the public examinations boards were wedded to translation as the main test form and undue concern with passing exams rather than learning French meant that it persisted as the main activity in teaching too. Specialists like E C Bearman and C V Russell were active within the examinations boards in pushing for more beneficent forms of testing. The latter in particular played a leading role in persuading the Associated Examining Board to break the mould: it was reluctantly permitted by the Secondary Schools Examinations Council to replace prose translation with a 'use of language' test in its O level exams in 1964. Since the AEB also simultaneously increased the mark value of the oral examination, it was hoped that the time freed from doing translations would lead to greater use of the target language in classrooms. However the continued use of translation as the principal means of language teaching in sixth forms and universities exerted a pull in the opposite direction and such over-use was still a major concern 20 years later at the seminal Bradford conference on oral skills in modern language degrees (Doble and Griffiths, 1985).

In summary, between 1945 and 1967 serious questions were being raised about how languages were taught in English secondary schools. Viable procedures were being developed for an active oral approach, the emphasis was shifting from grammar-grind to language structure in meaningful situations and the hegemony of translation was being challenged. These developments did not please traditionalists but neither did they match the behaviourist response to the innovations made possible by advances in technology nor the wish to introduce French into primary schools where it was assumed that unstructured 'naturalness' should be the order of the day. The resulting tensions and the massive change in clientele brought about by comprehensivization meant that post-1967 was to be a challenging period in which to teach modern languages.

Expansion, a modern language for all: 1967–1987

Imagine a continuum: at one end are the findings of academics representing linguistics, literary studies and psychological and social aspects of language, and at the other end are the classroom experience and practical common sense of language teachers in schools. Between the two is an important space in which neither 'pure' theory nor 'chalk-face' reality are completely at home and in which curriculum specialists have to work as bridge builders and mediators. The rapid expansion of language teaching in schools and the explosion of publications with titles including 'sociolinguistics', 'psycho-linguistics', 'stylistics' and 'pragmatics' demanded an increase in this mediating role and created a greater need for theoretical understanding.

The newly established Centre for Information on Language Teaching and Research (CILT) and the expanding university language centres, such as that directed by Professor Eric Hawkins at York, were invaluable players in this development and reinforced the practical guidance provided by international agencies such as the Institut Français and the Goethe Institute, the rich provision of resources from radio and television and the work of the growing body of locally appointed language advisers. The members of NALA (National Association of Language Advisers) became essential in making rapid changes in examinations, teaching materials and new theories comprehensible to language teachers. The Modern Languages Department at the Institute of Education, like all such centres, had to respond too. Its PGCE numbers expanded from 50 to 80 in the 1970s yet graduate teacher training ceased to be its almost exclusive preoccupation. It took responsibility for the 'method' element in the final year of the London Institute's new BEd degree, providing a weekly teaching session and tuition for some 60 languages students per year from the London colleges. A new taught MA course in modern language teaching was introduced, starting with three or four mainly part-time students and expanding fourfold to include full-timers by the mid-1970s. The course was innovative, setting theory firmly within the world of classroom practice and attracted part-time students from as far afield as Bristol and the Isle of Wight.

There had always been a steady flow of colleagues coming to work in London from universities abroad – London's resources are attractive – but now the department found itself teaching opinion-formers from abroad as full-time MA students. From the outset there was a policy of giving close supervision to dissertations, not only to ensure quality and to provide an initiation into research methodology but also to exploit fully the marriage of theory and the daily teaching experiences of the students themselves. This led to a library of work that did much to fill the space between the ends of the continuum described above. Several of the writers went on to do further higher degrees and by the 1980s other education departments, CILT and the languages inspectorate had a rich representation of former MA students.

An increasingly sophisticated profession recognized and debated the questions thrown up by the rapid changes in the activity of teaching languages. What could the new technology offer modern language teachers? How best could a subject area previously almost exclusively concerned with grammar school pupils adapt to expansion in both age range (primary school French) and ability range (comprehensivization)? How could those making slow and limited progress be motivated to continue? What shape should language work in the sixth form take and how should it be assessed since, despite the changed experiences and life-style of the learners and the changes in how languages were taught up to the fifth form, the A level examinations in the late 1960s were virtually indistinguishable from the Higher School Certificate examinations set 50 years earlier.

Developments in technology

Sophisticated projection and sound systems became the approved tools of the language teachers and the use of the word 'laboratory' as in 'language laboratory' gave language learning an apparent air of 'scientific' endeavour. Unfortunately the installation of the expensive equipment came first and the identification of its precise value was often either tardy or even bypassed. The change to such technology-driven teaching did not produce a coherent methodology and an aid was not infrequently described as a method. The problem was described in the report of a CNAA working party:

> Foreign language teaching makes more substantial use of resources other than teachers, chalk and books than it did twenty or even ten years ago. It is, however, clear that the hard work which has accompanied the change has not yet produced a coherent methodology. The points at which given aids can make a valuable contribution need to be identified, new possibilities need to be thought through. At the same time the use of expensive aids should not be

allowed to become an end in itself. Careful sequencing of materials and resource use is called for.

(CNAA, 1979)

If such a warning was needed in a report on higher education, it is hardly surprising that school teachers in less well-resourced settings and with less well-motivated pupils had difficulties. Rational use of language laboratories, for instance, was often thwarted by poor programmes, boring materials and unhelpful timetabling, not to mention physical problems like poor maintenance of the machinery and vandalism. The task of monitoring 30 pupils at a time was very ambitious and called upon the unjustifiable assumption that learners can necessarily hear their mistakes and are in a position to correct them. Content was particularly flawed, relying too heavily on repetition and mechanical drill. Learners could reproduce some of what they learnt by heart but they were unable to create their own appropriate statements or recognize the significant constituents of what they were repeating. Standard laboratory material was in those early days curiously free-floating, divorced from any reality:

> Apply the adjective used in the first half of each sentence to the noun suggested in the second half.
>
> 41. Cette jeune fille est intelligente. Et le garçon? STUDENT: Le garçon est intelligent.
>
> 42. Cette table est intéressante. Et le livre? STUDENT: Le livre est intéressant.
>
> 43. Cette maison est grande. Et le château? STUDENT: Le château est grand.
>
> (Stack, 1960)

The learner has to make statements about unknown and unseen people and things and simply follows the instruction that if a feminine object is big or interesting, then the following masculine one must have the same characteristic. The meaning is actually insignificant. All is intoned in a strangely stilted language, which apparently has no pronouns. Such work reached an even higher level of opacity when pictorial clues were given and learners were expected to understand 'this man has limited aspirations for his son' on the basis of a cartoon sketch of a man looking quizzical. Given the low value of such work and the high cost of the machinery, it was not difficult to think of better uses for the money involved (Rowell, 1974).

More and more language learners

From 1964 there was a growth in the teaching of French in primary schools and work in a pilot group of such schools was monitored by the National Foundation for Educational Research, which produced a critical report (Burstall *et al*, 1974). Unsurprisingly it found that the outcomes were best among girls in schools with enthusiastic heads in middle-class areas well away from disadvantaged urban centres. Despite criticisms, the work looked set to continue, largely because of a belief, based on only marginally relevant studies of first-language acquisition or of evidence from bi- or multilingual societies, that one of the strengths of younger children was an ability to pick up language and native-like pronunciation 'naturally'. This picking-up however had to be done in a couple of hours a week in a classroom saturated with English and possibly with a teacher whose own pronunciation was far from native-like. Use of writing to support and supplement the oral work was generally discouraged and grammar in a form that might have helped the learner to recognize basic patterns and syntax was not considered necessary. Many people actually supported an alternative drive, largely associated with Eric Hawkins at York, to give greater attention to developing children's awareness of language *per se* rather than spending primary school time on memorizing chunks of French of somewhat ephemeral value, often based on games, nursery rhymes and fairy-tales. In fact the languages inspectorate discouraged further expansion and all the questions, including those concerned with the availability of qualified teachers, were overtaken by other problems: falling rolls, comprehensivisation, a growing concern about the neglected mother tongues of an increasing minority of schoolchildren and the absence by default of a clear multilingual languages policy in schools. The absence of French from National Curriculum primary level provision in the late 1980s seemed to put an end to the debate but interestingly, in the cyclical way in which such issues recur, the whole matter has resurfaced in the 1990s and Beate Poole, a lecturer at the Institute of Education, has presented a substantial PhD thesis reviewing the literature and looking at current practice. Her conclusions again point to a lack of evidence that there is anything to be gained by an early start especially given that the unnatural setting of a classroom is not the arena of 'natural' language learning (Poole, 1999).

Comprehensivization brought with it the challenge of mixed-ability teaching, not an activity that accords easily with the cumulative nature of foreign language learning. There were frequent tussles over the need for setting modern language groups even among staff in schools where no streaming of teaching groups was tolerated. Students on teaching practice had to be helped through situations in which, for example, the use of the perfect tense in French or German was on their agenda, a tense that self-evidently presupposed some mastery of the appropriate auxiliary verbs (avoir/être, haben/sein), when these had not been grasped at all by slow learners in a group. A possible solution lay in the preparation of differentiated materials and much time was given to the question of grading and selecting input but in reality many teachers had neither the time for doing this nor the team support available, for example, to trainees. The latter were dismayed to find that the situation tended to lead to counter-productive short cuts – ignoring, for example, the constraints of the language itself by giving little attention to grammatical gender, pretending in German that case endings did not matter or avoiding past tenses by continuing and exclusive use of a historic present tense. All these activities were potentially damaging to the development of future language specialists.

A flood of new materials

As more and more children were included in learning a foreign language, teachers, trainees and course book writers were obliged to organize work with a very shallow gradient of progression. Work in many London classrooms had to blend with the content of *Eclair*, the Inner London Education Authority's specially designed course, which laudably aimed at a pace that did not exclude slow learners (ILEA, 1977). It was based on both structural and situational progression, setting grammar in recognizable simple locations like shops, schools, hotels and youth hostels. It was a useful model of a course that provided a complete package of pupils' books, teacher's notes and worksheets in an attractive and unthreatening layout. Perhaps its only drawback was that its modest objectives were hardly suitable for more able, highly motivated learners.

Already by the beginning of the 1970s the standard audio-visual courses like Crédif's *Voix et Images de France* and Tavor Aids' *Cours Audio-visuel de Français* were in decline and the following decade brought an upsurge in the number of new courses. *Longmans Audio-Visual Course* and Downes and Griffith's *Le Français d'Aujourd'hui* made a serious attempt to marry an oral approach and the new technology with a more conventional textbook style, and the Nuffield/Schools Council's *En Avant*, *Vorwärts* and *Adelante* produced comprehensive packages of materials of sometimes daunting complexity. These and the many other new courses represented an expensive investment for schools and critical analysis of courses became an essential feature of both in-service work and initial training to help teachers to make responsible choices. Every lecturer in the languages department of the Institute of Education consequently engaged in the task of writing course books (Russell,

1968; Hill, 1979, 1980; Hornsey, Hornsey and Harris, 1970, 1971; and Bennett, 1977, 1978, 1981) and the hands-on experience helped to keep our feet on the ground. We recognized that future courses would probably require teams of writers if only to produce the vast quantity of differentiated materials.

The efforts to produce useful materials did have one significant outcome, namely the development of the concept of 'documentary data'. The term, initially defined by Norman Hill (Hornsey, 1975: 143–53), quickly found its way into the vocabulary of language teachers. It focused primarily on the many everyday cues to language: jottings, symbols, notices, street signs, timetables, lists, statistics, recipes, instructions, plans, adverts, diary entries, pager messages. It presented learners with the language-rich talking points of their everyday lives – yesterday's football results (lots of past tenses), small ads, instructions for using or making things. David Swain, HMI, put it very succinctly: 'Inside every railway timetable, with its orderly rows of towns and times and symbols, there is a lot of language trying to get out' (Hornsey, 1975: 177).

The same is true of a football league table or a pop-music chart: they spawn cues to language without revealing it in a form of words that can simply be lifted from the page and they are things that secondary pupils actually do talk about. Eventually these became subsumed under the heading 'authentic materials' fashionable in the 1980s when sadly 'authentic' became the label for anything that really occurs in the foreign country regardless of its language potential, audibility or meaningfulness to learners – muffled railway station announcements, background music in restaurants, ephemeral slang were hardly edifying (Hornsey, 1994).

In 1975 the *Handbook for Modern Language Teachers* was published (Hornsey, 1975). It was not a reference book dominated by lists of useful information but a collection of 48 essays written by teachers, teacher trainers and linguists more than half of whom were, or had been, students or tutors at the Institute of Education. It was an attempt to place principles and theories firmly within the context of the classroom. It contained 10 sections covering questions of grammar, structure, teaching texts, documentary data, visual aids, pronunciation, reading and writing, drills and exercises and sixth-form work. A substantial bibliography was contributed by George Perren, then director of CILT. What clearly emerges from it is a rejection of a strictly behaviourist view of language learning. Rote memorizing and constant repetition are seen as inadequate. There is emphasis on the need to make language structure explicit but this does not signal a return to a Latin-based grammatical approach. The target language will be the main language of the classroom; it will be meaningful, tolerably accurate and, if not authentic, at least plausible.

Motivation: graded objectives and French studies

Coping with a wider range of pupils was not just a matter of finding appropriate materials. There was also the question of motivation. It could no longer be assumed, as it had been in the 1940s and 1950s, that the act of mastering the structure and overcoming the quirks of syntax and lexis would provide sufficient incentives. For English-speaking learners French did not appear to have much marketable value. Language teachers had to search for other attractions: sacrificing vacation time to take parties abroad, arranging exchanges of tapes and letters with school classes in Europe, using procedures pioneered by Barry Jones at Homerton College, Cambridge, and organizing pen-friend schemes. All of these were tried with varying degrees of success and some of the initiatives have survived to exploit fax and e-mail. The Central Bureau for Educational Visits and Exchanges (CBEVE) gave invaluable help with both arranging visits and making contacts. Ultimately however many learners never reached the point where their progress in the language matched the possibilities of such activities. Large numbers simply dropped French at the first opportunity. It was then in the late 1970s and early 1980s that the graded objectives movement (GOML) manifested itself. It was recognized that a promise of rewards only after a course lasting five years was too long-term and that short-term objectives were needed. Often led by local language advisers, *ad hoc* groups of teachers or even just the members of one school's languages department worked to identify a modest and rational progression of short-term goals. A record of achievement was kept, sometimes by the learners themselves, of goals reached both in speech and in writing – goals expressed in recognizable non-technical wording: 'I can now buy a newspaper in a French shop' or 'I can make enquiries about French bus or train times'. The accumulated attainment was then rewarded at intervals with certificates. Learners had tangible evidence of progress and clear goals to reach. The outcome was not a solution to all the problems but it was an imaginative step forward in a subject where for many years the best that was offered, in the absence of any syllabus provided by the examinations boards, was the contents of past exam papers as the only guide to what might be achieved (Harding, Page and Rowell, 1980).

The 1970s produced another initiative that filled the slot in timetables for 'French'. It was popularly known as 'French studies' and had less to do with the French language and more with the culture of everyday French life and interests. It could touch on French history, geography and politics but was more likely to be involved with shopping, travel, sport, television and the world of popular culture. None of this would be unworthy as a preliminary to learning the language or as a setting in which the language could be seen to operate. Unfortunately the clientele for such work was usually those pupils who were seen to be failing to learn French itself. The work became another preoccupation for the languages teacher, requiring new skills and materials, and by the end of 1983 was concerning a number of teachers on the MA course, as their choice of dissertation titles shows: 'Culture in foreign-language teaching', 'The presentation of culture in a selection of course-books', 'Images of France: the transmission of cultural messages'. Such work could have led to a correction of the outdated and romanticized background of many course books but the interest in culture was short-lived. It was not on the examinations agenda even though the stated aims of the National Curriculum stressed the value of cultural awareness. While it lasted, however, it was another distraction, taking up valuable time, for example in the nine-month PGCE course. A student on teaching practice doing too much study of labels on French food products, browsing with 4C through French travel brochures in English or trying to make a vinaigrette was not learning or practising much to do with teaching the language.

Sixth form work

By the 1960s sixth form language teaching, hampered by a form of examination that had persisted since long before the war, was overdue for reform. At its worst the A level gave scant reward for oral ability, overpractised the skill of translation and forced teachers to spend a lot of time training their pupils to write essays in English on literary texts. The latter did not necessarily reflect either current language use, as required in the translation papers themselves, or issues of importance to 18-year-olds living in the 20th century. These texts took up so much time that it left little space for any reading of non-literary language at all. In effect the exam was fulfilling its matriculation function and meeting the needs of entrants to the single-subject BA rather than providing a school-leaving certificate for all language learners even if they did not intend to study them at university.

Pressure for change came firstly from the pupils themselves. They needed a course more in line with their interests and they often did not have the reading background of their predecessors. Their oral skills no longer seemed as important as reading and writing and, for many, sixth form language work represented a lurch into a new subject rather than a development of what had gone before.

Secondly, the degree work itself for which A level had been a preparation was starting to change. Universities like Bradford, Bath and Aston and the polytechnics began to offer courses that led to unusual but very appropriate two-subject degrees such as French and physics or French and law. Even interpreting, previously regarded as not the business of a university, became possible as part of a language degree. This development became so popular that by the late 1990s the single subject language degree had been overtaken in student numbers by such joint degrees.

Thirdly, voices within the profession were being raised against the status quo. Although language teachers were by no means just giving in to buzz-words like 'relevance' nor accepting lower linguistic standards nor even rejecting the value for their pupils of experiencing examples of the very best writing, my criticism of the tendency to impose received views of literature on 18-year-olds and to set texts remote from their experience was generally met with sympathetic support (Hornsey, 1964, 1970). C V Russell was a leading figure in the moves of the AEB to shift the emphasis at A level to the study of contemporary writing – both literary and non-literary – set in a modest understanding of its social, political and linguistic context. His *Post O Level Studies in Modern Languages* (Russell, 1971) was a seminal work. Henry Widdowson also contributed usefully to the debate by advocating a stylistic approach to textual study in which the language became central instead of the pursuit of literary historical ideas (Widdowson, 1975). In schools, Whitmarsh and Jukes's *Advanced French Course*, the standard work since the war, was at last being replaced. Its random passages for translation were being overtaken by thematically more coherent courses like *Actualités Françaises* (Nott and Trickey, 1970). The whole development was greatly strengthened by the work of Frank and Heather Corless and Ralph Gaskell with the French 16–19 Study Group (1981) and in their subsequent publications *Aperçus* and *Vécu* (Corless, Corless and Gaskell, 1987, 1990).

Now and the future: 1987 onwards

The final chapter of the story is characterized by a growing seriousness of purpose in school language teaching as GCSE and the National Curriculum have become established, and by a renewed interest in theoretical issues. The latter has been a response both to the need to justify the position of modern languages in the curriculum and to the assertion that languages are taught for communication, an assertion that is self-evident but that at the same time devalues the cognitive value of the activity. After 30 years of growth and change a need is felt to consider which languages, if any, should be taught, to whom, for how long, with what intensity and to what purpose.

Examinations

The General Certificate of Secondary Education represents in modern languages a culmination of 40 years' efforts by teachers, advisers and examiners to drag language testing out of the 19th century. The traditional pattern of examinations – translation into and out of the foreign language, an essay and a perfunctory oral – had seemed in 1945 to be cast in stone. By the 1960s however orals were being upgraded and alternatives to translation devised, in particular by the AEB. The work of Lado (1961) and Valette (1967) in the USA and Otter (1968) in England encouraged the use of objective test forms and, despite the aberrations and overemphasis on recognition skills produced by the initial enthusiasm for multiple choice, attention was at last directed at identifying exactly which skills were measured by each test form. French dictation, for example, was unmasked: previously seen as a test of listening comprehension, it was recognized as primarily a test of grammar in which the many unsounded endings of words had to be deduced by the candidates. Listening and reading comprehension, previously downgraded by being called 'passive' skills, were re-established in CSE and, in more sophisticated forms, in GCSE. The use of prepared role-plays began to replace the artificial 'conversation' in oral exams. CSE even pioneered the offering of different examination modes giving the possibility of teachers' devising their own syllabuses or, for example, replacing the five-minute oral with continuous oral assessment.

In the 1970s and 1980s, with constant pressure from writers like Page (1973) and Buckby (1980), the changes gathered pace. Oral examinations in GCSE have been tape-recorded and this has made it possible to separate the role of interlocutor (the teacher) from that of assessor (the examiner). Much fuller syllabuses have been provided, replacing guesses based on the evidence of past papers and, with the introduction of different levels, candidates have been able to work at appropriate skills of the right level of difficulty. GCSE has obviated the need to label pupils prematurely as 'CSE' and 'GCE' according to ability. Even attitudes to marking have changed. Examiners in the past, perhaps too influenced by the model of the native speaker, had stressed what candidates could not do instead of using more explicit and more realistic criteria and then marking positively to reward what they could do.

Some problems still remain but they are not insuperable. It would be unfortunate if syllabuses with explicit vocabulary lists led to widespread return to the rote learning of alphabetical word lists regardless of the need for contexts and it would be disastrous if better forms of oral examining were abandoned because of the administrative burden, technological hazards and examiner boredom associated with the recording and marking of thousands of taped orals. The new examination forms are also notoriously difficult to set and need to be retained for reuse in test banks, an invitation, if not carefully monitored, to a culture of published examination cribs. These are all soluble problems. There is still however need to come to terms with the danger that an efficient languages examination needs to separate the different skills in order to do its job properly but language proficiency is more than a compilation of segments. Teaching to the exam can mean stifling genuine creativity and neglecting essential features like cultural awareness, which are very difficult to test. None of which denies that modern language examinations, which in 1950 were substantially the same as they were 50 years earlier, have changed beyond recognition by the 1990s, and for the better.

The National Curriculum

The National Curriculum has forced language teachers to think seriously about how languages are to be taught: the selecting and sequencing of content, the choice of vocabulary, the appropriate balance of speaking, listening, reading and writing. It has also provided for the first time a framework for a nation-wide syllabus. The language teaching community has recognized its undoubted value but its implementation, following hard on the heels of the introduction of the new GCSE examinations in 1986, caused a turmoil in schools, which took almost a decade to clear. Difficulties ranged from the details – the illogicality in the guidelines, for example, of introducing the first person of verbs in level 3 but the second person in level 4, though one could hardly function without the other – to major problems. The reordering of priorities necessitated by a change of emphasis from the supremacy of accuracy and of written skills to a prime aim of conveying and receiving messages in all four skills, the enormous increase in bureaucracy involved in recording hundreds of elements individually mastered by all pupils as they aspired to the next attainment level, the redrafting of schemes of work to match the prescribed 'areas' to be visited – a huge task of compilation from many different sources – and the risk of assessment taking up too much teaching time, all provided daunting challenges.

Fortunately, strong reactions to the prescriptions and considered comments and analyses from all over the country led to the Dearing Review, which brought a more reasoned approach to the implementation of the require-ments and an improved version of the syllabus.

For trainee teachers the details of the National Curriculum became a compulsory part of the PGCE. Its tables, lists, supplements and constant flow of emendations became a major preoccupation. Already by their first job interviews it seemed to be assumed that they would know chapter and verse and trainers found themselves having to give priority to its detailed study. Since there was no national agreement about the content of an ideal PGCE course, it was easy for the National Curriculum to take up time from work intended to help students develop a sound teaching method and appropriate classroom management skills.

The introduction of the National Curriculum coincided with the rapid developments in information technology and the use of computers was seen as essential in every subject. For language teachers it was neither a new dawn – it was in any case too reminiscent of the experience of language laboratories – nor was it a cure for the difficulties of boys whose general espousal of computers was expected to counter their notoriously poor performance in learning languages. PGCE students had to be given hands-on experience and to be shown examples of software. Once again they were faced, as in the early days of language laboratories, with a sophisticated aid that threatened to become a method in itself to be used according to a government-decreed schedule rather than as appropriate. A recognition of the need to be selective in the use of the technology was arrived at rather tardily in the final Dearing proposals after much loss of sleep by teachers faced with primitive software and the tension between the nature of machine-learning and the social and co-operative nature of the oral language-learning procedures they were being urged by the National Curriculum to adopt. It is clear that in language teaching computers will become an invaluable aid to systematic reinforcement and practice of material taught initially in language-like situations provided by a human teacher.

Theory and practice

Advances in technology and the developments in curriculum and examinations have combined to conceal a resurgence in the belief that learning a language in school could be reduced simply to imitating the surface forms of natural language acquisition. Not only has the idea of starting the process at primary level resurfaced but there has also been a dismissal of the value of the learner's awareness of language, with productive language being reduced to a matter of trial and error. Creations like 'je voudrais asseyez-vous' for 'I'd like to sit down' are manifestations of inadequate previous information on which some hypothesis has been based rather than an act of worthwhile creativity in a secondary school learner. Consequently, evening research seminars at the Institute of Education, attended by staff, research students, local teachers and invited guests have become preoccupied with the meaning of 'communicative methodology', with questions of language awareness and with the role of metacognition in foreign language learning (Roberts, 1991).

The assertion 'we teach languages for communication' needs to be examined carefully. Not only does it conveniently avoid the probability that many learners are not going to communicate in French but it also assumes, without clear evidence, that the aim (communication) requires necessarily that the means (what happens in the classroom) should be identical with it. Michael Salter, the chief inspector for languages, was dismayed by what he constantly saw as the result of these assumptions:

> Just as the audio-visual and audio-lingual revolutions were based on the highly commendable recognition of the need to give greater importance to the spoken language, but often led to 'Pavlovian' language learning, so the current emphasis on communicative competence, a very desirable accomplishment in itself, is too frequently resulting in excessive attention to low-level, transactional language. Whether through mechanical question and answer, acting out scenes or taking part in role-play, pupils spend a great deal of their time ordering drinks or meals which they never consume, purchasing items which they never own, seeking information about and buying tickets for journeys which they never make... For many pupils, much of what happens in the classroom is a rehearsal for what will never take place.
>
> (Salter, 1989)

What he describes is itself a cause for concern but it represents only one facet of a basically flawed method. The fusion of aims with means, the constant use of message-oriented language unrelated to precise structural or syntactical learning needs, the casual attitude to linguistic correctness as long as some kind of message is communicated, all seem to contribute to a kind of authenticity (Trim, undated) but the whole process presupposes that the position of a learner in a classroom for two hours per week is identical with that of young people actually living in the community where the target language is spoken all the time. Toddlers acquiring their mother tongue, immigrant children coping with a second language or even learners of English as a foreign language all represent poor models for school language learning in England. A teaching method based on such models means that learners not only fail to 'pick up' a foreign language, since time and motivation are against them, but also miss out on an awareness of the workings of language, which may well be the major justification for including a foreign language in the compulsory curriculum. Since it is impossible to identify one single language that will certainly be needed in the future, the prime function of the foreign language studied at school must be to introduce learners to experience and transferable strategies that will enable them to learn more easily any language that may become necessary to them in their adult life. In fact it could well be that it is the ability to read a language for business purposes that will be needed, precisely the skill that tends to be overlooked when spoken communication is stressed. The current neglect of written texts is now being seen as a cause for regret (Turner, 1994), whereas this history began with teachers' concern that the opposite was the case.

Envoi

The history of language teaching has been characterized by pendulum-like swings between direct methods and grammatical approaches and the last 50 years have run true to form. While teachers have usually found their own tentative compromises, opinion-formers have continued to take up 'either... or' positions: communication versus grammar; fluency versus accuracy; speech versus writing; situation versus structure; exclusive use of the target language versus mother tongue explanation. Calm consideration of how and where each of these putative opposites can fulfil a proper role has often been neglected. For example, in the 1960s, the *En Avant* course for primary schools initially rejected all writing for the first two years, not only failing to exploit its value as a support, summary and supplement to oral work but also imposing a considerable burden on the learners' memory. Many children responded by making up their own spellings. The extreme position had to be abandoned.

In the 21st century this pattern will have to be broken. Linguists will need to abandon 'either... or' extremes and respond to the inevitable advances in knowledge and technology by first clarifying aims and only then adopting the best available procedures and aids, regardless of orthodoxies, commercial pressures or the excitement generated by novelties. They will also have to face up to the problems of a school subject that lacks a self-evident justification for inclusion in the curriculum for all and show how learning a language can uniquely contribute to the education of future citizens of a language-saturated world. Then teachers and learners will be working purposefully towards an achievement that can genuinely compensate for trying to learn a language not perceived as necessary in itself in a location where the ease of natural acquisition is not possible.

References

Assessment of Performance Unit (1985) *Foreign Language Performance in Schools*, Report on 1983 survey, pp 208 *et seq*, Department of Education and Science

Bennett, A J (1977, 1978, 1981) ¡Buenos Dias!, Hodder and Stoughton, London

Buckby, M (1980) A graded system of syllabuses and examinations, Modern Languages in Scotland, 20, pp 75–81

Burstall, C et al (1974) Primary French in the Balance, NFER, London

Collins, H F (1930) A French Course for Schools, Macmillan, London

Corless, F, Corless, H and Gaskell, R (1987) Aperçus, Hodder and Stoughton, London

Corless, F, Corless, H and Gaskell, R (1990) Vécu, Hodder and Stoughton, London

Council for National Academic Awards (CNAA) (1979) Report of the Working Party on Resources for Language Learning, p 4, London

Doble, G and Griffiths, B (eds) (1985) Oral Skills in the Modern Languages Degree, University of Bradford 1984, CILT, London

Dutton, B (1965) A Guide to Modern Language Teaching Methods, Cassell, London

French 16–19 Study Group (1981) French 16–19: A new perspective, Hodder and Stoughton, London

Gilbert, M (1967) Cours illustré de français, University of London Press, London

Harding, A, Page, B and Rowell, S (1980) Graded Objectives in Modern Languages, CILT, London

Hawkins, E W (1987) Modern Language in the Curriculum, Cambridge University Press, Cambridge

Hill, N (1979, 1980) Across the Channel, Books 1 and 2, Hachette, Paris

Hodgson, F M (1955) Learning Modern Languages, Routledge & Kegan Paul, London

Hodgson, F M (1961) Language Learning Material, Educational Explorers Ltd, Reading

Hornsey, A W (1964) Wolfgang Borchert: Selected short stories, Pergamon, Oxford

Hornsey, A W (1970) Set books and sixth form studies, Modern Languages, 21 (4)

Hornsey, A W (ed) (1975) Handbook for Modern Language Teachers, Methuen, London

Hornsey, A W (1983) Aims and objectives in foreign language teaching, in Teaching Modern Languages, ed G Richardson, pp 1–19, Croom Helm, London

Hornsey, A W (1994) Authenticity in foreign language teaching, Languages Forum, 1 (2/3), February, ed A D Roberts, Institute of Education, University of London, London

Hornsey, A W, Hornsey, M and Harris, D (1970, 1971) On parle français, Parts 1, 2 and 3, Heinemann, London

Inner London Education Authority (ILEA) (1977) Eclair, Mary Glasgow, London

Lado, R (1961) Language Testing, Longman, London

Nott, D O and Trickey, J (1970, 1971) Actualités Françaises, English Universities Press, London

Otter, H S (1968) A Functional Language Examination, Oxford University Press, Oxford

Page, B W (1973) Another look at examinations, Audio-Visual Language Journal, 11 (2), pp 127–30

Poole, B (1999) Is younger better? A critical examination of the beliefs about learning a foreign language at primary school, unpublished thesis, University of London, London

Roberts, A D (1991) Towards a Learning Theory in Modern Languages, Occasional Papers, 2, Institute of Education, University of London, London

Rowell, S M (1974) Language laboratories in secondary schools in Great Britain, unpublished dissertation, Institute of Education, University of London, London
Russell, C V (1968) *Audio-Visual German*, Pergamon, Oxford
Russell, C V (1971) *Post O Level Studies in Modern Languages*, Pergamon, Oxford
Salter, M (1989) *Times Educational Supplement*, 3 March
Stack, E M (1960) *The Language Laboratory and Modern Language Teaching*, p 2, Oxford University Press, New York
Trim, J L (undated) *What is Meant by a 'Communicative Approach to Modern Language Teaching'*, CILT Information Sheet (late 1980s)
Turner, K (1994) Developing learner competence through written texts, *Languages Forum*, **1** (2/3), Institute of Education, University of London, London
Valette, R M (1967) *Modern Language Testing: A handbook*, Harcourt Brace, New York
Widdowson, H G (1975) *Stylistics and the Teaching of Literature*, Longman, London

Chapter 7

The evolution of music education

Charles Plummeridge

Introduction

In a wide-ranging and fascinating historical survey, Bernarr Rainbow (1989) has demonstrated that although music is often thought of as a relatively new addition to the curriculum it is, in fact, one of the oldest of school subjects. The ancient Egyptians, Greeks and Romans all considered musical studies to be of educational value, and due to the centrality of singing in religious practices over the past 2,000 years music has often been accorded a place in educational institutions. To appreciate modern patterns of curriculum organization and practice it is necessary to recognize that their foundations were laid during the course of the 19th century. Amongst many celebrated Victorian educationists, the names of John Hullah, Sarah Glover, John Curwen, William Hickson and John Turner stand out as forward-looking and imaginative teachers who promoted music teaching in the elementary schools. These innovators devoted their attention to class singing and the development of children's aural and music literacy skills. Their work rested on two closely related principles. Firstly, it was maintained that musical instruction in schools would lead to an improvement in the standard of congregational singing and thus the enhancement of divine worship. Secondly, many educators held a belief, inherited partly from classical ideals, in the power of music to cultivate moral awareness and a sense of decorum; there was a conviction that engagement in musical activity could become a worthy pastime for the lower orders and an alternative to those less desirable pursuits famously described by Hickson (1836) as 'vicious indulgences'.

Victorian thinking about musical education now seems rather quaint; the religious aims are no longer relevant and no doubt present-day choralists are slightly amused by the idea that singing would detract people from the pleasures (or evils) of the 'beer house'. However, several pedagogical techniques of the period survive in current practices, and the principle that music can and should be taught to all children as part of a general education has gradually won acceptance and finally official endorsement.

During the latter part of the 19th century a number of progressively minded headmasters in the reformed independent schools appointed directors of music to organize extra-curricular pursuits: individual instrumental tuition, choirs, orchestras and ensembles. These forms of music-making were also considered important in the growing number of private schools for girls. Music was treated as a 'cultural pursuit', which contributed to students' social accomplishments and the corporate life of the institution. Throughout the 20th century there was a gradual fusion of elementary and independent traditions of music teaching so that today music in the vast majority of schools is both a curriculum subject and a series of extra-curricular activities.

When referring to school music it is now customary to talk of music education. This is a slightly ambiguous term since it has come to include all forms of musical instruction that take place in schools, colleges, specialist music schools, conservatoires and universities. The intention in this chapter is to focus mainly on music as a component of children's general education and consider some of the factors that have contributed to its evolution as a school subject.

Developments in class music teaching

When the Subject Working Group for Music published its interim report in January 1991 (DES, 1991), outlining proposals for the National Curriculum, there were mixed reactions from different interest groups, which led to a surprisingly protracted and sometimes acrimonious public debate. Some of the most vehement criticisms came from certain philosophers and musicians who objected to the content of the proposed specification on the grounds that it represented a rejection of 'classical' values and an acceptance of popular culture. This interpretation was not only unjustified and inaccurate; it indicated how little these critics knew of developments in school music teaching. Even so, varying responses should not have been entirely unexpected, since one of the characteristic features of music education in British schools over the past 100 years has been its diversity in both theory and practice. Numerous 'experts' have introduced a plethora of rationales, pedagogical techniques, classroom resources and teaching materials. Consequently, there are, nowadays, alternative and often conflicting ideas about the place of music in the curriculum, what content should be selected and how the subject should be taught. What the Subject Working Group wisely attempted to do was produce a specification that reflected different strands of thinking and incorporate what they regarded as the best aspects of the many approaches to class music teaching. This was never going to be an easy task, but most music educators applauded the Group's efforts to take into account the variety of existing views and practices.

From 1945 until the 1960s, when music was becoming more firmly established as a curriculum subject in both primary and secondary schools, it was commonly accepted that children should learn something of the folk and classical musical traditions that constituted their cultural heritage. An examination of published schemes and materials reveals that programmes consisted typically of class singing, some recorder playing, skill development and musical appreciation. The popular and widely used course books by Priestley and Grayson (1947), Fiske and Dobbs (1956) and Horton (1969) are typical of the period: the content is carefully chosen, thoughtfully structured and beautifully presented, and always within the framework of classical tonality. There was an assumption that instruction in the arts should be part of an education that would equip young people for what the Newsom Committee (Central Advisory Council for Education, 1963) described as the 'life of work and leisure'. Music, designated as one of the 'practical' subjects, fitted in well with the concept of education for leisure. However, in spite of its practical nature, teachers in secondary schools sometimes attempted to make music more 'academic' by concentrating on historical and musicological aspects of the subject. People have speculated as to why teachers followed this much-frowned-upon course of action. It has been suggested that some did so because 'written work' was less demanding (and certainly quieter) than practical activity; others perhaps saw it as an outcome of the appreciation movement or a preparation for the fairly theoretical General Certificate of Education (GCE). For those who preferred sociological explanations, the academic study of music was interpreted as a way of raising the status of the subject (and the teacher) within the curriculum and the school. But learning 'about' music was condemned by several leading music educationists as unmusical and of little educational value.

In 1968 the Schools Council published the findings of a survey relating to secondary students' attitudes towards curriculum subjects; it was readily apparent that a large number of young people found music to be one of the least interesting. This naturally caused some consternation amongst members of the music education community who called for some fundamental and hasty practical reforms. However, significant changes were already occurring in class music teaching, which would have important effects over the next two decades. The ideas and teaching techniques associated with Orff Schulwerk became widely known through in-service courses offered by Margaret Murray (1957) and other Orff specialists. And there was a new interest in creative music-making generated through the innovative work of Murray Schafer (1965), George Self (1967), Tom Gamble (1976), Brian Dennis (1970) and John Paynter and Peter Aston (1970). The focus was now on encouraging children to explore and experiment with the basic materials of music, and compose in ways that often reflected the styles and techniques of contemporary, and especially avant-garde, composers. Those who supported this 'progressive' form of teaching emphasized that music in schools must be meaningful for all students; its main aim should be the education of feeling and the development of qualities of mind: imagination, creativity, sensitivity, aesthetic awareness. The best way of achieving genuine musical experiences for the majority was through direct musical encounters of a creative kind; less attention needed to be given to the acquisition of traditional aural and notational skills. This view was most clearly exemplified in the Schools Council Project *Arts and the Adolescent* directed by Malcolm Ross (1975). Some of the new ideas were thought to be 'revolutionary' although few innovators suggested that conventional styles of music teaching should be entirely abandoned. However, several music educators were very suspicious of these innovations and their underlying rationales. Arnold Bentley (1975) and Bernarr Rainbow (1985), both highly distinguished and respected figures, expressed reservations over what they considered to be fashionable but dubious trends. They regretted that there now seemed to be a neglect of essential aural skill development, which they saw as being at the heart of any genuine musical education. These different conceptions of music education were reflected to some extent in two Schools Council projects, namely *Music Education for Young Children* (Kendell, 1976) and *Music in the Secondary School Curriculum* (Paynter, 1982).

Teachers in schools throughout the 1970s and 1980s, always intent on finding activities that 'worked' and less bothered about ideological matters, were inclined to draw on both traditional and progressive methods in their everyday practices. An increasing number designed programmes that made provision for performing, composing and listening activities. The idea of a general musical education through different modes of experience had been advocated for many years by several well-known individuals including Percy Scholes (1935) and Kenneth Simpson (1968). One of the most detailed modern versions of this thesis is the CLASP model of curriculum design outlined by Keith Swanwick (1979); this subsequently proved to be popular with teachers and influential in curriculum planning. Composition (C), audition (listening in audience) (A) and performing (P) are main activities supported by the acquisition of skills (S) and knowledge about music, described as literature studies (L). The theoretical underpinning of Swanwick's model, which is further developed in his later writings (Swanwick, 1994, 1999), is a good example of how practice has been determined by changing views regarding the nature and significance of music itself. Following newer thinking in aesthetics, epistemology and developmental psychology, there is an emerging conception of the arts disciplines as ways of knowing or realms of meaning with a cognitive content equal to that of the sciences, mathematics and languages. At the same time, educators have questioned the dominance of Western classical traditions, and come to recognize the numerous styles and genres that constitute the 'world' of music. An inclusive view is taken to be a necessary condition for music studies that are part of an education in and for a pluralist society. The principle of basing school music programmes on the three experiential modes of performing, composing and listening and a broad conception of music received the official seal of approval from HMI in 1985 (DES, 1985a) and was incorporated into the national criteria for the General Certificate of Secondary Education (DES, 1985b). The same principle has informed the National Curriculum at all stages of its development.

Important changes in classroom practice have also been brought about by the growth of musical resources. In the 1920s, the availability of the gramophone and broadcasting led to the broadening of curricula, and the introduction of bamboo pipes, recorders and percussion instruments, well before the war years, marked the start of a move away from singing as the central classroom activity. The pitch and non-pitch percussion instruments originally designed by Carl Orff and brought to British schools during the 1960s enabled pupils to participate in new forms of instrumental music-making. Over the last 20 years, the rapid growth of technology has transformed the music classroom. Electronic instruments and computers with MIDI connections to keyboards facilitate sequencing, editing and notating, and enable access to a much wider range of performance and compositional activities. Most teachers welcome these technological advances, which are likely to revolutionize class music teaching in the coming years. However, Richard Hodges (1996), a leading authority in this field, has warned of the dangers of using the technology for little more than the development of basic skills. Technology has to be employed in imaginative ways that will contribute to students' *musical education*. As he rightly says, children can quickly learn 'how' to use computer software, but they also need to be taught how to use it musically and creatively.

Twenty-five years ago the prospect of a national curriculum for music would have seemed extremely remote to most people. However, it is not a new idea in musical circles. Walford Davies was recommending a national scheme for Wales in the 1920s, and in 1947 the Incorporated Society of Musicians (ISM) published an ambitious and detailed programme for use in primary and secondary schools. For reasons mentioned earlier, music teaching in British schools has never been uniform and some educators are unhappy about a centrally prescribed curriculum. However, others regard it as a way of ensuring that all children enjoy a musical education that provides for proper continuity and progression. In its conference report of 1999 the National Association of Music Educators refers to the findings of OFSTED supporting the claim that since the introduction of the 1995 Order there has been a marked improvement in the standard and quality of class music teaching. Many people will conclude that this information augurs well for the future. Those who have doubts about the advisability and viability of a centralized music curriculum might be slightly more sceptical.

The extra-curricular dimension

Although musical activities beyond the curriculum originated in the independent sector, it would nowadays be rare to find any school where music was no more than a timetabled subject. Usually, there are opportunities for children to receive additional instrumental tuition and to participate in choirs, orchestras, bands and other ensembles. These performing groups take place after normal school hours or at lunchtimes, and not infrequently at weekends and during holidays. Music teachers in both primary and secondary schools are expected to organize a variety of musical events throughout the year; indeed, concerts, productions and other presentations have become a standard feature of school life in this country.

There is a long tradition of instrumental teaching by visiting specialists, which can be traced back to the early part of the 20th century when much of the pioneering work was undertaken by the Rural Music Schools Association. Dorothy Taylor (1979) has pointed out that this aspect of musical education was further facilitated in the immediate post-war years following the appointment of advisers in most local education authorities. By 1968 Gertrude Collins was able to state that instrumental tuition in schools was an 'accepted fact', although conditions for teaching were often far from satisfactory. Individual and group instrumental lessons are now provided by local authority music services, private bodies, charitable trusts and self-employed teachers. One of the outcomes of this expansion has been the formation of orchestras and bands not only in schools but also in the local authorities. Many LEAs operate summer schools for young instrumentalists and singers, with youth orchestras and choirs frequently achieving very high standards of performance.

Some 10 years ago Caroline Sharp (1991) estimated that approximately half a million children were receiving instrumental tuition in schools. However, during the 1990s there was a decline in provision following the delegation of school budgets and changes in local authority funding of services. There are differences of opinion regarding the extent of the decline but the situation led to yet another public outcry and debate. Some well-known and influential members of the musical establishment protested that lack of opportunity for young people to learn musical instruments was not only educationally short-sighted and unacceptable, but would ultimately be to the detriment of the musical life of the nation. The government responded to these adverse comments and widely reported anxieties by launching the National Federation for Youth Music with substantial support for the improvement of music services. Even so, provision for instrumental tuition in schools across the country remains extremely variable and the recently appointed National Advisory Committee on Creative and Cultural Education (NACCCE, 1999) has recommended a national review of instrumental teaching services.

The 19th-century innovators in the independent schools were very conscious of a close relationship between artistic activities and social cohesion. They valued performances of choirs and orchestras as celebratory occasions that united staff and students and reinforced a community identity. Most teachers today in both independent and maintained sectors probably agree with such a view, but would also want to emphasize that extra-curricular activities are musically and educationally worth while in that they offer opportunities that are additional to (and in some ways different from) those of the regular curriculum. Unfortunately, throughout the 1960s and 1970s there was sometimes a tendency, especially in secondary schools, to devote a disproportionate amount of time and energy to this aspect of the music programme. Teachers were first gently chided and then severely criticized for 'neglecting' the class lessons. In an extensive survey carried out as part of the Schools Council Project *Music in the Secondary School Curriculum* (Paynter, 1982), it became apparent that over-concentration on highly accomplished groups of selected performers could lead to music being regarded as an exclusive pursuit and therefore of interest to only a minority. Consequently, teachers are now expected to ensure that curriculum and extra-curricular activities are properly related in a coherent music education programme that caters for all children.

Over the past 50 years 'public' musical events have become increasingly ambitious and sophisticated. Schools frequently mount performances of operas, standard choral works and musicals, as well as more modest concerts such as those featuring year-group work and student compositions. These presentations are seen as educationally valuable in that they provide further opportunities for students to develop their understanding and awareness of music and what it is to be a performing musician. The point has also been made by David Hargreaves (1982) that taking part in corporate artistic activities can be an important means of enhancing students' confidence and self-esteem. Hargreaves argues that because schooling often focuses on individual academic success, some less successful students acquire a poor self-image and a sense of personal failure. Through an arts production involving large numbers, the individual child who plays only a small part can nevertheless feel that he or she has made a contribution to the venture and thus develop a sense of achievement and personal dignity. On this view, extra-curricular activities in the arts are of value as forms of personal and social education.

Most teachers would probably subscribe to the musical and social values outlined above, but concerts and other musical presentations can be interpreted rather differently. It is sometimes said that they are used for the purpose of advertising a school's achievements and projecting its image in what is an increasingly competitive educational climate. There are plenty of stories about music being used by headteachers for the purpose of 'window dressing'. The extent of this practice is difficult to estimate, but findings from research conducted by Lawson, Plummeridge and Swanwick (1993) suggest that such observations are not entirely without substance. Of course, schools have always been proud of their artistic and cultural activities and public events are much welcomed and enjoyed by parents. The unease expressed by some educationists is that the promotion of school image could become the main reason for encouraging concerts and other artistic presentations.

There are, of course, many activities apart from those in music and the arts that take place outside school hours. Andrews, Vernon and Walton (1996) report that parents value and support these aspects of their children's schooling not simply as pleasant optional extras but as an essential part of a general education. Smith and Tomlinson (1989) suggest that pupils who participate in extra-curricular pursuits may make better overall progress in schools, and more recently, Michael Barber (Barber et al, 1997) has indicated that a flourishing extra-curricular programme is a characteristic feature of the 'effective' school.

Research, theory and practice

Although it may well be thought that music education research in Britain is in its infancy, an examination of Richard Colwell's (1992) comprehensive review of the field indicates that this is far from the case. There may be a slightly older tradition in the United States but British research has been steadily expanding over the past 50 years as music education has emerged as an area of educational study in its own right. The publication of another introductory text (Kemp, 1992), specifically for music educators, and the appearance of a new journal, *Research in Music Education*, are both signs of responses to the demands of a growing research community.

During the 1950s and 1960s a number of musicians, psychologists and educationists in Europe and America, influenced by the earlier work of Carl Seashore (1938), conducted investigations into the nature of musical ability. In Britain, the two best-known researchers were Herbert Wing (1948) and Arnold Bentley (1966). Bentley, at the University of Reading, concentrated on measuring competencies that were said to constitute the core of musical operations: pitch discrimination, tonal memory, rhythmic memory and chord (harmonic) analysis. His test battery can be easily administered to large numbers of subjects and has sometimes been used for diagnostic purposes, but more usually as a way of selecting children for instrumental tuition. There is now a general acceptance that this selection procedure has not been very satisfactory for both musical and educational reasons. It is an example of how psychological findings can be too readily applied in educational contexts and without sufficient regard to the complex relationship between research and practice.

Bentley's interests were by no means confined to psychometric studies. He encouraged research in many areas, organized conferences and in 1972 played a major part in establishing the Society for Research in the Psychology of Music and Music Education (SRPMME) and its journal, *Psychology of Music*. The society provided a national and international forum for researchers and curriculum theorists and continues to be one of the most active associations concerned with the psychology of music and the study of music education. Over the past 30 years psychological research in music education has broadened in its scope with greater emphasis on investigations into the developmental nature of musical operations and children's musical learning. The writings of Desmond Sergeant (1969), John Sloboda (1985), David Hargreaves (1986), Anthony Kemp (1996) and Keith Swanwick and June Tillman (1986) are illustrative of the variety of studies in the psychology of music related to education.

A second area of research, namely historical studies, arose initially from an interest in past methods of teaching. Kenneth Simpson (1976) and his colleagues in London revisited the ideas and practices of some 'great' music educators and sought to show how a knowledge of their methods could be useful in a practical sense and also help to shed light on current policies and practices. One of the outstanding researchers in the history of music education has been Bernarr Rainbow (1989) whose seminal writings over some 40 years have made a major contribution to the field. In general, historical research has not received wide acknowledgement, perhaps because it seems to be a scholarly area of enquiry and removed from the concerns of contemporary practitioners. However, there are signs of renewed interest. Articles on music education are now published more frequently in the historical journals, and the recent work of researchers including Christopher Turner (1997), Gordon Cox (1993), Stephanie Pitts (1998), David Allsobrook (1992) and Vic Gammon (1999) shows how historical investigations can be of both academic interest and practical relevance.

The publication of Bennett Reimer's (1970, 1989) *A Philosophy of Music Education* signalled an approach to music education that placed importance on aesthetic theory as a basis for practice. Greatly influenced by the philosophy of Suzanne Langer, Reimer was one of a number of arts educators to subscribe to the notion of *aesthetic education*, which has since been taken further by Malcolm Ross (1989) and Peter Abbs (1994). The connections between musical aesthetics and music education are most powerfully illuminated in the writings of Louis Arnaud Reid (1969, 1986), who is one of the few leading philosophers of education in Britain to have focused on the teaching of the arts subjects. One of the outcomes of work in the philosophy of art has been a support for the idea of the arts as a 'generic community'. For Abbs (1994), what unites the arts is the aesthetic mode of understanding and certain common practical procedures. Such a view is sometimes used to justify proposals for combined arts programmes and the establishment of arts departments in secondary schools. However, combined arts teaching and the concept of aesthetic education have not received universal approval; both are strongly challenged on philosophical grounds by David Best (1992) and David Elliott (1995).

Studies in the sociology of music during the 1970s supported new thinking regarding the choice of curriculum content and methods of teaching. Of particular note is the theoretical work of John Shepherd (1977), Graham Vulliamy (1977) and Christopher Small (1977), who in different ways drew on the 'new wave' sociology of education and the sociology of knowledge; in so doing they questioned many of the aesthetic theories that had often been taken as 'given' by music educators. Empirical investigations within a sociological framework, carried out by Lucy Green (1988, 1997), indicate changing attitudes on the part of teachers as to what 'counts' as music in an educational context, and a growing rejection of the principle that the Western classical tradition represents the paradigm of musical achievement. Conceptions of music have also been modified by research in the field of ethnomusicology and especially through the writings of John Blacking (1973). Several educationists including Robert Kwami (1998), Trevor Wiggins (1993), Gerry Farrell (1990) and Jonathon Stock (1996) have used their ethnomusicological research findings as a basis for the production of classroom activities designed to introduce children to a variety of world genres.

In his excellent introduction to research in music education, Kemp (1992) outlines some standard methods and provides illustrative examples. However, he and Adelman (Kemp and Adelman, 1992) could find no instances of British music educators adopting action research strategies. This is perhaps surprising since one of the outcomes of the Schools Council Project *Music in the Secondary School Curriculum* (Paynter, 1982) was that teachers were encouraged to reflect on their practice, meet together and enter into a pedagogical dialogue. Such procedures are at the heart of action research methods and one might expect that this would have been an area of developing interest. Although more teachers are registering for research degrees it may be that a research orientation does not, at present, inform the wider music education community. It might also be argued that government policies militate against the 'teacher as researcher' movement.

Music is school and community

There have always been links between school music educators and professional musicians since many composers, conductors and performers take part in different kinds of educational work and teach in educational institutions. Over a long period composers have written music for children: Gustav Holst, Ralph Vaughan Williams, Benjamin Britten, Peter Maxwell-Davies, Imogen Holst and Elizabeth Poston are amongst the many British composers who have contributed to the large instrumental and vocal repertoire for young performers. Live performances for children are encouraged by musicians and educationists. Robert Mayer and Earnest Read, in the 1920s and 1940s respectively, organized orchestral concerts for schoolchildren that proved popular, and with the growth of local education authority music services after 1945 there were new opportunities for students to experience high-level professional performances at first hand. One of the first LEAs to develop music programmes was the West Riding of Yorkshire. The music organizer, Edmund Priestley, founded first a small professional demonstration orchestra and later a string quartet to give concerts in the authority's schools. Paul Mann (1991) has provided a detailed and most enlightening account of Priestley's untiring efforts to bring music to the children of Yorkshire. The West Riding became famous for its imaginative and adventurous music policy. It was often taken as a model for initiatives in other local authorities with professional concerts for students becoming a regular feature of music education schemes in many parts of the country.

At the beginning of the millennium there are many opportunities for children to have more direct contact with professional musicians. Opera companies, national orchestras and other bodies now appoint education officers to promote outreach and partnership programmes so that performers are able to share their expertise with young people. There are also organizations that set up school and community projects and employ specialists in jazz, rock and non-Western genres. Support for music in the curriculum from agencies beyond the school has increased considerably over the past 10 years; an informative coverage of these developments is given by John Stephens, Jillian Moore and Julian Smith (1995). On the whole, moves to encourage professional musicians to work in schools have proved very successful, although Saville Kushner (1991) has shown that these innovations, like any others, are not always straightforward and unproblematic.

A glance at the *Music Education Yearbook* (Head, 1999) reveals a large number of professional associations and societies for music educationists. Many of these have been, and continue to be, influential in the creation of school policies and practices. The associations fall into three main categories. First, there are those that have been formed for the purpose of studying and disseminating the principles of national and international figures in music education, the most prominent being Kodaly, Suzuki, Curwen and Orff. These societies organize teachers' courses, summer schools and conferences; some award certificates and diplomas. Their influence has been widespread although members have sometimes been criticized for being rather narrow in their outlook and overzealous in their commitment to one approach to music teaching. On occasion, such criticism may be justified but the overall impact of these societies has been mostly positive. A second category consists of those societies set up by musicians and educationists who share a particular specialism: instrumentalists, choralists, conductors, therapists, composers, handbell ringers and piano tuners. Their general aim is to maintain high standards of professional practice through courses and conferences. In different ways all have had direct and indirect influences on the growth of school music. The third category of professional associations comprises those national bodies that cater for a wide cross-section of the music education community and includes the Incorporated Society of Musicians (ISM), the Schools Music Association (SMA), the Music Education Council (MEC) and the National Association of Music Educators (NAME). These organizations offer a range of services to their members and aim to support teachers and disseminate good practice through their courses, conferences and journals. Throughout the post-war years the professional societies have advised governments and official bodies on music education policies; recently, they have been particularly active in monitoring the National Curriculum and participating in consultation exercises at all stages. And in the increasingly political educational climate these societies have ensured that government and the general public are constantly reminded of the importance and value of music in education; they have also drawn attention to the economic benefits of a strong musical culture in a post-industrial society.

Teacher education and training

In 1839 Dr James Kay, Secretary of the Committee of Council on Education, appointed John Hullah as music teacher at the newly founded teachers training college in Battersea. So began the tradition of including music studies in the training of elementary schoolteachers that was to last until the 1930s. Students received instruction in sol-fa and many had regular piano lessons. According to Rainbow (1985) this policy ensured that children's singing in the elementary schools was kept at a good standard. After 1945 music became an optional subject in training courses for primary teachers. Where students were able to opt for music they usually followed a musically demanding course of study and were well equipped for their roles as music specialists or co-ordinators. But the policy of making music optional meant that in some schools there was no teacher with substantial musical expertise and the subject was given little attention or even ignored. Many teachers relied on school broadcasts such as *Singing Together* and *Time and Tune*, which were well designed, musically attractive and effectively presented. Unfortunately, those teachers without sufficient musical know-how could often not carry out the necessary follow-up work. In 1986, Shirley Cleave and Caroline Sharpe reported that 75 per cent of postgraduate courses for general primary teachers included a compulsory music element but usually amounting to no more than 20 hours. Large numbers of students following BEd courses received little or no musical tuition. Inadequate musical training for primary school generalists has been a problem for 50 years and with ever greater prominence being given to the core subjects it seems most unlikely that the situation will improve in the foreseeable future.

The shortage of qualified music teachers for the secondary schools in the 1940s led to the introduction of graduate diplomas in the colleges of music that included an element of professional training. Some college and university music graduates completed general courses at the training colleges but for many this proved to be of only limited value. This somewhat unsatisfactory situation was greatly improved by the establishment of specialist one-year postgraduate courses for musicians. The first commenced in 1949 at the University of Reading under the direction of Arnold Bentley. Ten years later Kenneth Simpson was appointed Head of the newly formed Department for the Teaching of Music at the Institute of Education in London to set up a similar course. This pattern of consecutive education and training for secondary music specialists was subsequently offered in other university departments of education and the colleges of education.

With the introduction of the BEd degree in 1964 many of the concurrent music courses in the colleges for intending primary and secondary teachers became rather more academic and performance-oriented, with less attention given to music teaching skills. When in the 1970s the Schools Council (Paynter, 1982) reviewed the training of secondary music teachers it was concluded that many had not acquired the range of musical techniques required for class teaching. Students embarking on training programmes were often accomplished musicians, but with a very narrow expertise. It was suggested that although high standards in individual instrumental performance, conducting and academic knowledge were obviously valuable and, indeed, necessary, teachers also needed further opportunities to develop as composers and arrangers. What is not clear from the report is whether or not these reservations about teacher education applied to both concurrent and consecutive courses. The vast majority of secondary specialists now follow the one-year programme and have to acquire a much greater range of musical and professional skills than was the case in the early 1980s. But how much new musical knowledge can be assimilated in one postgraduate year remains questionable. It is interesting to note that OFSTED (1999) report that while student subject knowledge is good, most need support in one or more of the following areas: music technology, world music repertoire, vocal music, composing.

There has, of course, been a major expansion of in-service education and training (INSET) with courses covering every aspect of music teaching being provided by the LEA advisory services, the colleges of education, university departments, professional associations and consultants. At the present time there is a particular demand for INSET from generalist primary teachers who are required to teach music but are lacking in confidence and the necessary skills. However, because of the new emphasis on numeracy and literacy fewer primary schoolteachers see music as a priority in their personal development plans. For secondary specialists, courses in world musics and music technology continue to attract large numbers of applicants. An important new in-service initiative is the introduction of training courses for private instrumental teachers. Following an extensive survey Louise Gibbs (1993) concluded that these teachers constituted a 'forgotten group' of music educators. Private teachers clearly make a valuable contribution to music in society but their educational function has not always been fully appreciated. These teachers are aware of the need for professional development and the advisability of obtaining recognized teaching qualifications. The University of Reading in collaboration with the Incorporated Society of Musicians now offers a diploma course of continuing professional education for private instrumental and voice teachers; on successful completion some may proceed to higher degree studies. A similar course is run by the Associated Board of the Royal Schools of Music (ABRSM).

Since the establishment of the Council for the Accreditation of Teacher Education (CATE) in 1984 and more recently the Teacher Training Agency (TTA) there have been major changes in initial teacher training. A series of government circulars has set out defined policies and instructions, and control of courses has been removed from the training institutions. Schools play a much larger part in the training process with subject mentors having increased responsibility for introducing beginning teachers to methods, classroom materials and resources. The training institutions, closely monitored by the Office for Standards in Education (OFSTED), are required to focus on trainees reaching required 'standards' in subject knowledge, planning and management, communication skills, assessment, reporting and recording. Following a secondary subject inspection (SSI), OFSTED (1999) has reported on 25 PGCE music courses. The quality of training is judged to be good or very good in a large number of cases but some providers do not make sufficient provision for the development of trainees' subject knowledge. Whilst this may be a valid criticism the inspectors fail to address the complexity of the subject knowledge issue. The best trainees are said to be outstanding although a significant minority need to improve the monitoring, assessing and recording of students' progress. This is perhaps hardly surprising when one considers the difficulty of such tasks, which even the most experienced music teachers find extremely taxing. The inspectors report that recruitment is good but institutions find it difficult to meet targets. Overall, the standards and quality of music teacher training are judged to be high. These findings are reassuring for the training institutions and will obviously be welcomed by members of the teaching profession.

There has been much criticism of teacher training over the past 20 years especially on the part of politicians and right-wing groups like the Centre for Policy Studies (Lawlor, 1993). Staff in colleges and university departments are accused of peddling specious theories; it is frequently said that this is one of the causes of a decline in educational standards. Little evidence can be found to support these claims. What is also conveniently overlooked (or ignored) is that teacher educators have had a major impact on curriculum innovation and development throughout the 20th century. This is particularly so in music education. Roger Fiske and Jack Dobbs (1956), Kenneth Simpson (1975), John Paynter (Paynter and Aston, 1970), George Self (1976), Janet Mills (1991) and Robert Kwami (1998) are but a few of the many teacher educators who through their innovative teaching materials have injected new life into classroom practices. Without these curriculum innovations the teaching of music in schools would have been much the poorer. What effect changes in the role of teacher educators will have on curriculum development in the 21st century remains to be seen.

The international context

Music educators in Britain have for long shown interest in, and been influenced by, policies and practices from abroad. During the 1770s, Dr Charles Burney travelled widely throughout Europe and reported on musical provision in a number of countries. A hundred years later John Hullah and John Spencer Curwen were engaged in similar missions. Many of the recognized 'methods' of music teaching employed in British schools are modified imports from other systems. In the mid-19th century Hullah was greatly impressed by the singing classes of Guillaume Bocquillon Wilhem in Paris and adopted the 'fixed doh' system. At the same time John Curwen was perfecting the method of sight singing using the 'movable doh' that had previously been recognized by the French teacher, Pierre Galin, as an effective way of understanding the mysteries of tonality and standard notation. Curwen's tonic sol-fa was subsequently taken up by teachers in Australia, Canada, the USA and several parts of Europe; it has also been widely used in African countries. The great international teachers of the 20th century were Dalcroze, Orff, Kodaly (much indebted to Curwen) and Suzuki. Their principles and techniques have undoubtedly made an impression across the world, although lack of awareness of the problems of cultural borrowing has sometimes led to frustration and disappointment. The ideas of modern British music educators, including John Paynter at York, Keith Swanwick in London and Arnold Bentley at Reading, continue to have an international influence. Their research, teaching and publications have been universally acknowledged, and a large number of educationists from all parts of the world have subsequently come to this country to study for specialist diplomas and to teach masters and research degrees.

Because of the nature of music itself it is inevitable that music education should have a fairly strong international dimension. During the post-war era it has become common practice for groups of school musicians to participate in overseas concert tours and often to make music with their contemporaries in other countries. Academic and professional contacts between music educators were greatly advanced by the formation, in 1953, of the International Society for Music Education (ISME). The society, which is affiliated to the International Music Council and UNESCO, now has members from over 60 countries. It makes provision for international exchange and dialogue through its numerous conferences and publications, including the *International Journal of Music Education*, and seeks to further all aspects of music education. Over the past 10 years ISME has been particularly active in promoting world musics and supporting moves to make educational research more relevant to classroom practitioners.

From a survey of national educational systems it becomes apparent that it is nowadays quite unusual to find schools where children do not receive musical instruction at some stage of compulsory schooling. Research studies by Laurence Lepherd (1995) and Martin Comte (1994) confirm that many of the issues occupying the minds of music educators in Britain are also under consideration in other countries. A number of governments are moving towards national curriculum frameworks as a way of providing for more structured and coherent music programmes. However, the tight prescription and legal status seem to be largely confined to England and Wales; national schemes in the United States, Australia, Japan and Denmark allow for far more flexibility. There appears to be international concern over the supply and training of music teachers, particularly at primary school level. Debates about the most suitable way of organizing music in the primary schools and the issue as to whether music should be taught by generalists or specialists are certainly not confined to Britain. Many teachers express concern that with an increasing world-wide tendency to relate education to economic advancement there is a danger of music being marginalized or included as a component of expressive arts programmes, thereby diminishing its educational significance. However, it is also clear that there is now much more publicity for music and a greater recognition of its value in a contemporary liberal education. In spite of their doubts and worries the international community of music educators seem to retain a fairly optimistic outlook.

Present and future challenges

Although there is a long tradition of music in education, its place in school programmes has often been rather insecure and there are today those who question its educational value. As previously stated, with so much attention to the raising of standards in the core subjects some people feel that the arts subjects are, once again, being pushed to the edges of the school curriculum. How far there is a legitimate cause for concern is uncertain, but one of the outcomes of this sense of insecurity is that both individuals and professional bodies seem to feel the need to turn increasingly to extrinsic justifications for music in education. In particular much importance is attached to a supposed relationship between music studies and general academic achievement. During the 1960s and 1970s there was much excitement over the findings of Hungarian music educators, reported in a famous book by Frigyes Sandor (1966). It was stated that researchers had gathered 'overwhelming evidence' to show that children attending the special music schools in Hungary attained better academic standards than their contemporaries in the regular primary schools. Surely, people said, this must be the indisputable reason for including music in the curriculum. However, the research evidence has seldom been questioned or scrutinized in any systematic manner. Recently it has been resurrected and features prominently in a booklet entitled *The Fourth R*, published by the organization The Campaign for Music in the Curriculum (1998). This claim about the 'power' of music is, of course, by no means new. It is often maintained that as well as developing cognitive abilities the study of music will also help learners to acquire agreeable dispositions such as tolerance, perseverance, co-operation and even kindness. Whatever the strengths and weaknesses of these views, transfer claims do not provide a very sound justification for music in education. In fact, they might even prove to be quite dangerous. If music is to be part of children's education because it improves general intellectual performance and personal skills then, logically, the evaluation of music programmes would have to be undertaken with these things in mind. What counted as good or bad music education would depend on children's achievements in non-musical areas. Attempting to judge music curricula in these terms would obviously be quite absurd. There is a need for a proper rationale for music in the curriculum since this is the determinant of practice, but justifications that arise from spurious arguments, however well intentioned, are fraught with difficulties. It could be that the strongest justification for music is to show through good practice that it is a meaningful subject for the majority of children. Elegant and seemingly convincing justificatory arguments are of little value if the subject is not being effectively taught. In fact, when it is being well taught questions of justification seldom seem to arise.

Some music teachers nowadays sometimes find themselves working as members of a combined arts team or an arts department. The theoretical basis for this type of organization is that the arts are united by a distinct mode of aesthetic meaning and understanding. Reference has already been made to the notion of the generic community (and the philosophical objections to this position), but how far curriculum organization is ever underpinned by this sort of theoretical ideal is very uncertain. Combined arts departments are likely to arise from rather more practical considerations, which will include the management of staff resources, timetabling or often the wish of individual arts teachers to work together. One of the objections to combined arts programmes is that they further marginalize the separate disciplines. Teachers hold different views on this issue. Many would argue that the existence of an arts team is likely to strengthen the position of their subjects. Others may interpret a move from subject specialism to membership of a larger group as a threat to their status within the social structure of the school. However, as schools seek more efficient and financially secure organizational patterns, the notion of combined arts is likely to feature more prominently in school's action plans. It will perhaps be necessary for all arts educators to give greater attention to the philosophical, pedagogical and professional issues related to this form of curriculum organization.

Post-war developments in music education have inevitably led to growing demands on teachers. Some 40 years ago, Her Majesty's Staff Inspector for Music (quoted in Brace, 1970) expressed concern that teachers with their responsibilities for both curriculum and extra-curricular activities had acquired a dual role, which might in some cases become unmanageable. The situation has not really changed. Many teachers will point out that increasing bureaucratic demands obstruct their teaching and inhibit their musical, personal and professional development. Traditionally, teachers have participated in a range of activities beyond education, which have enhanced their own musicianship and consequently their work as school practitioners. There is a genuine fear, not infrequently expressed, that increasing administrative duties will be detrimental to both their musicianship and creativity. No doubt, teachers of all subjects have similar concerns.

In a detailed study of over 30 schools carried out at the London Institute of Education in 1987 (Swanwick et al, 1987) it was found that a large number of teaching and non-teaching staff took a considerable interest and pride in their schools' artistic activities. They welcomed concerts, productions, carol services and other musical events, which they regarded as occasions that had a special meaning for all the members of the school community. And this, of course, is the true power of music and the arts; they bring with them a certain excitement, brighten people's lives and add a particular quality to the environment. Nowhere is this more apparent than in schools. The challenge for the school music educator is, as it has been for the past 50 years, to preserve the extra-curricular dimensions and at the same time ensure that music is also in a healthy state as a curriculum subject. As always, the success and future growth of school music is dependent on teachers. In many ways their task seems more daunting than ever before but those of us who work with the young men and women preparing for careers in the teaching profession cannot help but be impressed by their enthusiasm and sense of commitment. They believe in the value of their subject and share the same vision that has inspired generations of music educationists. The future of school music is surely safe in their hands.

Acknowledgements

My colleagues at the Institute of Education – Professor Keith Swanwick, Dr Lucy Green, Dr Robert Kwami and Dr Ashley Kent – kindly read an early draft of this chapter and made many helpful comments and suggestions. I am grateful to Dr Gordon Cox for his generous assistance in providing information about developments in music education at the University of Reading.

References

Abbs, P (1994) *The Educational Imperative*, Falmer Press, London
Allsobrook, D (1992) *Music for Wales*, University of Wales Press, Cardiff
Andrews, K, Vernon, G and Walton, M (1996) *Good Policy and Practice for the After School Hours*, Financial Times Pitman Publishing, London
Barber, M *et al* (1997) *School Performance and Extra-Curricular Provision*, Department for Education and Employment, London
Bentley, A (1966) *Music Ability in Children and its Measurement*, Harrap, London
Bentley, A (1975) *Music in Education: A point of view*, NFER, Slough
Best, D (1992) Generic arts: an expedient myth, *Journal of Art and Design Education*, **11**, pp 27–44
Blacking, J (1973) *How Musical is Man?*, Faber, London
Brace, G (1970) *Music and the Secondary School Timetable*, Themes in Education, 24, University of Exeter
Campaign for Music in the Curriculum (1998) *The Fourth R*, Campaign for Music in the Curriculum, London
Central Advisory Council for Education (1963) *Half Our Future*, HMSO, London
Cleave, S and Sharpe, C (1986) *The Arts: A preparation to teach*, NFER, Slough
Collins, G (1968) Visiting specialist teachers, in *Handbook for Music Teachers*, ed B Rainbow, Novello, London

Colwell, R (ed) (1992) *Handbook for Research in Music Teaching and Learning*, Schirmer, New York

Comte, M (ed) (1994) *Music Education: International viewpoints*, Australian Society for Music Education, Nedlands

Cox, G (1993) *A History of Music Education in England, 1872–1928*, Scolar Press, Aldershot

Dennis, B (1970) *Experimental Music in Schools*, Oxford University Press, Oxford

Department of Education and Science (DES) (1985a) *Curriculum Matters 4: Music from 5–16*, HMSO, London

DES (1985b) *General Certificate of Secondary Education: The national criteria – music*, HMSO, London

DES (1991) *National Curriculum Music Working Group Interim Report*, DES, London

Elliott, D (1995) *Music Matters: A new philosophy of music education*, Oxford University Press, Oxford

Farrell, G (1990) *Indian Music in Education*, Cambridge University Press, Cambridge

Fiske, R and Dobbs, J (1956) *The Oxford School Music Books*, Oxford University Press, Oxford

Gamble, T (1976) Creative music at Manland, *Music Teacher*, **55** (12), December, pp 9–10

Gammon, V (1999) Cultural politics for the English National Curriculum for music, *Journal of Educational Administration and History*, **31** (2), pp 130–47

Gibbs, L (1993) Home and away, *Music Teacher*, **72** (5), pp 12–13

Green, L (1988) *Music on Deaf Ears*, Manchester University Press, Manchester

Green, L (1997) *Music, Gender and Education*, Cambridge University Press, Cambridge

Hargreaves, D (1982) *The Challenge for the Comprehensive School*, Routledge, London

Hargreaves, D J (1986) *The Developmental Psychology of Music*, Cambridge University Press, Cambridge

Head, L (ed) (1999) *Music Education Yearbook*, Rhinegold, London

Hickson, J (1836) *The Singing Master*, E Wilson, London

Hodges, R (1996) The new technology, in *Music Education: Trends and issues*, C Plummeridge, Institute of Education, University of London, London

Horton, J (1969) *The Music Group*, Schott, London

Incorporated Society of Musicians (1947) *An Outline of Musical Education*, Curwen, London

Kemp, A (ed) (1992) *Some Approaches to Research in Music Education*, ISME, Reading

Kemp, A (1996) *The Musical Temperament: Psychology and personality of musicians*, Oxford University Press, Oxford

Kemp, A and Adelman, C (1992) Case study and action research, in *Some Approaches to Research in Music Education*, ed A Kemp, ISME, Reading

Kendell, I (1976) *Music Education for Young Children*, Arnold, London

Kushner, S (1991) *The Children's Music Book*, Calouste Gulbenkian Foundation, London

Kwami, R (1998) *African Songs for School and Community: A selection from Ghana*, Schott, Mainz

Lawlor, S (1993) Classrooms are the place to learn, *Observer*, 14 March 1993

Lawson, D, Plummeridge, C and Swanwick, K (1993) Music and the National Curriculum in primary schools, *British Journal of Music Education*, **11**, pp 3–14

Lepherd, L (ed) (1995) *Music Education in International Perspective: National systems*, University of Southern Queensland Press, Toowoomba

Mann, P (1991) *The Robe of Gold*, West Riding Music Education Collection

Mills, J (1991) *Music in the Primary School*, Cambridge University Press, Cambridge

Murray, M (ed) (1957) *Orff Schulwerk: English edition*, Schott, London

National Association of Music Educators (NAME) (1999) Conference report '99, *NAME Magazine* (3)

National Advisory Committee on Creative and Cultural Education (NACCCE) (1999) *All Our Futures: Creativity, culture and education*, DfEE Publications, London

Office for Standards in Education (OFSTED) (1999) *Secondary Initial Teacher Training Subject Inspections, 1996–99: Overview report*, OFSTED, London

Paynter, J (1982) *Music in the Secondary School Curriculum*, Cambridge University Press, Cambridge

Paynter, J and Aston, P (1970) *Sound and Silence*, Cambridge University Press, Cambridge

Pitts, S (1998) Looking for inspiration: recapturing an enthusiasm for music education from innovators' writings, *British Journal of Music Education*, **15** (1), pp 25–36

Priestley, E and Grayson, J (1947) *A Music Guide for Schools*, Nelson, London

Rainbow, B (1985) *Onward from Butler: School music, 1945–1985*, Curwen Institute, London

Rainbow, B (1989) *Music in Educational Thought and Practice*, Boethius Press, Aberystwyth

Reid, L A (1969) *Meaning in the Arts*, Allen and Unwin, London

Reid, L A (1986) *Ways of Understanding and Education*, Heinemann, London

Reimer, B (1970, rev edn 1989) *A Philosophy of Music Education*, Prentice Hall, Englewood Cliffs

Ross, M (1975) *Arts and the Adolescent*, Schools Council Working Paper No 54, Evans, London

Ross, M (ed) (1989) *The Claims of Feeling: Readings in aesthetic education*, Falmer Press, London

Sandor, F (1966) *Musical Education in Hungary*, Boosey and Hawkes, London

Schafer, R Murray (1965) *The Composer in the Classroom*, Canada BMI, Ontario

Scholes, P (1935) *Music, the Child and the Masterpiece*, Humphrey Milford, London

Schools Council (1968) *Inquiry 1: Young school leavers*, HMSO, London

Seashore, C (1938) *Psychology of Music*, Dover Publications, New York

Self, G (1967) *New Sounds in Class*, Universal Edition, London

Self, G (1976) *Make a New Sound*, Universal Edition, London

Sergeant, D C (1969) Experimental investigation of absolute pitch, *Journal of Research in Music Education*, **17**, pp 135–43

Sharp, C (1991) *When Every Note Counts: The schools instrumental music service in the 1990s*, National Foundation for Educational Research (NFER), Slough

Shepherd, J et al (1977) *Whose Music? A sociology of musical languages*, Latimer, London

Simpson, K (1968) The teacher's task: aims, in *Handbook for Music Teachers*, ed R Rainbow, Novello, London

Simpson, K (1975) *Music Through the Recorder*, Thomas Nelson, London

Simpson, K (1976) *Some Great Music Educators*, Novello, London

Sloboda, J (1985) *The Musical Mind*, Clarendon Press, Oxford

Small, C (1977) *Music – Society – Education*, John Calder, London

Smith, D and Tomlinson, S (1989) *The School Effect: A study of multiracial comprehensives*, Policy Studies Institute, London

Stephens, J, Moore, J and Smith, J (1995) Support for the music curriculum, in *Teaching Music in the National Curriculum*, ed G Pratt and J Stephens, Heinemann, London

Stock, J (1996) *World Sound Matters: An anthology of music from around the world*, Schott Educational, London

Swanwick, K (1979) *A Basis for Music Education*, NFER, Slough

Swanwick, K (1994) *Musical Knowledge: Intuition, analysis and music education*, Routledge, London

Swanwick, K (1999) *Teaching Music Musically*, Routledge, London

Swanwick, K and Tillman, J (1986) The sequence of musical development: a study of children's compositions, *British Journal of Music Education*, **3** (3), pp 305–39

Swanwick, K et al (1987) *Music in Schools: A study of context and curriculum planning*, University of London, Institute of Education, London

Taylor, D (1979) *Music Now*, Open University Press, Milton Keynes

Turner, C (ed) (1997) *The Gallery Tradition: Aspects of Georgian psalmody*, SG Publishing, Ketton

Vulliamy, G (1977) Music as a case study in the new sociology of education, in *Whose Music? A sociology of musical languages*, ed J Shepherd, Latimer, London

Wiggins, T (1993) *Music of West Africa*, Heinemann/WOMAD, London

Wing, H (1948) Test of musical ability and appreciation, *British Journal of Psychology*, Monogram Supplement, 27, Cambridge University Press, Cambridge

Chapter 8

Religious education: Soul-searching in an era of 'supercomplexity'

Ruth-Anne Lenga, Michael Totterdell and Vanessa Ogden

No boy or girl can be counted as properly educated unless he or she has been made aware of the fact of the existence of a religious interpretation of life.

(Board of Education: 1938)

The greatest single achievement for RE within the half-century from1944– 1994 is that in a society which on the surface appeared to discard religion as a majority preoccupation and to have lost much of its educational sense of direction, religious education as a curriculum subject persisted at all.

(Copley, 1997: 194)

Introduction

The challenges religious education has faced and the developments it has undergone can only be understood against the background of the wider changes of our era. With this in mind, this chapter will consider the changing aims and distinctive concerns of religious education, and discuss the implications of some of the controversies and complexities that surround it. It will discuss the growing impact of the national guidelines for syllabus content, programmes of study and assessment mechanisms for religious education at all key stages and assess the effect of this on a subject that has always been locally defined. It will also consider the future contribution of religious education at the post-16 level and the opportunities that it can offer in developing and strengthening vocational education in terms of social well-being, self-actualization and empowerment. Finally it will discuss the immediate and emerging challenges for those who must lead the way forward.

A complex era of change

We live indeed in challenging times: an era of continual change, of constant flux and of extensive technical mastery. Modern consciousness is alive with conflicting, proliferating and multi-faceted frameworks of understanding. It is a condition of our time that Ronald Barnett (2000) has summed up in the idea of 'supercomplexity' – a term for the 21st century that encapsulates the problems of multiple discourse in our contemporary world.

Life is unquestionably a fast-moving process, where even the most mundane and ordinary daily tasks are made 'simpler' by technology. Information and perceived knowledge can be 'downloaded' from around the world in an instant. Yet, ignorance is made ever more explicit. It is the contradiction of progress; the more we know, the more we are aware of how much we don't know (Lukasiewicz, 1994). Learning is increasingly 'distant', communication increasingly 'virtual'. The pervading language is that of '.com speak', electronically transmitted at the click of a mouse. Science and its sibling technology have indeed reached a pinnacle in jointly constituting the dominant force in everyday life.

So within all of this, what place is there for thinking critically about religion, religious meaning and the contribution of religious language? What does it mean to be religiously literate and educated? In addressing such questions – and a host of related issues – perhaps more than ever before religious education has a central and serious role to play.

In *The Hungry Spirit*, Charles Handy (1997), economist, educationalist and one of the seminal thinkers on business in its social context, writes that much of humanity is confused by the modern world and its consumerist values, and that a hunger exists for something that transcends the pragmatic concerns dominating modern life. He confesses, 'I am concerned by the absence of a more transcendent view of life and the purposes of life, and by the prevalence of the economic myth which colours all we do... there must be something we can do to restore the balance' (Handy, 1997: 3). Critical of the 'false lures of certainty' that are offered by the competing traditions of science, economics and dogmatic religion, he states that, in searching for a philosophy of our time, the key question rests with: 'What ultimately is the real purpose of life?' (Handy, 1997: 5). He acknowledges that answering this perennial question is as much about values and belief as anything else is. 'Beliefs begin when the facts run out. Nobody can prove their beliefs are right to anyone else's satisfaction. But when they click with other people's sense of what is true, they can be very powerful' (Handy, 1997: 5).

Handy advocates individuals and organizations engage in an ongoing redefinition of who and what they are, reaching out as well as reaching in, to grasp a sense of personal and collective purpose and destiny. He is, perhaps, describing something of what it might be to be religiously educated. For religious education does not seek to compel a rule book of creeds or religious and moral absolutes; nor does it aim to impose a learning strategy that puts thinking on hold. But rather, it endeavours to encourage knowledge, understanding and intelligent thinking about religion and the influence of beliefs, values and the traditions of individuals and communities. As a curriculum subject, it aims to enable pupils to make reasoned and informed judgements about religious and moral issues and to enhance their spiritual, moral and social development. It looks to arousing awareness of the fundamental questions raised by human experiences, with pause for careful reflection by pupils on their own beliefs and experiences in the light of their study. It is perhaps the only area within the current school curriculum in the UK that provides allocated space, albeit only 5 per cent of the timetable, for this crucial activity.

Religious education, seriously conducted, can develop both cognitive and emotional intelligence at a sophisticated level. It is a subject that extrapolates from pupils' ability to critique, by providing a platform for pupils to stand back and critically analyse what is going on in their world and the society within which they operate. It can equip them with the necessary skills for a particular type of discourse that asks existential questions and relates these to a personal understanding of the human condition. The questions probed are those relating to the deeper purpose and meaning behind the mechanical, technical and material processes that are negotiated in daily life. Through this reflective process, critical awareness of the diverse authorities (including market forces) that jostle one another for a position of dominance can be cultivated. The subject can empower students by fostering self-responsibility and discernment whilst recognizing and respecting the position and ultimate authority of others. In this way it champions learning to live with our deepest differences without compromising a personal search for truth. It recognizes that however secular and technically advanced our society may be, the need to address the most profound of human questions remains critical (Grimmitt, 1987; Watson, 1991).

The complexity of pluralism

This task is made all the more challenging owing to the complexity of pluralism in contemporary British society. The era of rapid technological growth in society and consumerist expansion has been accompanied by radical change in the ethnic mix and cultural patterns of our society. No longer the monoculture rooted in Anglo-Saxon Christian identity, perceived to be the measure of society in the Education Act of 1944, our nation now constitutes a diverse heterogeneous tapestry of multi-faith and non-faith life stances, ethnic groupings and cultural diversity (Parsons, 1994).

Interestingly, multiculturalism, like globalization, has brought about a degree of separatism or particularism as a counterpart to cosmopolitanism. The Anglicization and assimilation of second, third and now fourth generation migrants in this country has intensified the desire for separate, religious and community-based schools in order to inculturate young people back into their traditional frameworks, and to ensure community cohesion. This unexpected sociological change reflects changes in the perceived needs of ethnic minority communities. For example, the needs of first-generation Yiddish-speaking Jewish immigrants in the early 1900s were to absorb their Jewish children into the established English environment, so that they could 'fit in' and become an accepted part of society. Religious development and learning were transmitted through family life and focused on the home environment. Ordinary schools were the places to transform young immigrants into indigenous citizenry. Nowadays, the inculturation and integration process for Jews in this country is fairly firmly set, and the need for becoming part of English society is superseded by the concern for what is being lost through growing assimilation. Chief Rabbi Sacks (1994: 3) states the depth of this concern:

> Anglo Jewry, estimated at 450,000 Jews in the 1950's, now numbers barely 300,000. That means we have lost more than ten Jews a day, every day for the last forty years… It means that young Jews are disengaging, disaffiliating and drifting away from Judaism… It is this that marks our time as a new era in Jewish History.

For the Jewish community of Great Britain, the ensuing decrease in religious and cultural identity threatens its very survival. Education for 'continuity' is the new priority. The thinking is that only with knowledge, identity and affiliation can the chain of tradition continue and thrive. Full-time schooling, where religious nurturing and education can be provided with professional integrity in order to instil knowledge and values of the faith and generate a strong religious identity, is now seen by many in the community as 'the' way forward. This is increasingly the pattern of other minority communities as evidenced by the fast-growing interest in establishing new voluntary-aided schools with religious foundations. Such faith schools appear to be showing, for whatever reason, a value-added dimension, reflected in OFSTED, LEA and diocesan inspection reports, low exclusion rates, examination results, league tables, and parental approval and support. This in turn has attracted crucial government legislative and financial support (Sullivan, 1999).

Notwithstanding the plural nature of society, the idea of society being *pluralist* does not necessarily follow. Pluralism suggests a collective and positive attitude that society holds towards its diversity. Haydon (1987: 9–10) argues the point as follows: 'Pluralism is a matter both of institutions and of ethos... it must involve some approximation to equality of standing between different cultural, ethnic and religious groups... Pluralism then is not so much a condition we are already in, as something to be attained.' It is not yet clear that our society is pluralist, that is, a society that has fully accepted its new character. Religious education can play a pivotal role in the state school curriculum in educating for pluralism by taking the connection between religion and culture seriously and promoting knowledge and understanding of others, leading to appreciation of their point of view and spiritual home beyond the point of mere tolerance.

Faith schools too, of course, have a responsibility to educate for pluralism. It would be worth examining the ways in which faith schools and the religious education delivered in them deal with the potential problem of inculcating sectarian values. The handling of conflicting truth claims of religious and non-religious life stances within a nurturing environment is one example of the complexities involved. The King David Jewish Primary School in Birmingham faces the challenge perhaps more explicitly than most, with 66 per cent of its intake being Muslim, Hindu, Sikh, Rastafarian and Orthodox children. Keen to send their children to a 'good' school, which respects the spiritual dimension of life and nurtures faith, religiously committed, non-Jewish parents look to the Jewish school as a better alternative than the regular state system. Schools with a religious ethos and explicit moral code are clearly therefore regarded by some 'outsiders' as less of a threat than the perceived secularist values permeating maintained schools (Davie, 1995: 131). A school that embraces and respects the existence of a religious interpretation of life can therefore be a de-indoctrinatory force from prevalent rationalistic, materialistic and consumerist values.

Contrary to the idea that faith schools must promote separatism, they may, in fact, do much to inculcate inclusivity by cultivating principled pluralism among those of 'thick' religious–moral persuasion. Sullivan (1999) argues that such schools can act as 'constitutive' communities. Drawing on the works of Fowler (1992) and Golby (1996), Sullivan's (1999: 112–14) understanding of a constitutive community is one that is 'identity-building' and fundamental to 'self description', where memory, membership, responsibility and conscience are integrated without neglecting critical thinking or imagination. From this position, children strong in their self-understanding of their religious identity and community are more able to 'reflect critically on this tradition and reach out to and work with others outside it' (Sullivan, 1999: 113–14).

Supercomplex; but post-religious and secular?

Notwithstanding increased religious diversity, the place of religion in society has changed. Since 1890, regular attendance at a place of worship has greatly fallen. Likewise, where once religion commanded centre stage of political activity, it now absorbs little parliamentary time. The past once saw the Church as the status symbol of local prominence. Now the life of a town has come to be identified more with its shopping centres and supermarkets. They are the new weekly sanctuaries, the new sites of family involvement providing retail rather than spiritual therapy. Even the architecture of such centres of consumerism takes on ecclesiastical features, with spires and arches and Gothic windows (Barnett, 2000: 13). One might say it is the superstore that is the place of contemporary worship in a culture absorbed by the telos of economism. Added to this is the fact that where once the Church provided care for the elderly and poor, now the Welfare State absorbs these functions. Moreover, religion is not regarded as being as significantly important within the education structure as it once was. Thus from this perspective the place of religion has, in some ways, been superseded by secularism. Arguably the 'fall-out' of the Enlightenment and industrialization, secularization has been seen as the major influence of our contemporary age, which is characterized by 'an immense shrinkage in the scope of the sacred' (Berger, 1969: 111). Yet this may simply reflect only part of the story – a secularized history of ideas (Chadwick, 1975). The cunning of the secular is to play down the unusual dynamic potentialities of religion by camouflaging the transfusion of sacrality into ordinary life so that 'axiomised ambiguity' becomes 'stable legibility' (Gauchet, 1997) in our discourse of human being. As such, it conceals the way in which the modern invention of the secular both redefines 'religion' and conceals the religious import we accord to 'the system' (Lasch, 1996). It also overlooks the provenance of the secular and is insensitive to the profoundly religious recesses of our political order and thought world

(Gauchet, 1997). It manoeuvres us too readily into falling hostage to the imprisoning constraints of modern cliché and prevents us appreciating that the principle of change has been a spiritual rather than a material one in the progress of Western civilization; it is intimately related to the dynamic ethos of religion as restorative in nature and comprehensive in scope (Dawson, 1947; Pannenberg, 1994). Religious education professionals should therefore be at the forefront of those now rethinking the architectonic divides between the religious and the secular, Christendom and modernity, the spiritual and the material.

Research amongst both adults and children indicates that society is still a society of believers, if not one that 'belongs' (Davie, 1995). For example, the European Values Study of 1991 confirmed that 71 per cent affirm the existence of God, while those remaining express doubt rather than unequivocal disbelief. A more implicit religiosity therefore exists (Parsons, 1994: 78; cf Hay 1987, 1990). Amongst people with an outward show of a 'thorough-going practical approach to life' there appears to exist a 'persistence of religiosity' rooted in belief that 'there is a point more profound than transient personal pleasure' (Cox and Cairns, 1989: 81). Parsons's (1994) view is that this religiosity manifests itself in personal feelings, emotions and experiences, even though the more traditional indicators (affiliation to organized religion, regular worship, for example) are the ones currently most affected by secularism. We may be an increasingly 'unchurched' and 'post-denominational' society, but we nevertheless retain a high interest in spiritual things, while playing down the connection between personal spirituality and institutional religion. But the idea that we are living in a post-religious, spiritually vacuous, secularized society is in fact largely mistaken. One could go so far as to argue that the spiritual dimension is a natural, indeed essential aspect of being human. So, for example, Abraham Maslow (1967: 139) claimed that: 'The spiritual life is part of our biological life. It is the highest part of it, but yet part of it. The spiritual life is part of human essence. It is a defining characteristic of human nature. It is part of the Real Self, of one's identity, of one's inner care, of one's specieshood, of full humanness.' If education is to be holistic and organic there is good reason to think we need the discursive space of religious education within it to explore the nature of our spiritual consciousness – a ubiquitous reality that resources both individuals' aspirations and communal life, whether or not it is manifest through formal religious affiliation (Totterdell, 1995: 10).

The debate about the extent to which tradition is giving way in our society with a consequent shift in cultural authority from 'without' to 'within' remains lively (Halpin et al, 2000). The 'post-traditional' world advocated by Robert Bellah (1970) in the 1970s has given way to one in which he has more recently expressed the belief that 'only living traditions make it possible to have a world at all' (1990: 122). As diverse as the religious traditions undoubtedly are, the insights into human being that they embody and the common and self-critical relevance they offer hold great promise in the search for a usable future (Marty, 1969).

Perceptions and misconceptions

Religious education is perhaps the most misunderstood area of the curriculum. This is due to the fact that the subject, as it is known today, is relatively new to the curriculum. A subject of various incarnations, religious education has emerged from former subjects such as scripture, theology and religious knowledge or instruction. Associations relating to the aims and style of teaching of these subjects have, to some degree, remained in the minds of many. Moreover, the constant link of religious education with collective worship by government legislation and documentation conjures up inappropriate connotations of religious education being in the business of 'doing' religion, or worse, indoctrinating pupils. The subject is also seen to be closely associated with moral development and moral education. Whilst acknowledging the potent and distinctive contribution that religious education can make in this area of personal growth, the subject is not synonymous with imbuing morality. Similarly, the development of the spiritual dimension of human experience has been regarded by many as one and the same as religious education. Religious educators would, no doubt, hold firm views that their subject is uniquely conducive to this aspect of personal growth, that it allows and develops the tools for expression and serious reflection on this dimension of human experience. But they would also claim that the subject does not hold a monopoly on moral or spiritual development, and neither should these be its sole responsibility, but that of the wider curriculum.

Whatever the misunderstandings, the long and turbulent history, the changes in attitude towards religion, and legislative directions that have left religious education to some extent marginalized within the school curriculum, the relationship of religious education with schooling has endured in time (Copley, 1997). A look at the history of the subject will reveal some of the significant reasons for religious education's struggle and survival. It may, though, be fair to say that in general many would see a curriculum without a religious education component as one crucially inadequate. Indeed both religious and non-religious people have argued for the presence of religious education in the school curriculum and it is possibly this social fact that has enabled the subject to survive. The findings of a poll carried out by NOP in 1993, amongst 625 parents with children aged 5 to 16 for the *Independent*, revealed that most parents support the broad legal obligation placed on schools to teach religion and hold religious assemblies (even though only 18 per cent affiliate to a place of worship themselves). A large majority (82 per cent) supports teaching children about different faiths (Hughes, 1993).

Whilst religious education is seen as important, confusion exists in the public's mind as to the nature and intentions of the subject. Religious education professionals believe theirs is an academically rigorous and intellectually challenging subject; it is philosophical and theological, requiring the disciplined mastery of the tools of religious literacy (Wright, 1993). It demands a critical capacity, questioning and responding (with respect and empathy) to different and sometimes conflicting claims about reality, whilst not negating the possibility that an ultimate truth exists. But religious education is not only this. It is partly an aesthetic exploration, where creativity, imagination and emotion can fuse and integrate around inspired insights and visions (Starkings, 1993). It is also, in part, a historical encounter with tradition and heritage, an appreciation of one's place in relation to time, and identification with a context. The subject is also about a process of discovery and awareness of selfhood. It is where pupils can acquire the tools to discern, interpret and judge for themselves that which is significant in experience (both cognitive and non-cognitive) in developing their life-style and acquiring values. Josephine Cairns conceptualized this process as the theory of world-view development (Cairns, 1991: 85–87). Intrinsically connected to this idea, but none the less distinct, is an understanding of the self *in relation to* the frameworks of beliefs and values of others. Engagement in the discourse that can be aroused from encountering these frameworks and being able to negotiate a path through this landscape of multiple horizons and hidden inner spaces is a highly skilled intellectual and *emotional* task. It arouses the sensitivities and sensibilities necessary for an authentic proclivity towards social inclusion and cohesion. Those overly keen for religious education to be seen as essentially 'critical thinking' may lose sight of its distinct role in building a community of citizens through injecting an antidote to social fragmentation, fear, the predisposition of 'difference' in relation to the 'other', and xenophobia. Religious education in post-Holocaust times cannot and must not risk losing its grip on this pivotal goal (Lenga, 1998).

To understand the nature of the subject, the complexity of its teaching, is to find oneself embroiled in a history of peaks and troughs, high politics (governmental, Church and interest groups) interwoven into the context of a country's desperate and ongoing search for national identity. But, like religion, little is straightforward when it comes to religious education.

Nowhere else in the curriculum is there a subject more laden with misunder-standing, controversy, status ambiguity and paradox (Day, 1985; Kay and Barnes, 1999).

The history of religious education: pre-1944

In other parts of the world it is illegal to teach about religion in schools. This has never been the case in this country. Religious education has always been a part of our educational tradition. The exact reason for this is not clear, but there are factors that have had their influence. Firstly, our earliest schools and universities grew from the Christian monastic tradition. Secondly, the Church of England had a significant stake-holding on school buildings. Thirdly, religion has been used as political leverage to rebuild a spirit of national identity. Fourthly, the Victorian belief in the inextricable link between morality and religion ensured the presence of religious education in the curriculum.

The first schools in Britain, provided by religious institutions, aimed to induct children into the Christian faith and adopted a confessional approach to its religion teaching. Since many of the schools were attached to a particular Christian denomination, teaching was seen as a way of recruiting members into the Church. Disputes (and they were fiercely acrimonious) about religion in school were concerned primarily with the *denominational form* of Christianity to be taught. Queen Victoria herself relished a tolerant approach to the religious education, writing in 1846: 'A good, moral, religious but not bigoted religious education is what I pray for... but where to find exactly what one wants?'(Arnstein, 1986, 5: 101).

The Liberal MP W Cowper Temple resolved the denominational dispute with a clause in the 1870 Education Act, repeated in the 1944 Act and continued on into the Education Reform Act of 1988. It stated that religious teaching in school must not include any catechism or formulary that was distinctive of any particular religious denomination. This led to the adoption of heavily Bible-focused teaching with its associated historical and geographic studies of 1st-century Palestine. The confessionalist intention for instructing religion in school remained the same, only now it had to be impartial with respect to Christian denominations.

In the era immediately prior to the Second World War, religious education gained renewed attention. Mindful of the powerful influences of scientism and positivism on education and society, religious education was seen as a way of galvanizing Christian spirit back into the lives of children. In so doing it would stem moral decline and facilitate pupils' propensity to see 'that the Christian faith not only made sense but also made more sense than any other philosophy on offer' (Angel, 2000: 217). This was a vision shared by an influential body of Christian educationalists and intellectuals who saw schools as Christian societies in pursuit of reversing the tide of corrosive forces such as materialism and totalitarian political philosophies (Reeves, 1999).

Religious education, 1944 and the spirit of restoration

The debate, dialogue and conjugations that preceded the religious provisions of the 1944 Education Reform Act took place in the very difficult circumstances of war. By 1944, the Church still had a powerful influence on the new Education Act and a degree of 'horse trading' between government and Church in relation to schools and the provision of religious education took place in the pre-Act negotiations. It would be fair to say that the prominence of religious education within the framing of the legal statutes resulted from ecumenical agreement (Hull, 1982: xv). Politicians at the time saw the need to generate a spirit of hope and renewal out of the despair and depression of the war years. In a sense their vision was rooted in nostalgia. Imbuing the young generation with religion and a religious attitude was seen as the apparatus to achieve this goal. They hoped to recreate a myth of the 'good old days' of colonial achievement when Britain was a 'green' and Christian land, echoing the spirit of the anthemized hymn, *Jerusalem*. Government yearned for a return to the climate of Victorian England, when religion occupied so large a part in the nation's life (Kitson Clark, 1962: 50). Churchill himself was committed to the idea of religious instruction in school, which he referred to as 'the fundamental element of school life', although he spoke with some reservation of the perceived 'authority' of institutionalized religion, identifying more with the idea of an individual spiritual quest. The overall mood of the time is well captured in the 1943 White Paper, which preceded the Act: 'a general wish not confined to representatives of the churches that religious education should be given a more defined place in the life and work of the schools, springing from the desire to revive the personal and spiritual values of the nation' (Board of Education, 1943).

Politicians were convinced the populace wanted Christian virtues upheld and valued the Christian principles perceived to be undergirding the national psyche and social life of the nation (see Wedderspoon, 1966; Copley, 1997). Legislators were in no doubt that Christianity would restore the soul of the nation, empower democracy and knit society together in unity and identity. This association of the Christian religion with the cause of democracy was one background factor that helped secure a more widespread acceptance of the religious clauses than it might otherwise have had (Niblett, in Wedderspoon, 1966: 20).

But there were those who could foresee problems. In a piece in *The Times Educational Supplement* entitled 'What is religious education?', Hamilton (1942) argued that:

> ...if it is by no means certain yet that the basic philosophy of England will be in the future a Christian philosophy which not unimportant sections of the community consciously and deliberately reject – any attempt to capture the schools for the systematic inculcation of the Christian view of life will be wrong and might well precipitate embittered conflict between rival religious and political parties for possession of the schools.

This was indeed a sharp prediction of the difficulties that were to follow religious education in the decades ahead.

Religious education and the 1944 legal statutes

The 1944 Act made religious education the only compulsory subject in the school curriculum. It remained that way until the 1988 Education Reform Act introduced the basic and National Curriculum. The outcome of the 1944 law was that religious *instruction*, as it was known then, became the only named subject in the Act and thus was accorded a unique position. Together with the legal obligation to a daily act of collective worship at the beginning of each school day, religious instruction would provide the nourishment and scaffolding for a moral and decent education for future generations. Religious education was the name given to the combined elements of the religious instruction and collective worship; thus was born the guilt by association that would haunt religious education over the years ahead.

Parents, in addition, could request (with certain conditions) that their children be given a form of religious instruction, different from that normally provided by the school. Despite retaining the Cowper Temple clause, which prohibited any formulary distinctive of any denomination, conscience clauses were introduced that gave parents the right to withdraw their children from religious instruction and collective worship and granted the teachers the right to refuse teaching the subject or leading assemblies without prejudice to their career aspirations.

The local education authorities were to frame their own agreed syllabus or adopt one designed by another local authority. The syllabuses were to be written by an Agreed Syllabus Conference consisting of four panels representing the following interests: the Church of England, other religious denominations (assumed to be Christian), the local education authority and teachers associations. Aided schools (of which the majority were Anglican or Roman Catholic) and special agreement schools were exempt from this obligation. Such schools retained the right to provide denominational instruction for their children under the control of governors and without obligation to adopt the agreed syllabus of the local education authority, but were free to choose a diocesan syllabus. The Act did not identify the amount of time and how regularly religious instruction should take place. This was to prove quite problematic in the future. Religious instruction was subject to formal inspection and the local education authority could choose to establish a Standing Advisory Council on Religious Education (SACRE) to advise them on matters connected with religious instruction in accordance with the agreed syllabus, the methods of teaching, provision of teachers and resources. The role of SACRE was strictly advisory and it had no real power (Cox and Cairns, 1989: 2–3).

The Act, in itself, did not lay down the content of religious instruction, nor did it specifically require it to be of a Christian nature, but it is fair to say that this was tacitly accepted. The presence of a 'conscience clause' made this abundantly clear. Although efforts were made to safeguard against denominational indoctrination through the Cowper Temple clause, the Act gave support to a confessional Christian approach with an emphasis on the examination of New Testament scripture. It was assumed that Britain was a Christian country and that its schools were Christian communities. But in making this assumption, the scene was being set for the troublesome times ahead for religious education.

Impact of the 1944 Education Act on religious education: proliferating problems and loss of credibility

Syllabuses produced after the 1944 Act, such as those of the City of York in 1948 and the East Riding of Yorkshire in 1950, did not reflect the ambivalence toward Christianity that appeared to exist in society. Thus the implicit, but none the less influential, confessional message had a significant impact on the syllabuses that were produced after the Act and this continued into the 1960s. However, the Christian nurture model underlying the confessional approach was open to abuse by untrained religious 'enthusiasts' (Parsons, 1994: 168) and during the years that followed a number of changes in society, including the further decline of Christian commitment and the impact of immigration, forced those leading the way forward in religious education to reconsider its aims and direction, or risk loss of credibility and demise.

With hindsight, the 1944 Act missed an important opportunity in failing to recognize the need of young people growing up in post-war Britain (Cox and Cairns, 1989). It is not that a religious education had no possible relevance of purpose at the time. Quite the contrary. It simply failed to help young people in such a way that it met with their needs, their problems and life questions after the trauma of war (Cox and Cairns, 1989; cf Copley, 1997). It also failed to engage with Judaism as other than an 'extinct prologue to Christianity' despite a vibrant Jewish community with a living faith long-established in England and the atrocities arising from anti-Semitism fresh in people's memories. Copley (1997: 32ff) has speculated about the reasons for this, but in retrospect it is difficult to appreciate how a serious endeavour to educate for democracy could overlook this aspect of European and British complicity in the prejudice that issued in such appalling consequences for fellow citizens.

Religious education in the 1950s and 60s: from Bible-centred to child-centred

By 1950 it was clear that the Act had little success in nurturing 'lost souls' back to Christian religious observance. Church attendance continued to wane and society appeared to be increasingly one of secular priorities. Parsons writes:

> The 1944 Education Act was arguably less realistic and successful in its assumptions about the nature of religious education which was appropriate and suitable for the post war world. Granted that the respect for and residual allegiance to formal Christian commitment and belief were undoubtedly much greater in the ... 1940's and 1950's, the extent of that commitment and allegiance was already markedly less than the 1944 Education Act had assumed implicitly in its provision for religious instruction and worship.
>
> (Parsons, 1994: 168–69)

Greater recognition of this might have led to a more critical engagement with the varieties of religious belief and post-religious humanism emergent in the populace at large.

The research of Harold Loukes (1961) showed that a decade and a half after the Act, the religious instruction being taught in schools was in a sorry state and that it was often rejected and ridiculed by pupils. Religious instruction did not appear to be making sense for pupils, and much of the lesson content was forgotten. Loukes remarked that one of the major problems was 'the passivity of the over instructed class', a reference to the rigid 'Bible-bashing' style of instruction. The Bible was known in parts 'too well, to the point of vain repetition'. Many pupils were bored and viewed religious instruction as childish and dull: 'It makes me disbelieve in God more when we are taught the same "drooy" speech every week.' As Loukes (1965) opined:

> We should be alarmed if the teaching of mathematics resulted in a generation of young people who not only got their sums wrong (which does not matter when sums are very difficult) but did not know how to begin to think about them and we must view with equal alarm a religious education that results in a total inability to think about religion. The orthodox appealing to one authority and the atheists appealing to another are in no better state than the bewildered trying hard to think but denied the tools of thought.

Bible history, church history and doctrine were seen by pupils as a total irrelevance yet they evinced much interest in the related issues and questions when they were allowed to engage in debate. Loukes set about designing curriculum materials that were based on 'life themes' and were problem-centred. The materials reshaped religious instruction in a way that sought to give pupils the skills and disposition to discover for themselves significance and meaning in their lives. This innovative model became known as the 'implicit approach'.

About this time, Edwin Cox (1966) wrote a seminal book, *Changing Aims in Religious Education*, which was to have considerable influence. The book marked a turning-point in thinking regarding the aim of religious education in an increasingly pluralist society. He regarded religious education as the response of the individuals to the mystery of life, and the attempt to solve these in symbolic language. Ultimately, Cox argued that children must be allowed to make their own value judgements on the religious material presented and that religion should be presented as response to the mystery inherent in life. Other thinkers including Acland (1963) and Hyde (1965) contributed actively to the debate at the time. The main aim was to make religious education more child-centred and relevant to the feelings and issues of pupils' lives (Parsons, 1994: 170). With this emphasis, ideas of an open-ended approach, life themes and experiential learning entered the discourse. This demonstrated a shift in the aims of religious education from being rooted in the authority of Christianity to being rooted in the authority of the child's experience.

Ronald Goldman (1964, 1965) looked to stage development theory to shed light on children's aptitude for religious thinking. He concluded that religious thinking followed broadly the schema defined by Piaget. He claimed that while children are capable of feeling emotions associated with religion they are not able to understand the conceptual complexities of symbol, myth and religiously esoteric language. To teach abstract concepts and Bible narrative before children are suitably mature might well lead to misunderstanding. It might even conflict with their 'logical–scientific' world-view causing them to reject religion as infantile. Goldman, Cox and others were advocating a pedagogical approach that abandoned 'instruction' of Christianity, doctrine, or Bible stories or history in favour of starting with the child. However, it was less than clear whether this was conceived of as a pedagogic principle concerned with the process of learning or a curricular one concerned with its content.

At the corresponding time, dramatic developments were taking place within theology. The 'new theology' (eg Robinson, 1963; Tillich, 1969) broke with tradition by advocating personal quests in search of meaning, rather than revealed truths. Cox (1983: 18) later wrote: 'This redefinition of religion suggested what the new content of religious education was to be, namely helping pupils to discover their deepest concern and to think out their personal and social problems in the light of it.'

Again critics were unsure whether such thinking represented an agenda for adaptation by religious educators or one of accommodation to the sirens of modernity in the guise of so-called secular theology (Howkins, 1966). This, along with the progressive social, moral and educational outpourings of the 1960s, paved the way towards rocky turbulence and change in religious education. Critics of Christian religious instruction in schools such as Paul Hirst (1965) and humanist A J Ayer (1968) advocated replacing the subject altogether with secular moral education. The objections were powerful and may have helped to shape the religious education that followed, but the implication for religious education of the increasing pluralism in society was developing the thinking of religious educators in another direction. The Plowden Report (DES, 1967), the Newsom Report (Ministry of Education, 1963) and the Schools Council Working Paper 36 (Schools Council, 1971) recognized the different educational needs of children from different ethnic backgrounds and gave support to a multi-faith perspective.

The 1970s: a complex plural society

The Jewish community has been present in Britain since medieval times, but it was the mass wave of Jewish immigration from the anti-Semitic pogroms of Eastern Europe (1881–1910) that gave British society its first real glimpse of 'foreign' cultures, languages and alternative religious perspectives. The 1940s saw Jewish refugees and survivors of Nazi tyranny flee to this country in pitifully few numbers looking for sanctuary and a new start. Included in this period of immigration was a transportation of 10,000 Jewish and non-Aryan children of the 'Kindertransport' in 1938–39 – a desperate late bid on the part of the UK to find a safe haven for them in the midst of grave danger. But immigration to this country from Commonwealth states in the 1950s to 60s brought further change to the demographic, cultural and religious character of Britain. The 1950s saw an influx of Caribbean and Irish, the latter extending the numbers of Roman Catholics. The 1960s witnessed immigration from India and Pakistan bringing Hindus, Sikhs and Muslims. This posed several questions for religious education teachers to ponder:

- Could the aims of religious instruction remain the same?
- Were immigrant children to be taught Christianity like the other children or were they to be educated in the faiths that they practised at home? How could this be done?
- Was there a need for some inter-faith education so individuals could learn and understand about their neighbours from whichever faith background they might be?

By the late 1960s, another debate was circulating in educational thought and was to reverberate forcefully into religious education. Educationalists were becoming increasingly concerned about indoctrination and looked to 'rational autonomy' as a key aim for education. With this in mind, concern spread to issues of neutrality and commitment in religious education. How should teachers deal with questions of truth without plunging into indoctrination, consciously or unconsciously motivated? If teachers were to reflect the increasing plurality represented in society and in the classrooms, would it be possible to teach multi-faith religious education with authenticity, balance and impartiality? Educators realized the need to find a way of addressing these significant concerns (Grimmitt, 1978). The Schools' Council Working Paper 36 (Schools Council, 1971) emphasized the need for a religious education that would reflect society and a multi-faith approach to teaching. The aims and content of new syllabuses began to change. The Hampshire syllabus of 1978 captured this in its preamble: 'It is no part the responsibility of a county school to promote any particular religious standpoint neither can an exclusive Christian content do justice to the nature of the subject.' The challenge that faced religious education was the need to refashion itself in such a way as 'would be faithful to its own content, and which would be impartial but not arid, personal but not proselytising' (Hull, 1982: xiii). Along with this redefinition of aims, a powerful pedagogical approach emerged that would influence considerably the teaching of the subject throughout the following years.

A new pedagogy of religious education: phenomenology

By the 1970s teachers were attempting to respond to the needs of the new religious pluralism that they found reflected in their classes by teaching about a variety of world faiths. It was not just syllabus content that was affected but also the attitude and teaching of religion (Cox and Cairns, 1989). The syllabus that most notably marks this shift of emphasis was the Birmingham Agreed Syllabus of 1975. Entitled 'Living together', it raised considerable controversy due to the inclusion of 'non-religious' life stances such as humanism and Marxism as well as a wide coverage of different religions. A growing number of new syllabuses followed suit and rejected the confessional stance, adopting a radically new approach to teaching religion. The new pedagogic model was called the explicit or phenomenological approach and was based on a rationale for critical enquiry that withheld judgement.

Compared to the confessional approach, this new model appeared revolutionary and refreshing. Religious education ceased to seek to nurture any particular religion but aimed to develop a sympathetic and yet critical understanding of the variety of religions, religious life and practice. Expounded by its protagonist, Ninian Smart (1968, 1973), each religion studied was to be respected and seen as holding truth from the believer's perspective. The aim of the approach is to 'try to understand what a religion means to its adherent, to see it through the eyes of a believer, and to sympathize with how a believer feels when being religious' (Cox and Cairns, 1989: 19). The issue of whether the religion holds ultimate truth was not to be raised in the classroom. In order to understand and think about religion students should attempt to 'bracket out' their own views and beliefs. Smart drew upon the earlier work of Rudolph Otto (1923) as well as phenomenology (Surin, 1980); the concept of the 'numinous' was enlisted to emphasize the experiential as one of the dimensions of his typology of religion.

The approach, however, was often misunderstood. A simplistic fact-based application in the classroom led to a superficial 'Cook's tour' of religions squeezed into a very limited curriculum time. In doing so it lost much of its empathetic element. Critics accused teachers of having inadequate knowledge to do justice to each faith and that a confused 'mishmash' study often resulted. Critics also concluded that excluding issues of truth inherent within many faiths could induce a relativistic notion of religion, and observed that the experiential dimension appeared to be largely lost in classroom application. Whilst this approach *may* have avoided confessionalism, it failed to address the questions pupils were interested in exploring and suggested that no type of religion could have any deep significance except for a peculiar few. Although recognition was given to the unique role religious education played in promoting understanding and tolerance of racial diversity, criticism strengthened that religious education was dominated by facts and that the spiritual or experiential essence of religion had disappeared from the learning with a consequent loss of a balanced curriculum as advocated in the government report, *Curriculum 11–16* (DES, 1977). In some cases this had led to a 'dumbing down' to the point of irrelevance or inadvertent stereotyping. Despite these weaknesses, the 1970s proved to be a growth time in religious education. There was a proliferation of new texts and resources, but the prevailing problems persisted – what were the educational aims of religious education and how were these to be achieved?

- Is its role to promote religious tolerance and social harmony?
- How far should religion be taught from any one religious stance?
- Can a teacher adequately and authentically teach a religion other than his or her own?
- Can you be an agnostic or atheist and teach religious education?
- How should a teacher respond to the question 'Is this true?'
- How can the inner dynamic of religions be portrayed in the classroom beyond the merely descriptive?

The next decade would see further soul searching as the subject sought to grapple with these questions (Day, 1985; Slee, 1989).

Religious education in the 1980s: the attempt to reform religious education

Informed understanding about the beliefs and values of others, the promotion of tolerance, good inter-community relations and social cohesion must have been the hope of those in favour of the study of world religions in schools. Indeed the Swann Report (1985: 178), which endorsed multi-faith religious education, suggested that this was 'the best and only means of enabling all pupils, from whatever religious background, to understand the nature of religious belief, the religious dimension of human experience and the plurality of faiths in contemporary Britain'.

By the 1980s, sophisticated accounts of the need to recover breadth, balance, perspective, inspiration and insight through religious education were circulating (Cox, 1983; Hull, 1984; Grimmitt, 1987) culminating in the Westhill Project (Read, 1992). There was a growing feeling that religious education had outgrown its Cinderella past and was emerging into a new era of respectability as a curriculum subject in its own right. A degree of professional consensus was evident that had hitherto been lacking. All this was to change with the arrival of the most important piece of educational legislation in the second half of the 20th century.

The Education Reform Act 1988 revised the requirements as stipulated in the 1944 Act requiring in particular a prominent place for Christianity in revised locally constructed syllabuses and a balanced exposure to other major world faiths (see Cox and Cairns, 1989). According to the Education Reform Act (Section 7), religious education in schools should 'reflect the fact that the religious traditions of Great Britain are in the main Christian whilst taking account of the teaching and practices of the other principal religions represented in Great Britain'. This, together with the stipulation that religious education should be accorded reasonable time in the curriculum, was designed to strengthen the place of religious education, but it had the effect of weakening it by exposing it to politicization. The emphasis on Christianity in the wording of the statutes, although vague, led for a while to a campaign to enforce predominantly Christian content, reinforced by the issue of DFE Circular 1/94, which in paragraph 35 stated, 'As a whole and at each key stage, the relative content devoted to Christianity in the syllabus should predominate.' Commenting on this Robson (1996: 16) notes, 'Parliamentary debates about religious education have rarely considered it in educational terms; almost invariably the subject has been caught up in the unfinished debate on British national identity... The clear implication of the Cox lobby in 1988 was to give religious education a deliberately Christianizing role.' Reactions amongst some in the professional world of religious education were intense and the subject was in danger of becoming a vehicle for culture wars. But the professionalism of the majority of religious education teachers surmounted the politicization saga, indicating perhaps that the subject had exchanged the 'shifting sands' of its former position for firm ground.

National consensus for locally framed religious education

As the legislation for regular schools' inspection began to take force after the 1992 Education (Schools) Act was passed, religious education had, almost imperceptibly at first, begun to reclaim some of its sense of positive achievement. This was helped in part by the requirement that OFSTED should inspect the provision schools make for the spiritual, moral, social and cultural development of pupils as one of the four main areas of inspection. Although clearly all curriculum subjects were expected to contribute to this, it was perceived by many that religious education specialists would provide the means to unlock the creative potential of others in schools, through their unique understanding of a dimension to educational practice into which their training provides a window. Thus, there arose a demand for teachers who were specialized in religious education to take a lead and build on established good practice. This in part led the Qualifications and Curriculum Authority (formerly SCAA), INSET providers, LEA inspectors and advisers and university schools of education to take seriously the need for a methodological framework for the subject, which promotes rigour, continuity and progression country-wide.

On the other hand, from the analysis of OFSTED inspection findings in religious education, it had become clear that a number of serious concerns needed to be addressed: standards of teaching and learning; standards of attainment; and continuity and progression. It seemed that religious education had proceeded on an almost *ad hoc* basis, areas of good practice being confined to counties and London boroughs where LEA advisory provision was strong. Primary religious education in particular was identified as a weakness in many areas.

Responding perhaps in some degree to this, SCAA produced national (non-mandatory) guidelines for syllabus conferences in July 1994. It was the first serious attempt to centralize religious education syllabus content. The content of the syllabuses emerged from the in-depth work of Barbara Wintersgill at SCAA, other educationalists, government representatives and members of the faith communities. Working parties representing the faith traditions set out to find consensus as to what should be taught about their faith in any given key stage. This provided a much-needed authorization of the selection of content and tried to ensure that cognizance was taken of the diversity within faith communities. The Faith Communities' Working Group reports, a glossary of terms (that standardized the translations, spellings and meanings of religious terms) and two different model syllabuses were eventually published.

The LEA syllabus conferences were encouraged to use the guidelines in the writing or adoption of new syllabuses. The syllabuses use a systematic approach as opposed to the use of themes to direct the learning. This is to emphasize the importance of pupils acquiring a coherent understanding of individual religions, and to clarify for conferences the knowledge and understanding recommended at each key stage. This did not preclude a thematic strategy being used within the systematic framework or a compara-tive approach being adopted when deemed appropriate. The approach implied that the data of religion belonged primarily to the communities of belief and that theological concepts intrinsic to each religion should help to construct and classify religious materials. In effect, each religion was to be allowed to present itself authentically and was to be studied in terms of its distinctiveness rather than allowing educationalists to appropriate religious materials or ideas and refashion them into themes or topics that appeared to have educational validity.

The rejection of a third model syllabus, one that was thematic in style, led to consternation amongst those religious educators who took issue with the systematic approach's projection of religions as distinct entities and favoured a generic and unitive notion of religion, which emphasized similari-ties, connections and shared spiritual response. This led Baumfield *et al* (1994) to promulgate an 'unofficial' alternative, *A '3rd' Perspective*, which set out a thematic model for religious education along the lines that had been common practice. About the key skills, attitudes and dispositions pupils should develop, there was less debate. Perhaps this is unsurprising since those identified are characteristic of other curriculum subjects. Key skills include investigation, interpretation, reflection, empathy, evaluation, analysis, synthesis, application and expression. Key attitudes and dispositions include commit-ment, fairness, respect, self-understanding and enquiry.

The syllabuses introduced two national attainment targets. These were identified as: 1) learning about religion; and 2) learning from religion. Attainment Target 1 includes the ability to:

- identify, name, describe and give accounts, in order to build a coherent picture of each religion;
- explain the meanings of each religious language, stories and symbolism;
- explain similarities and differences between, and within, religions.

Attainment Target 2 includes the ability to:

- give an informed and considered response to religious and moral issues;
- reflect on what might be learnt from religions in the light of one's own beliefs and experiences;
- identify and respond to questions of meaning within religions.

These attainment targets recognized the cognitive and affective, external and internal domains of learning in religious education, but also defined to some extent the subject's methodological framework. It was to be a mutual relationship between the academic, ethnographic and phenomenological approach in Attainment Target 1 and the dynamic, living and experiential approach of Attainment Target 2.

The creation of a national framework for teaching and learning in RE, albeit a non-compulsory model, was a significant step forward in the drive to resolve concerns about rigour, content and methodology. But this in itself did not promote raised standards of attainment or continuity and progression, despite the inclusion in the syllabuses of end-of-key-stage statements of attainment. Concerns over standards and continuity remained. At this point, however, SCAA turned its attention to RE at Key Stage 4 and thought to address another problem: the provision of accreditation for compulsory core RE at this level. Expecting all pupils to study for and sit examinations in a full GCSE course at the end of Key Stage 4 was considered to be inappropriate and impracticable; only one of many prohibitive factors was the pressure on school timetables. A way forward was urgently needed. Compulsory core religious education at Key Stage 4 without the acknowledge-ment of status that accreditation lends to any subject area at this level had led to disaffection amongst pupils and was seriously undermining the subject's indispensable contribution.

In 1994, The John Templeton Foundation and the Christian Education Movement jointly held a conference with SCAA to identify possibilities for a GCSE short course (half of a full course) qualification. Together with the work of Angela Wright (1994, unpublished report), then the Halley Stewart Teacher Fellow in RE, a case was made for improved provision and the GCSE short course was launched in 1995. This has led to a 12-fold increase in the numbers taking RE, and fears about a possible negative impact on the take-up of the full GCSE have proved unfounded.

As these developments were proceeding, inspection was having an impact on primary religious education. This had improved to the extent that in 1998 Barbara Wintersgill, now HMI, pointed out that at Key Stage 3 pupils were often engaged in a repetition of the contents and learning styles now prevalent at Key Stage 2 (see Wintersgill, 2000). The QCA (1998) began to address standards of attainment and issues of continuity and progression in RE and published *Exemplification of Standards in Religious Education*. This was an important document in that it provided a gauge for RE teachers against which to measure the standards of their pupils' work. Practical in nature, the document supplied teachers with examples of pupils' work graded against the end-of-key-stage statements of attainment specified in the model syllabuses, and a commentary that explains the rationale behind each grading.

However, the assessment of standards in RE has remained an area of deep uncertainty for the classroom practitioner and it was felt that there was a need for teachers to have a more concrete definition of standards for attainment in RE. With Curriculum 2000, there appear two further model frameworks for RE: the National Expectations in RE and the Model Schemes of Work for RE. The importance of the provision of a model eight-level framework for attainment in RE, comparable to National Curriculum subjects, should not be underestimated. Whilst there will doubtless be debate about setting levels of attainment in the more experiential dimensions of learning inherent in AT2, the contribution of the framework to raising standards in RE through assessment and supporting continuity and progression (particularly in the Key Stage 2 to 3 transition) could be immense.

In themselves, of course, the national expectations will not resolve the problems of continuity and progression. This will depend on effective implementation by Agreed Syllabus conferences and most importantly of all by teachers in the classroom. The next stage in the national development of RE must be concerned with the rigour of the training of religious education teachers and the impact of continuing professional development on their professional practice. There must be a suitable academic under-pinning to this; to fail to provide the academic basis for what is a highly specialized field in education, requiring sophisticated in-depth knowledge and advanced pedagogic skills, is to do it a major disservice.

Further research is needed into the pedagogy of religious education. Here a tribute must be paid to the invaluable work of the trusts – Sainsbury's, the Family Trust, St Gabriel Trust, Farmington Trust, Culham College Institute and the United Jewish Israel Appeal – in the development of religious education through the funding of research projects and the professional development of teachers. The need for a professional register of research in the subject area together with a digest of research evidence and findings is paramount.

Religious education is maturing into a flexible curriculum subject and it has largely lost the aura of defensiveness and preciousness that at times characterized its rhetoric of inclusion. It remains distinctive, because of its locally determined nature, but it bears many of the hallmarks of a National Curriculum subject. This naturally begs the question of its future inclusion in the National Curriculum with the wider ramifications for subject identity, including the extent to which the conscience clause is deemed to remain appropriate. A voluble lobby of religious education professionals thinks the subject is worthy of foundation status; they argue on the basis of analogy with other subjects that religious education's impeccable educational credentials now make the option of 'withdrawal' redundant. Others, perhaps with a greater sense of the history of modernity (Toulmin, 1990), or because they hold a conviction that membership and participation in society, both civil and religious, are best when they are voluntary, or because they believe that religious assumptions always intrude into the study of religion, are more hesitant.

The legacy of the 1990s

If the National Curriculum's apparatus has imposed something of a consensus on the subject's working practices, the same cannot be said about its underlying methodological assumptions and subject philosophy. Here the 1990s have witnessed the break of the regnant 'orthodoxy' of the 70s and 80s. Epistemological notions of professional participants in a community of practice being united in a *universitas* – a group united by mutual interests in achieving a common end – have given way to hermeneutical views of them being in a *societas* – individuals whose paths through life have fallen together, united by contract and civity rather than a common goal, much less common ground. It is unlikely that any return to a conceptual scheme that provides a single vocabulary or normal discourse will occur and therefore improbable that a common definition or understanding will emerge upon which religious education can build (Cairns, 1998).

With the loosening of the ties to Enlightenment rationality, religious education has spawned a number of interesting theoretical models, many of which have been successfully translated into good classroom practice. Amongst the more notable are the 'experiential approach', which seeks to connect with the interiority of pupils' spiritual selves and draws eclectically on religion as a stimulus, resource and framework for myth-making, or constructing narratives of the self (Hammond *et al*, 1990). This is essentially an affective approach to religious education and is in part a reaction to the imbalance that can occur when education lays stress solely on the cognitive and is suspicious of the language of transcendence (Hay, 1985). It has developed into a broader movement that claims spirituality provides the wherewithal for a broadly progressive, holistic education that focuses upon the child and its inherently creative powers as against a content-based 'traditional' curriculum (Priestley, 1996; Hay and Nye, 1998; Starkings, 1993). Spiritual intuition is seen as being at the heart of all authentic religious, moral, aesthetic and educational commitments; as a capability and response-orientated dimension of human being it is therapeutically efficacious (Erricker *et al*, 1997), as a cognitive sensibility it is evaluative of all putative life stances (Lealman, 1986). Such claims in the context of intervention by central government and its agencies (see, for example, SCAA, 1996) have naturally stimulated a debate about the proper interpretation of spiritual experience in relation to both religion and education and the overall thrust of experiential–spiritual development has been subjected to critique (Thatcher, 1991; Wright, 1998; Copley, 2000).

Another approach, sometimes described as 'concept-cracking', endeavours to break down the key ideas of religions into their component parts in such a way as to 'buy purchase in the experience of the child' (Cooling, 1994; Wright, 1993). This approach is designed to provide young people with an appreciation of religious concepts and their related perspectives and practices. It gives children materials with which to philosophize and theologize and immerses them in the project of interweaving their vital interests with perspectives from the world's wisdom traditions. It is underpinned by a critical realist perspective of the practical indispensability of truth that is doubly 'related' to the personal and to culture on the one side and to actuality or reality on the other. On this basis one cannot approach truth in terms of 'true for each at different times' or in terms of a power-balancing act of compromise between positions, but only in falliblist terms as a goal that constantly beckons us even whilst it transcends our best efforts. These remain provisional and incomplete whilst cumulative, progressive and increasingly reliable, necessarily trusted in practical living.

A third approach, grounded in extensive ethnographic studies of (and partnership with) religious communities in Coventry and Birmingham and which draws on theory from cultural anthropology, is the 'interpretive approach' (Jackson, 1997). This was developed in 1994 by the Warwick RE Project at the University of Warwick Religious and Education Research Unit, which sought to reassess the way in which religions are represented. Concerned that existing approaches to understanding religion rested heavily on Western, academic constructions, paradigms or essences reducing or even contorting the interpretations of distinctively different religions, the new approach sought to establish a more authentic representation. What emerged is a pedagogy of interpretation for understanding religion and the religious lives of individuals. With close attention to the tools of interpretive anthropological methodology, the approach attempts to 'bridge' the experience of the learner and that of the children represented in the curriculum materials devised by the team (Warwick RE Project, 1995). It sought a way of representing each religious community from within the insiders' terms and frames of reference, embracing its changing nature, complexity and diversity. The project also introduces a further challenging idea in its notion of edification. Jackson understands this as a 'transformative' concept in that learners engaging in conversation with their own spiritual tradition or, perhaps, others' self-understanding of theirs, are taken out of themselves for potentially enriching change.

In sum, religious education's role, as defined by its historical past and the present context, has come to be seen as:

- structuring an informed introduction to the knowledge and under-standing of world-view beliefs and major religions;
- developing self-consciousness and a sense of identity in young people;
- providing concepts, skills and attitudes of use to achieving both the critical distance and a general capacity for sympathy or fellow-feeling essential to free society.

Its character is rich, vibrant and plural, with an emphasis on Christianity; it is working to engage with young people's needs, to enhance their reflective capacity for self-knowledge and conscious respect or tolerance for others as the basis for social cohesion. It is making its own inimitable contribution to 'visioning' the future.

The role of religious education in the ascendancy of work-related learning

Education is essentially teleological in nature; it reflects what society believes about the future and destiny of the nation. Increasingly, the idea that learning should be work related has gained support from those with a vested interest in education for lifelong learning and is reflected in policy documents: 'The education and skills of all our people are crucial to our prosperity and national success... A motivated, flexible and highly skilled workforce is vital to the UK's competitiveness' (Department of Trade and Industry, 1995: 2). Subjects must consider the contribution that they can make to a framework for education that takes work-related learning seriously (Dearing, 1996), and religious education is no exception. Within this context religious education must reconsider its position.

Those who take a utilitarian view of human purpose will see no more value in religious education than as a means to the enhancement of interpersonal skills in multinational, multicultural working contexts, or communication skills in the workplace. However, those who balance this attitude with a view of human purpose that respects the dignity and autonomy of the human person will wish for more. In this respect, religious education will be valued as a significant contributor to the promotion of 'critical being' (Barnett, 1994) personal flourishing (White, 1997) and investment in social capital (Kennedy, 1997). The significance of a subject like RE, which is concerned with such skills as critical analysis, isolation of truth, transformation of ideas into rationally refined argument, and accepting and making sense of ambiguity should be transparent in this broader matrix.

Religious education as a discipline contributes to the development of many of the dispositions and skills that employers require, but particularly in certain key areas: where adaptability and flexibility are at a premium; where work requires the ability to recognize and cope with ambiguity, diversity and conflict; where collaboration and breadth of perspective are required to work with cross-cultural and international sensitivity; where work requires employees to make sense of, express and develop complex ideas and solve conceptual problems while remaining attentive to the human dimension involved.

Religious education also has a 'prophetic' concern about pedagogy, counterbalancing the predominance of 'vocationalism' in education, with its concentration only on procedure and competence in employment as an overarching goal for learning. The concern is to point out what could be a consequence of human existence in an age governed by technological and industrial objectives: the loss of the sensitive, creative, spiritual quintessence of human nature in subjugation to mechanization, where human value is reduced to economic productivity. Do we want, as Richard Hoggart (1996: 22) writes in *The Way We Live Now*, 'vocationalist policies in education [which] have convinced people that they should only learn what is immediately useful'? What are the 'survival' prospects for a nation of people with increasing economic and human capital but a deficit of social capital (Kennedy, 1997: 5–6)?

Barnett's (1994) powerful discussion of the limitations of the dominant paradigm of critical thinking offers us a model for the reconstruction of pedagogy in work-related learning. He replaces critical thinking with the notion of 'critical being', which comprehends a much deeper conception of what it means to think and act critically. Critical being unites critical reason, critical self-reflection and critical action, leading the individual to a state of being where critical thought steps out of the confines of its operational relationship with knowledge and into the domains of self and the world.

If Barnett's 'life-world becoming' leading to critical being is required in vocational education as a counterbalancing force to economic utilitarianism, then religious education is an invaluable resource in redefining vocationalism.

Through good religious education one has the chance to gain insight into the complex systems of beliefs, cultural and social sensitivities, and often deeply felt, unarticulated senses of spiritual identity. Moreover, because it is so closely connected with the way societies work, religious education is of great significance in the effort to combat social fragmentation (Islamic Academy, 1990). Religious education is concerned with bridge building and ambassadorship, working alongside faith communities in an atmosphere of shared understanding and mutual respect despite difference in belief. The importance of understanding religious and secular beliefs and their interaction in social, political and work-related contexts should not be underestimated.

The intimate connection of religious education to each of these aspects of a healthy learning society – work-related skills, critical being and social cohesion – is a clear indication of the role that the subject, in its multi-faith character, can play. It obviously has significance and worth. Religious education's distinctive worth lies in its capacity to engage and interact with the subtleties and intricacies of belief in a diverse and conflicting society. It deals with the sensitive inner world of others' spiritual expression that displays itself in belief, practice and action, in both private and public life – the one essentially affecting the other. No other subject is directly concerned with this; the true recognition and appreciation of the life stances of others depends on the understanding of formative beliefs.

Work-related learning within a flexible structure for education enables religious education to broaden out, especially in post-compulsory education, serving diversity of interests, aptitudes and aspirations and liberating it from the restrictions of an exclusive subject-based approach at post-16 when it can only be studied at A level. It could even facilitate the partnership dimension between business, the education establishment and individuals that has been highlighted as an important future concern by the CBI and others. Religious education could offer a variety of programmes of study in the form of modules within a flexible qualification framework at different levels (Ogden, 2000).

This is a new vision of religious education that embraces work-related learning, viewing it in a positive light. The 'privatization' of religion in Britain has had the effect of divorcing religious education from its living context: public and community life. The very valuable contribution of work-related learning to religious education is to draw it back into the arena of modern daily life, empowering society to appreciate the dynamics of belief as crucial to social structure and human interaction (Gates, 1996). Through a more flexible framework, which embodies reciprocity between the goals of invest-ment in economic capital and investment in social capital, religious education may both contribute to this reconciliation and gain from it (Ogden, 1997a, 1997b).

The complex task ahead

If one were to characterize the religiously educated person in the most general sense, it might be as someone who is religiously literate and who also develops a level of integrity, constancy and yet openness to the 'other' in a supercomplex world of conflicting ideas and ideals, which often exhibits prejudice and bigotry, with the courage to care, the capacity to understand and the desire to search for ultimate meaning and human purpose. In a society where values are so often seduced by instrumental reasoning, religious education is a counterbalancing conduit for the necessary soulcraft.

There are three immediate agendas for religious educators in our contemporary era. First is to clarify the ways and extent to which religious education can be a potent force in developing young people's understanding of their world and the world of others, and their evaluative capacity to critically affirm some enduring concept of what it means to be human. Second is the identification and implementation of teaching and learning processes that can bring about an awareness of spiritual and moral growth. Hogan's (1995) timely reminder that teaching and learning as a courtship of sensibility rather than a custodianship of experience should be our goal is particularly apposite in the case of religious education. As he puts it (1995: 15), 'teaching is then characterised as a special kind of cultural and communicative art, which seeks to get the epiphanies of learning under way and to sustain them in practice'. Third is the discovery of effective ways of developing discourse(s) for inter-faith dialogue, conversation between participants in different world and life views, conflict resolution and the appropriate expression of civil affection as the emotional basis of society in the modern age.

In effect this means that there is unfinished business to be done: first, in delineating a philosophical framework in which religious education can overcome the prevailing fact/belief divide and function to build a macro-morality, an ethics wide-reaching enough to ground belief in the religious meaning of secular experience, be concerned with the larger problems of democratic society and give witness to the social dimension of religious experience; second, in revisiting the curricula options and pedagogic strategies available to us in the light of lessons learnt from earlier eras in the subject's history, which must be refined and appropriated for the challenging context of the new learning age (Eisner, 1994; Mortimore et al, 1999); third, to carry forward the burden of conversation without which we lack the necessary means to discern those new meanings of community and common good proper to our particular age. For example, the announcement in 1999 by the Labour Government of the creation of a national Holocaust Memorial Day, to be launched in January 2001, denotes finally a recognition of the unprecedented scale of inhumanity that took place and the profundity of its universal lessons. In terms of Jewish–Christian relations, a new era may have begun since the momentous visit to Israel by Pope John Paul II and his words of reconciliation at the Yad Vashem Holocaust memorial. At a time when governments have become over-ideological, religious education could be a catalyst in helping a rising generation have the propensity to cultivate the lattice-work of collective humanness in a world characterized by supercomplexity.

References

Acland, R (1963) *We Teach Them Wrong*, Gollancz, London

Angel, A (2000) Religious education and moral education, in *Learning to Teach Religious Education in the Secondary School*, ed A Wright and A-M Brandom, Routledge/Falmer, London

Arnstein, W L (1986) Queen Victoria and religion, in *Religion in the Lives of English Women 1760–1930*, ed G Malmgreen, Croom Helm, London and Sydney

Ayer, A J (1968) (ed) *The Humanist Outlook*, Pemberton, London

Barnett, R (1994) *The Limits of Competence: Knowledge, higher education and society*, Open University Press, Buckingham

Barnett, R (2000) *Realizing the University in an Age of Supercomplexity*, SRHE/Open University Press, London/Milton Keynes

Baumfield *et al* (1994) *A '3rd' Perspective*, School of Education, Exeter

Bellah, R (1970) *Beyond Belief: Essays on religion in a post-traditional world*, Harper & Row, New York

Bellah, R (1990) Finding the Church: post-traditional discipleship, in *How My Mind has Changed*, ed J Wall and D Heim, Eerdmans, Grand Rapids, MI

Berger, P L (1969) *The Sacred Canopy*, Doubleday Anchor Books, New York

Board of Education (1938) *Secondary Education with Special Reference to Grammar Schools and Technical High Schools* (The Spens Report), HMSO, London

Board of Education (1943) *Educational Reconstruction*, HMSO, London

Cairns, J (1991) Religious education and the humanities, in *Teaching the Humanities*, ed P Gordon, The Woburn Press, London

Cairns, J (1998) Placing value on consensus: an elusive goal, *The Curriculum Journal*, **9**, pp 23–29

Chadwick, O (1975) *The Secularisation of the European Mind in the Nineteenth Century*, Cambridge University Press, Cambridge

Cooling, T (1994) *Concept Cracking: Exploring Christian beliefs in school*, Stapleford Project Books, Nottingham

Copley, T (1997) *Teaching Religion: Fifty years of religious education in England and Wales*, University of Exeter Press, Exeter

Copley, T (2000) *Spiritual Development in the State School,* University of Exeter Press, Exeter

Cox, E (1966) *Changing Aims in Religious Education,* Routledge & Kegan Paul, London

Cox, E (1983) *Problems and Possibilities in Religious Education,* Hodder & Stoughton, Abingdon

Cox, E and Cairns, J M (1989) *Reforming Religious Education: The religious clauses of the 1988 Education Reform Act,* Kogan Page, London

Davie, D (1995) *Religion in Britain since 1945: Believing without belonging,* Blackwell, Oxford

Dawson, C (1943) *The Judgement of the Nations,* Cambridge University Press, Cambridge

Day, D (1985) Religious education forty years on: a permanent identity crisis, *British Journal of Religious Education,* **7** (2), pp 55–63

Dearing, R (1996) *Review of Qualifications for 16–19 Year Olds: Full report,* SCAA, London

Department of Education and Science (DES) (1967) *Children and their Primary Schools* (The Plowden Report), HMSO, p 207

Department of Education and Science (DES) (1977) Curriculum 11–16: A contribution to current debate, working papers, HM Inspectorate, London

Department of Education and Science (DES) (1977) *Curriculum 11–16,* HMSO, London

Department of Trade and Industry (1995) Competitiveness: forging ahead, White Paper, HMSO, London

Education Reform Act 1988, HMSO, London

Eisner, W (1994) *Cognition and Curriculum Reconsidered,* Teachers College Press, New York

Erricker, C *et al* (1997) *The Education of the Whole Child,* Cassell, London

Fowler, J (1992) *Character, Conscience and the Education of the Public in the Challenge of Pluralism,* eds F Clark Power and D Lapsley, University of Notre Dame, Notre Dame

Gates, B (ed) (1996) *Freedom and Authority in Religions and Religious Education,* Cassell, London

Gauchet, M (1997) *The Disenchantment of the World: A political history of religion,* Princeton University Press, Boston

Golby, M (1996) Communitarianism and Education, Papers of the Philosophy of Education, Society of Great Britain conference, Institute of Education, University of London, London

Goldman, R (1964) *Religious Thinking from Childhood to Adolescence,* Routledge & Kegan Paul, London

Goldman, R (1965) *Readiness for Religion,* Routledge & Kegan Paul, London

Grimmitt, M (1978) *What Can I Do in RE?,* Mayhew-McCrimmons, Great Wakering

Grimmitt, M (1987) *Religious Education and Human Development,* McCrimmons, Great Wakering

Halpin, D *et al* (2000) Maintaining, reconstructing and creating tradition in education, *The Oxford Review of Education,* forthcoming

Hamilton, H (1942) What is religious education?, *Times Educational Supplement,* 18 November, in (1997) *Delivering and Managing Effective RE in the Secondary School,* C Wright and I Vale, Courseware Publications

Hammond, J *et al* (1990) *New Methods in RE Teaching,* Oliver and Boyd, London

Handy, C (1997) *The Hungry Spirit: Beyond capitalism, a quest for purpose in the modern world,* Random House, New York/London

Hay, D (1985) Suspicion of the spiritual: teaching religion in a world of secular experience, *British Journal of Religious Education,* **7** (1), pp 140–47

Hay, D (1987) *Exploring Inner Space,* 2nd edn, Mowbray, London

Hay, D (1990) *Religious Experience Today*, Mowbray, London

Hay, D and Nye, R (1998) *The Spirit of the Child*, HarperCollins, London

Haydon, G (1987) *Education for A Pluralist Society*, Bedford Way Papers, London

Hirst, P (1965) Morals, religion and the maintained schools, *British Journal of Educational Studies*, **14** (1), November

Hogan, P (1995) *The Custody and Courtship of Experience: Western education in philosophical perspective*, The Columbia Press, Dublin

Hoggart, R (1996) *The Way We Live Now*, Chatto and Windus, New York

Howkins, K G (1966) *Religious Thinking and Religious Education*, Tyndale Press

Hughes, C (1993) Parents reveal league of favoured subjects, *Independent*, 6 September

Hull, J (ed) (1982) *New Directions in Religious Education*, The Falmer Press, Lewes

Hull, J (1984) *Studies in Religion and Education*, Falmer Press, Lewes

Hyde, K E (1965) *Religious Learning in Adolescence*, Oliver and Boyd, London

Islamic Academy (1990) *Faith as the Basis of Education in a Multi-Faith, Multi-Cultural Country*, Cambridge

Jackson, R (1997) *Religious Education: An interpretive approach*, Hodder & Stoughton, London

Kay, W and Barnes, L P (1999) Developments in religious education in England and Wales (Part 1): Church and state, the 1988 Education Reform Act, and spirituality in schools, *Themelios*, **25** (1), pp 23–38

Kennedy, H (1997) *Learning Works: Widening participation in further education*, FEFC, London

Kitson Clark, G (1962) *The Making of Victorian England*, Cambridge University Press, Cambridge

Lasch, N (1996) *The Beginning and End of Religion*, Cambridge University Press, Cambridge

Lealman, B (1986) Grottoes, ghettos and city of glass, *British Journal of Religious Education*, **8** (1), pp 65–71

Lenga, R-A (1998) Holocaust education: the search for a suitable pedagogy, *Journal of Holocaust Education*, **7** (3), Winter, pp 51–60, Frank Cass

Loukes, H (1961) *Teenage Religion*, CEM, London

Loukes, H (1965) *New Ground in Christian Education*, SCM, London

Lukasiewicz, J (1994) *The Ignorance Explosion*, Carton University Press, London/Ottawa

Marty, M (1969) *The Search for a Usable Future*, Harper & Row, New York

Maslow, A H (1967) The good life of the self-actualising person, *Humanist*, July/August

Ministry of Education (1963) *Half Our Future* (The Newsom Report), HMSO, London

Mortimore, P (ed) (1999) *Understanding Pedagogy and Its Impact on Learning*, Paul Chapman, London

Ogden, V (1997a) The future role and importance of religious education 16–19, Part 1, *Resource*, **19** (3), pp 12–15

Ogden, V (1997b) The future role and importance of religious education 16–19, Part 2, *Resource*, **20** (1), pp 17–21

Ogden, V (2000) Establishing and enriching religious education at 16-plus, in *Learning to Teach Religious Education in the Secondary School*, in ed A Wright and A-M Brandom, Routledge/Falmer, London

Otto, R (1923) *The Idea of the Holy*, Oxford University Press, Oxford

Pannenberg, W (1994) Christianity and the West: ambiguous past, uncertain future, *First Things*, **48**, December, pp 18–22

Parsons, G (ed) (1994) *The Growth of Religious Diversity in Britain from 1945*, Routledge, London

Priestley, J (1996) *Spirituality in the Curriculum*, Hockerill Educational Foundation, Frinton

QCA (1998) *Exemplification of Standards in Religious Education: Key stages 1 to 4*, QCA, London

Read, G et al (1992) *The Westhill Project, RE 5–16: How do I teach RE?*, Stanley Thornes, Cheltenham

Reeves, M (ed) (1999) *Christian Thinking and Social Order: Conviction politics from the 1930s to the present day*, Cassell, London

Robinson, J (1963) *Honest to God*, SCM, London

Robson, G (1996) Religious education, government policy and professional practice 1985–1995, *British Journal of Religious Education*, **19** (1), pp 13–23

Sacks, J (1994) *Will We Have Jewish Grandchildren? Jewish continuity and how to achieve it*, Vallentine Mitchell & Co, Essex

School Curriculum and Assessment Authority (SCAA) (1996) *Education for Adult Life: The spiritual and moral development of young people*, SCAA, London

Schools Council (1971) *Religious Education in Secondary Schools*, Working Paper 36, Evans/ Methuen Educational, London

Slee, N (1989) Conflict and reconciliation between competing models of religious education: some reflections on the British scene, *British Journal of Religious Education*, **11** (3), pp 126–35

Smart, N (1968) *Secular Education and the Logic of Religion*, Faber & Faber, London

Smart, N (1973) *The Phenomenon of Religion*, Macmillan, London

Starkings, D (1993) The landscape of spirituality, in *Religion, Spirituality and the Arts in Education*, ed D Starkings, Hodder & Stoughton, Abingdon

Sullivan, J (1999) Catholic schools and the common good, in *Values and the Curriculum: The school context*, ed D Lawton, J Cairns and R Gardiner, pp 104–16, Curriculum Studies Academic Group Occasional Paper No 1, Institute of Education, University of London, London

Surin, K (1980) Can the experiential and the phenomenological approaches be reconciled?, *British Journal of Religious Education*, **2** (2), pp 99–103

Swann Report (1985) *Education for All: The report of an inquiry into the education of children from ethnic minority groups*, HMSO, London

Thatcher, A (1991) A critique of inwardness in religious education, *British Journal of Religious Education*, **14** (1), pp 22–27

Tillich, P (1969) *The Shaking of the Foundations*, Penguin, Harmondsworth

Totterdell, M (1995) The spiritual rights of children: some considerations in the context of education, *Paideia*, **9**, pp 6–19

Toulmin, S (1990) *Cosmopolis: The hidden agenda of modernity*, The Free Press, New York

Warwick RE Project (1995) *Bridges in Religion*, Heinemann, London

Watson, B (ed) (1991) *Priorities in Religious Education*, Falmer Press, Lewes

Wedderspoon, A G (ed) (1966) *Religious Education 1944–1984*, George Allen and Unwin, London

White, J (1997) *Education and the End of Work: A new philosophy of work and learning*, Cassell, London

Wintersgill, B (2000) Task setting in religious education at Key Stage 3: a comparison with History and English, *Resource*, **22** (3), pp 10–17

Wright, A (1993) *Religious Education in the Secondary School: Prospects for religious literacy*, David Fulton Publishers in association with the Roehampton Institute, London

Wright, A (1998) *Spiritual Pedagogy: A survey, critique and reconstruction of contemporary spiritual education in England and Wales*, Calham College Institute, Abingdon

Chapter 9

Art and design: Developments and dislocations

Roy Prentice and Tony Dyson

Introduction

> In order to understand what art education is today it would be useful to examine some of the developments which have occurred in its history...
>
> With a clearer view of the present those responsible for art education programs will be better prepared to make intelligent decisions regarding its future.
>
> (Eisner and Ecker, 1966: 1)

This chapter traces the changing nature of art and design education. It does so in the spirit of the above remark by Eisner and Ecker and invites the reader to explore connections between past experience, the present situation and future possibilities at the beginning of a new century. At different times and in different institutions this area of the curriculum has been known variously as art and crafts, art, and art and design. In some situations terms such as visual studies, visual education, aesthetic education, creative studies, design education and expressive arts have also been applied. In the interests of consistency throughout the present discussion the term art is used to cover a continuum of art, craft and design activity, and references to artists are intended to embrace craftspeople and designers unless otherwise stated.

It is widely acknowledged that 'Ideas in art education change, develop, become modified in response to pressure and needs from inside and outside' (Field, 1970: 47). Of central importance in this process of change is the nature of the perceived relationship between professional practice in art and in art education. However, this relationship is complex and changing views of art education are not based on 'some notion of art as evolving progressively through critical refinements', as Addison and Burgess (2000: 327) make clear. As they go on to stress, the changing nature of art is driven by a series of 'critical relationships, revisions and revolutions as it simultaneously responds to and produces the needs of any one time or context'. In recognition of the constant state of flux in which art thrives it is necessary to establish at the outset that its educational potential is wide in scope and complex in nature. Given the constraints of a single chapter what follows is, unavoidably, a selective account. It is also an account that reveals the particular contribution of the Institute of Education to teaching and scholarship in the field of art education.

The area of the curriculum under discussion accommodates a broad spectrum of theoretical positions and professional practice. It is this diversity – which can be regarded as both a strength and a weakness – that has influenced the development of art in schools. It has been shaped by curious juxtapositions of cherished beliefs and strongly held views, creative energy and imaginative practice as well as by conflicting ideologies and debilitating orthodoxies. By its very nature creative activity, if it is to retain integrity, is complex, challenging, risky and often contentious. Thus art, like creativity itself, is often perceived as *difficult* to pin down and to accommodate within a formal education system. On the one hand it could be argued that the contribution of art within the curriculum over many years has been uneven and undervalued, its purpose largely misunderstood and its position marginalized in many schools. On the other hand, however, it is widely recognized that art educators have generated innovative approaches to curriculum development and pedagogy. From whatever position the story of art education is reviewed, it is apparent that landmark achievements are the outcomes of the driving force of a succession of committed individuals and groups with a vision to secure for art a central role in the *mainstream* of educational provision.

Curriculum development

Philosophies and approaches

Unlike any other group of curriculum subjects the arts are repeatedly required to justify their existence (Gulbenkian Foundation, 1982; NACCCE, 1999).

For art educators the skills of advocacy have always been of central importance. Such advocacy has generally been based on sets of ideas and beliefs associated with individuals or small groups of practitioners, and exemplified by their pupils' work, rather than based on formalized approaches and agreed directions informed by research. As a result of the freedom that traditionally art teachers have enjoyed, a wide range of attitudes and approaches has simultaneously had an effect on the teaching of art. Alternative rationales for the inclusion of art in the school curriculum coexist. At one extreme the place of art is justified in terms of its instrumental function. This might be seen as developing self-confidence and citizenship or enhancing academic achievement in more high-status subjects such as English and mathematics. At the other extreme art is justified for its intrinsic value, for the unique contribution it makes as a way of knowing.

Teachers of art are expected to be able to respond to a range of views about the nature of art activity, the various forms it has taken and functions it has fulfilled in different cultures and at different times. A narrow view of art based exclusively on a male-dominated Western European tradition (significant though this tradition is) tends to overemphasize the importance of practical skills and verisimilitude. Sometimes approaches to art in schools are based on notions of the innate talent and giftedness of a minority of individuals rather than on strategies for effective teaching of all pupils. The problems inherent in such an elitist approach are exacerbated when fuelled by the misapplication of ill-defined concepts such as creativity, imagination, discovery, expression, freedom and child-art.

The 'child-art revolution'

The 'child-art revolution' with which such pioneering educators as Franz Cizek, Marion Richardson and R R Tomlinson are associated had a huge impact in a growing number of schools in the 1930s. The post-war optimism, of which the 1944 Education Act was a foreshadowing, provided new opportunities for imaginative teachers in both primary and secondary schools to build upon and extend pre-war achievements. However, it should be pointed out that alongside innovative developments there remained in a significant number of schools prescriptive approaches to teaching informed by certain attitudes towards the subject, particularly in relation to neatness and accuracy, that had hardly changed since the early years of the 20th century (Carline, 1968; Macdonald, 1970). In the 1950s most pupils participated in practical art and craft activities each week for periods of time that ranged from 45 minutes to an entire morning or afternoon. It is important to remember that this area of the curriculum was perceived as being practical in nature and reflected models of professional practice in the fine arts and crafts. Children were expected to function as artists and craftspeople. The qualities and properties of available materials – along with a new-found curiosity about how they might be used, combined, experimented with – provided a powerful and refreshingly uninhibiting source of motivation for exploration by pupils and teachers alike. The philosophical and psychological underpinning of such practice can be found in a number of seminal texts that draw upon the fundamental ideas about art and the development of each individual's response to experience as expressed by Dewey (1934). The work of Read (1943) and Lowenfeld and Brittain (1947) presented intellectually stimulating ideas about the centrality of art in education and the relationship between children's general growth and creative development respectively. The publication of Marion Richardson's *Art and the Child* (1948) disseminated more widely her ideas about art teaching. Her influence in London was particularly strong as a result of an exhibition of her pupils' work held at the Grafton Galleries (1920), through her association with the critic Roger Fry, through her appointment in 1924 as the first lecturer in art at the London Day Training College (later to become the Institute of Education, University of London) and in her role as District Art Inspector from 1930 for London County Council where her senior colleague was R R Tomlinson.

The 1950s

In the hands of knowledgeable teachers 'new' materials provided liberating opportunities for children's creative responses with which connections could be made with the experimental approaches to materials and processes adopted by many modern artists. However, the 1950s are also remembered for the non-interventionist approach of many teachers and for a belief in self-expression, autonomous image-making and individuality at the expense of skills, contextualization and critical evaluation. The situation in the mid-1950s is described by Field as follows:

> …in art classes in junior and secondary schools up and down the country, children were happily toying with all sorts of materials, and they and teachers alike were immersed in some at least of the problems inherent in such untraditional activities. Many teachers soon realised that new media might serve as a stimulus for failing interest or as a compensation for lack of success in other directions. For many teachers and children during that period there was a great enthusiasm, an opening of doors, a fresh realisation of true and genuine aspects of art.
>
> No revolution can be sustained and by the early 1960s this one, rooted in progressive ideas about child-centred education and a recognition of Child Art had 'long lost its first glow'.
>
> (Field, 1970: 15)

During the 1950s a major change occurred in the way art students were taught in colleges of art and in due course this had an unintended impact on the art curriculum in secondary and to some extent in primary schools. The ideas explored by a group of artists involved in the teaching of foundation course students became the basis of innovative curriculum development in several colleges of art. Victor Pasmore, Richard Hamilton, Harry Thubron and Tom Hudson provided the leadership for what became known as the basic course movement. Inspired by Bauhaus philosophy, lively basic courses were developed in London, Leeds, Newcastle and Bath and the approach to which Pasmore *et al* subscribed was made more widely accessible through a series of exhibitions they mounted at the Institute of Contemporary Arts, London.

The 1960s

The basic courses were introduced to develop in art college foundation course students an understanding of visual phenomena through analysis of visual form. Visual exercises were designed that required students to investigate and experiment with materials, processes and the basic elements of visual communication and expression that include form, pattern, shape, texture, line, tone and colour. The aim was to provide future artists, craftspeople and designers with a shared grounding in visual understanding from which work in either an abstract or figurative vein could develop. The essential characteristics of this approach to art college teaching are clearly articulated by Maurice de Sausmarez in his richly illustrated and influential book, *Basic Design: The dynamics of visual form* (1964). He reaffirms that Basic Design should be: 'an attitude of mind, not a method... primarily a form of enquiry, not a new art form... not exclusively abstract (and) emphatically not an end in itself' (de Sausmarez, 1964: 11–12). Unfortunately, in its wider application by less inspired teachers than the originators of the basic course approach it often did become reduced to a formula to produce a range of abstract images and visual effects that were all too often regarded as ends in themselves. During the 1960s, the misapplication of basic course exercises in the secondary school art curriculum, for which they were never intended, was commonplace.

Eventually further diluted versions of this approach filtered down to some primary schools. Whilst work of this kind at its most banal was reduced to a series of exercises with little meaning for children, at its best it promoted visual analysis and encouraged a planned approach supported by positive teaching and critical evaluation. It could be argued that for all its shortcomings the basic course movement helped to move art college teaching into a more imaginative era; and this in turn had an influence on future generations of art teachers. The impact of such ideas on schools in the 1960s and 1970s is encapsulated by Field (1970) who says:

> The protagonists of the Basic Course have made determined efforts to dissem-inate their ideas through the secondary schools. Here, on the whole, they have been unsuccessful, partly because of the difficulty of securing under-standing of their principles, and partly because of the difficulty of relating basic course exercises with other work. On the one hand, as in the schools of art, they have woken teachers to the fact that the art teacher can – should – be active and not passive; and they have broken in upon the entrenched idea that children must make art. The ambiguous exercise, that can be looked at in two ways, is another weapon in the attack on the picture; a potent element for change.
>
> (Field, 1970: 64)

The 1970s

From the vantage point of the early 1970s it is possible to identify key factors that played an important part in shaping the curriculum for art for the decade. The publication of the Plowden Report brought sharply into focus the desirability of direct experience, personal discovery and creative activity in the primary school curriculum. It heralded art as 'a form of communication and a means of expression of feelings which ought to permeate the whole curriculum and the whole life of the school' (CACE, 1967: 247). Where the Plowden Report inspired teachers to exploit the potential of art as a tool for learning, work of quality using a wide range of media was often witnessed. The case studies included in the Department of Education and Science Survey 11 *Art in Schools* (1971) based on HMI inspections undertaken between 1967 and 1971 confirm this to be so.

Whilst acknowledging the uneven quality of provision and practice in art in primary schools this survey is optimistic in tone. Seven years later a survey of HM Inspectorate, *Primary Education in England* (DES, 1978a) revealed a somewhat different reality. In a majority of primary schools art was rarely seen to make a proper contribution to the development of children's perceptual skills through carefully considered programmes of work designed to encourage drawing, painting and modelling from direct observa-tion. Art educators expressed their growing concern about the lack of art activity derived from first-hand experience, together with the apparent relegation of art to a peripheral position in the curriculum of a significant number of primary schools.

An attempt to strengthen the teaching of art in primary schools was made by HM Inspectorate through the presentation of 'good practice' in the publication *Art in Junior Education* (DES, 1978b). Reference is made to 'three major elements that stand out' in the schools under discussion: 'conviction', 'care' and 'expectation'. Concern for the quality of the learning environment, to include interpersonal relationships, is stressed. The ideas and feelings of individuals are valued and tools and materials are well organized and handled with sensitivity. Activities are carefully planned, imaginatively presented, well resourced and progressively more demanding as later learning builds upon earlier learning. Attention is also drawn to the importance of whole-staff discussion about this area of the curriculum to achieve continuity through a whole-school policy for art supported by the appointment of a subject co-ordinator. In the same year, the Schools Council Art Committee published *Art 7–11* (Schools Council, 1978). It offered practical advice to classroom teachers through which issues were raised about the functions and value of art at different stages of children's development. In particular it addressed the perceived deterioration in the quality and challenge of art experiences available to children as they progress from infant to junior schools. Extreme approaches to art teaching that are clearly identifiable in a large number of schools are highlighted as 'two traps' into which it is easy for 'the uncertain teacher' to fall:

> One is heavily prescriptive, directing the children's work step by step and thus rejecting the creative process in art…
>
> The other is to be so committed to 'free expression' as to be unwilling to intervene in the expressive process; the teaching of skills is left severely alone and the teacher acts mainly as a facilitating agent.

> (Schools Council, 1978: 7)

Most importantly this publication helped to establish drawing as a fundamental means of investigating and recording experience and provided frameworks within which projects could be planned as a sequence of lessons rather than as a disjointed set of practical activities. The developing emphasis being placed on drawing in both the primary and secondary art curriculum was further enhanced by a large-scale touring exhibition, 'Learning Through Drawing', that was accompanied by a book of the same title that served as an informative catalogue (Art Advisers Association, 1979). The aim of this enterprise was to stimulate a wider interest in children's drawings and foster a deeper understanding of the educational potential of drawing. Drawing is presented as a process to be harnessed to promote learning, rather than as a technique to be acquired. Furthermore, in an effort to erode the widely held stereotype of drawing – associated with accuracy, neatness and photographic likeness – the cross-curricular implications of a broad concept of drawing are explored In many schools the art curriculum reflected a concern for the development of children's visual perception through drawing.

The art curriculum in secondary schools was influenced by the combined impact of the expansion of secondary schools, the restructuring of courses in colleges of art and the vibrant world of popular youth culture in which new overlapping relationships between art, design, fashion and popular music were promoted through the mass media. With the development of comprehensive schools came more firmly established and more lavishly equipped art departments, often accommodated in purpose-built specialist suites of studios and workshops. Between the mid-1960s and the mid-1970s the social, educational and economic climate prompted many forward-thinking local education authorities to appoint specialist advisers for art in order to support the work of developing departments in secondary schools that were often based on models of art college foundation courses. Indeed at their best large comprehensive school art departments produced work of a more ambitious nature, of a higher quality and in more lavishly resourced accommodation than some colleges of art.

In such departments staffed by teams of specialist teachers each with expertise in a particular area of work – painting, graphics, ceramics, textiles, printmaking or photography – it was possible for opportunities in such areas to be available to pupils to an advanced level of study. Organizational patterns included those that provided pupils in the first three years with opportunities to study different specialisms in rotation on a termly basis as a broad-based foundation for examination courses that could focus on, say, printmaking and painting or ceramics. Experiences of this kind enabled potential art students to prepare high-quality portfolios to support their applications to colleges of art. Within many secondary schools art departments were an energizing source of activities, clubs and societies that involved exhibitions, music and drama events and, increasingly, visits to museums and galleries and involvements with practising artists through artists in residency schemes. Exhibition modes of assessment for the Certificate of Secondary Education examination resulted in often ambitious displays of work that provided focal points for in-service courses and conferences. During this period teachers gained ever more control over curriculum content and examinations at 16-plus. For a more detailed picture of art education in secondary schools between the late 1960s and 1980 the reader is referred to a series of revealing case studies based on HMI inspections (DES, 1971; DES, 1983). Writing in 1983, HMI refer to 'an unusual, and in some ways surprising, consensus about the purpose of art education in the junior school' (DES, 1983). Given the complexity of the subject at secondary level, however, it is claimed that 'It is expected that there would be great variety in practice and in the underlying principles of art education which inform it' (DES, 1983: v).

For secondary school teachers of art two publications provided important reference points in the developing debates about curriculum rationales for art. In the UK, from his position as head of the art department at the Institute of Education, Field (1970) was well placed to offer an overview of developments in the subject and comment on their implications for the future. The centrality of art as a means of organizing experience, the relationship between practical studio-based work and a critical understanding of the work of other artists, plus a concern for continuous learning in art, are examples of prominent themes. Two years later art teachers in the UK gained access to a wide range of ideas explored by Eisner (1972) at Stanford University. Eisner's expertise enables him to bridge the worlds of curriculum studies and art. As a result his ability to conceptualize approaches to art – particularly in terms of intrinsic and instrumental rationales – has helped vast numbers of teachers to locate themselves in the curriculum debate. It could be argued that the long-lasting influence of these two landmark publications of the early 1970s is due to the academically rigorous way in which fundamental issues are interrogated in a context of professional practice. Following the Ruskin College Speech in 1976 by Prime Minister James Callaghan, those involved in and concerned about the arts in a wider sense in the school curriculum were alarmed by the absence of well-informed comments on the arts as the vocationally orientated national curriculum debate rapidly gathered momentum.

The 1980s

In 1982 the Gulbenkian Report *The Arts in Schools* was published and provided a focal point for teachers, headteachers, administrators and parents involved in discussions about the idea of a national curriculum and the place of the arts within it. The Report addressed issues relating to 'principles, practice and provision'. It stressed that any arts curriculum should encourage a dynamic relationship between two kinds of experience: 'participation' and 'appreciation'. Traditionally art in schools had been predominantly practical in nature apart from the teaching of art history for examination courses. Certainly, at the primary stage children rarely (if ever) engaged in work of a critical or historical nature, in art lessons. The Gulbenkian Report heightened awareness to the possibilities offered by the study of work by a wide range of artists from different cultures and different periods. It is recognized that from the earliest years of schooling the erosion of boundaries between school and the world beyond school can be aided by professional artists, arts organizations and museum and gallery education staff working closely with children and teachers. Whilst the Report and the curriculum development project of the same name that followed promoted a concept of a balanced arts curriculum, this idea was strongly rejected by the National Society for Education in Art and Design in favour of retaining a separate identity for art education. During the 1980s there developed a growing commitment to a hitherto largely neglected aspect of art education: critical, historical and contextual studies. The contribution to this development of the Schools' Sub-Committee of the Association of Art Historians, which promoted a salutary dialogue about knowledge and understanding in art between teachers and art historians, is discussed more fully below.

Between 1981 and 1984 a national curriculum development project, *Critical Studies in Art Education*, raised the awareness of a large number of teachers to the value of a critical and contextual dimension to art education. This widely publicized project grew out of pioneering work at Drumcroon Education Art Centre (Taylor, 1986). The high profile enjoyed by this curriculum project was achieved through the driving force of Taylor and his ability to involve a wide range of teachers, artists, museum and gallery educators, local education authority advisers and representatives of the arts, crafts and design councils. This initiative was well timed. It provided a focus for the fundamental debate about the relationship between making art and learning about art in the school curriculum. In doing so it explored a key issue to which attention had been drawn by the Gulbenkian Report (1982) and HM Inspectorate (DES, 1983) and the outcome was to have a strong influence on the thinking that underpinned the first National Curriculum for Art.

The 1990s

For most of the last decade of the 20th century the twin concerns of the National Curriculum and school inspections dominated art teachers' agendas. With the implementation of the third version of the National Curriculum (September 2000) it seems inconceivable that until 1992 teachers were 'responsible for deciding what to teach in art lessons and why to teach it' (Robinson, 1995: 124). Given the diverse nature of art education the implementation of a centrally imposed curriculum presented teachers with a challenging task — to meet the required criteria while retaining their creativity and professional integrity. There were also opportunities to be grasped to address fundamental issues of unevenness of practice and provision, continuity and progression along with the problem of marginalization within the curriculum in many schools. Above all the National Curriculum was optimistically regarded by most teachers as a means through which they could secure for all children a broad-based experience of art, craft and design as an entitlement. The centrality of *making* was reaffirmed but with the expectation that practical work would be informed by investigative studies and greater knowledge and understanding of the work of others. Heated arguments were triggered by what many regarded as an unacceptable degree of political intervention to determine the structure and content of the statutory requirements for art (1992). A high-profile debate focused on three main points: firstly, the exclusion of Key Stage 4 from the statutory require-ments for the teaching of art; secondly, the rejection of the Art Working Group's proposed structure of three attainment targets (DES, 1991) in favour of two attainment targets was seen as a political rather than an educational decision (Robinson, 1995: 124); thirdly, controversial views fuelled a highly politicized debate about the concept of cultural heritage as a result of the inclusion of an *approved* list of examples of artists, movements and periods for children to study.

The revised version of the National Curriculum for art (1995) retained the two-attainment-target structure but attempted to simplify and clarify the requirements particularly with generalist primary teachers in mind. Further revision of the requirements for art in the National Curriculum to be introduced in 2000 has resulted in a single attainment target to embrace knowledge, skills and understanding, plus the inclusion of the term 'design' in its title. Whilst the framework provided by the National Curriculum has done much to help teachers articulate their ideas and focus more clearly on lesson planning and intended learning outcomes, overall familiar short-comings remain in many schools. These include a lack of a systematic approach to the development of skills, knowledge and understanding, the copying of reproductions of a narrow range of predominantly male Western European artists' work and poorly developed three-dimensional work (OFSTED, 1995). Based on a large number of school inspection reports the positive features of current practice in art are identified in *The Arts Inspected* (OFSTED, 1998). When considered alongside *Art in Secondary Education 11–16* (DES, 1983) and *Art in Schools* (DES, 1971) it is fascinating to see how a legitimized model of what is considered to be 'good practice' has been reinforced over a period of over 30 years. Within the field of art education there is growing awareness that change is needed to ensure that art education not only meets the complex demands of the 21st century but also fosters and channels the creative energy and vision of the children who as adults will shape it. Current orthodoxies are criticized for clinging to a 19th-century tradition (Hughes, 1998) and further challenged by those who propose an alternative approach to art education informed by postmodern ideas that emphasize 'difference, plurality and independence of mind' (Swift and Steers, 1998: 3).

Since the introduction of the National Curriculum the government's provision for headteachers to 'slim down' the art curriculum in primary schools from September 1998 has resulted in a serious impoverishment of art experiences available to many 5–11-year-olds. Clearly the pressures on schools to raise standards of literacy and numeracy have further eroded time formerly available for art activities. Among the numerous critics of this contentious shift in policy, Lord Puttnam (1998) has drawn attention to 'the danger of allowing arts education to be marginalized, unnecessarily sacrificed at the altar of numeracy and literacy targets'. At secondary level many committed art teachers have used the framework of the National Curriculum to advantage to promote challenging, intellectually rigorous courses. Highly creative and energetic teachers have often far exceeded the requirements of the National Curriculum and extended the scope of the subject field. Opportunities have been grasped to explore relevant contemporary (often contentious) issues through a range of processes and procedures in art that bring together in creative relationships traditional media, skills and new electronic technologies. Personal responses to experience are located in wider social, cultural, historical contexts and ideas are articulated through sophisticated annotated sketchbooks, portfolios and critical language. Pupils' making is informed by contemporary art practice and an extended agenda of visual and material culture. Resources available to many learners and teachers include living artists, craftspeople and designers, and museums and galleries.

A wider professional context and international developments

In Britain, art teaching in general education received early encouragement through the ideas of William Morris and John Ruskin. Ruskin's *The Elements of Drawing* (1857) contained one of the earliest manifestations of a respect for children's natural aptitude for drawing. Subsequently, T R Ablett built upon this interest in children's creative ability, energetically propounding the notion of 'drawing for delight' and founding in 1888 the Royal Drawing Society, which held its first exhibition of children's art two years later. At the turn of the century, the inspirational R Catterson Smith, placing an emphasis rather on 'remembered observation' than on the direct recording of observation, numbered among his students Marion Richardson. The enthusiasm generated by these influential pioneers led to the formation of the New Society of Art Teachers and the Art Teachers' Guild, and further stimulus was provided by Herbert Read's seminal *Education Through Art* (1943) and R R Tomlinson's significantly titled *Children as Artists* (1944). In 1946 the New Society of Art Teachers and the Art Teachers' Guild amalgamated to become the Society for Education in Art (SEA), which published regularly the journal *Athene* and which had Read as its chair and president for 28 years (Barclay-Russell, 1967). The title of Read's book, a work that he saw as embodying revolutionary proposals affecting the whole curriculum, sprang from his passionate conviction of the potency of art education, and it was largely as a result of his persuasiveness that the name of SEA was in 1953 changed to the Society for Education *Through* Art, a title more properly reflective of the aspiration, still enduring today, to establish for art a central place in the curriculum.

The aftermath of the Second World War saw the foundation of the United Nations Educational, Scientific and Cultural Organisation (UNESCO) during whose early general conferences (in 1946 and 1947) resolutions to inquire into art education were adopted. In 1948 Herbert Read chaired an international exploratory committee whose deliberations resulted in a UNESCO art education seminar in Bristol in 1951. Twenty countries were represented and the International Society for Education through Art (InSEA) was conceived. Incidentally, John Steers (1999) points out that the idea of such an international organization was not entirely new: a society with similar aims held its first congress in Paris in 1900 and eventually, in 1963, merged with InSEA. Ever since its foundation, InSEA has held almost without interruption world or regional congresses each year in major cities in every continent. The Society has by and large pursued its original ideals of the fostering of education through art, extending and developing the world-wide association of art educators at all levels, co-operating to mutual advantage with those in disciplines outside the teaching profession, and encouraging better understanding between peoples of different cultures. But it has also recognized the opportunities and the potential pitfalls of the rapidly developing communication technologies: opportunities for the efficient dissemination of ideas, none the less accompanied by the need to 'encourage and appreciate diversity... [and avoid] a stultifying international uniformity devoid of all individuality, originality and creativity' (Steers, 1999). Equally vigorous are the activities of the National Society for Education in Art & Design (NSEAD), whose name is yet another example of the need carefully to reflect a philosophy. In 1982 it launched its *Journal of Art & Design Education* with the stated aim of providing an international forum for the dissemination of ideas, practical developments and research findings in the field. Guided by an editorial board composed of members representing the subject in all its aspects and at all levels of education and by an international consultancy team, it has been impressively successful in these various respects.

As we have indicated above, after several decades of evident neglect (Brazier, 1985) there emerged in the late 1970s and the 1980s a new interest in the possibility of fostering art–historical and critical studies in schools. It should be acknowledged, of course, that certain School Certificate and GCE examination boards had, over the years, offered examination syllabuses in history of art, but these examinations had attracted relatively small numbers of candidates in the later years of their schooling. The new democratizing aspiration was to make historical and critical studies accessible, as an integral part of art education, to all pupils throughout the primary and secondary levels of schooling (Dyson, 1991). Naturally, this was to have its effect in the training of specialist art teachers, the majority of whom embarked on their professional courses having gained a degree in art or design that, as a result of the recommendations of the National Advisory Council on Art and Design (appointed in 1959 under the chairmanship of Sir William Coldstream) contained a mandatory element of history of art or some related study complementary to their studio work (Bell, 1964).

However, among these graduates there began to appear some with degrees in history of art or design, so the new importance being proposed for their field seemed opportune. The Association of Art Historians, formed in the early 1970s and hitherto concerned mainly with the subject in higher education, became alert to these developments in general education and formed a Schools Sub-Committee late in the decade. The Sub-Committee held its inaugural conference at the Institute of Education in 1980. It was attended by over 350 delegates representing many spheres of education: the Department of Education and Science; the Arts Council of Great Britain; the Schools Council; the Association of Art Advisers; local education authorities; the Association of Centres of Art and Design Teacher Education; colleges and departments of education; museum and gallery education departments; and schools (Dyson, 1981). There was a further large conference at the Victoria and Albert Museum in 1983 (Dyson, 1984) and, with the collaboration of the ILEA Art and Design Inspectorate, the Open University and other bodies, a succession of courses and seminars for teachers. The work of the Association of Art Historians Schools Sub-Committee under the successive leadership of Howard Hollands and Nicholas Addison has continued to influence inquiry and practice. It is heartening that the recently established Arts and Humanities Research Board has chosen to fund a research project directed by Addison, the purpose of which is to investigate ways in which art critics and art historians in schools can contribute more widely to pupils' critical understanding of visual and material culture.

All these initiatives have been strongly supported and enriched by museum and gallery education departments. The main contribution of these departments has obviously been to make original works of art and artefacts directly accessible to pupils and students, though they have also produced valuable resource material and in some cases have contributed significantly to teacher training and to higher degree programmes. For example, in the early 1970s strong links were established between the art teacher training course at the Institute of Education and four major London establishments: the National Gallery; the Victoria and Albert Museum; the Tate Gallery; and the British Museum. These links have been further consolidated at the Institute by the introduction in 1994 of a master's degree in museums and galleries in education that is taught in collaboration with the education departments of the British Museum and the Victoria and Albert Museum.

Teacher education

A few years before it assumed the title of Institute of Education, the London Day Training College played an important part in providing a category of teacher previously hardly known in state education at school level: in December 1923, the government's Board of Education approved the College's proposal for the establishment of a course of training for specialist teachers of art (Institute of Education archives). Presumably with an eye to local need, the Board stipulated that the course should cater for no more than six students and that amongst these there should be a sufficient number of Londoners. The course was to begin in August 1924, and was to follow preliminary training at approved schools of art. This art school training would be designated Part 1 of the aspirant teacher's preparation and would culminate in the Board of Education's drawing examination; Part 2 would be a combined professional and art course. The professional component would be taught at the London Day Training College, which, though administered by the London County Council, had from 1909 been affiliated to London University; and the continuing art training would be provided by the relevant school of art. Part 2 would lead to the Board's examination in: a) painting; b) modelling; c) pictorial design; d) industrial design; and e) principles of teaching. Successful candidates would be qualified to teach both in schools and in schools of art, and the examination in principles of teaching and school management provided for this. The first paper contained such questions as 'In what ways would you interest the pupils of an Elementary or a Secondary School in their surroundings from an artistic point of view?' and invitations to 'Describe... adequate equipment for a) an Etching Room or b) a Painting Room or c) an Embroidery Class in a School of Art.'

As may be imagined, there was considerable debate concerning the distribution of students' time between the schools of art and the London Day Training College. The Slade School of Fine Art (which, as part of London University, was a principal provider of the new teacher trainees) insisted upon three years' full-time art training plus a component of continuing art school attendance during the fourth year of professional preparation. A letter dated 21 November 1924 (Institute of Education archives) from London County Council relates to the staffing of the new course and, incidentally, gives us an early glimpse of Marion Richardson. She was appointed to teach for two hours and to supervise teaching practice for one day per week. She was currently developing her philosophy of art education as a teacher at Dudley Girls' High School and continued in this work alongside her new teacher-training commitment until 1930, when she moved to the inspectorate. Other institutions were quick to follow the example of the London Day Training College. In 1927 Hornsey School of Art, under the auspices of Middlesex County Council, proposed a scheme for the training of art teachers. The Hornsey course seems to have materialized by the following year, judging by a slightly petulant letter (Institute of Education archives) from the London County Council to the Board of Education, pointing out that it might have been more economical to expand the London course beyond the Board's stipulation of six students rather than institute a new course. No one could at the time have envisaged the dramatic increase in the numbers of specialist art teachers that was to take place over the next 30 years.

The London Day Training College assumed the title of Institute of Education in 1932, and in its annual report for the academic year 1933–34 the newly named institution noted that a certain Clarence Waite, formerly a part-time art teacher at Alleyn's School, had been appointed tutor in charge of the art teacher training course from which he had recently graduated. (This would turn out to be a highly significant appointment, perhaps principally for political reasons.) By now, the Board of Education had relented to the extent of allowing 12 students, who were required to have gained a diploma of the Slade School of Fine Art or the specified Board of Education examination, to enter the one-year course of training, which consisted of two-thirds pedagogical and one-third 'technical' studies (the latter presumably a continuation of training in some aspect of art or a craft). Most of the teaching was divided between Waite and John Alford, an art historian who, though paid by the Institute of Education, counted officially as a member of staff of the Courtauld Institute of Art, the University's major institute for the study of history of art. This is not without significance; nor is the fact that in the 1930s Marion Richardson, despite the burden of her inspectorial duties, was giving art appreciation lectures at the Institute and that another colleague was Margaret Bulley, who was doing much to promote an interest in art history at school level through radio broadcasts. As we have seen, the historical and critical aspects of art education were, except under the wing of certain regional examination boards, inexplicably to suffer a decline and a virtual disappearance until reinstated in schools of art in the 1960s following the recommendations of the Coldstream Committee (Bell, 1964), in the newly established BEd courses during the same decade, but not in schools until the 1980s.

By 1944 the status of the subject in the Institute – and probably nationally – was reflected in Clarence Waite's elevation to the post of full-time Head of the Art Department. There was further enhancement in the rapid post-war increase in the numbers of art teacher trainees: 46 by 1947. By the early 1950s there were four centres awarding the Art Teacher's Certificate under the auspices of the Institute of Education: the Institute's own art department, Goldsmiths' College, Hornsey College of Art and Brighton College of Art. By the mid-1950s they had nearly 150 students between them (Institute of Education archives). Other important centres had also appeared in such cities as Birmingham, Leeds, Leicester, Liverpool and Manchester. Furthermore, 35 London area colleges of education (formerly known as teacher-training colleges) had by this time become constituent colleges of the Institute of Education. All had art departments that offered courses of two kinds: curriculum courses dealing principally with the pedagogy of the subject; and 'main field' courses aiming at the personal artistic development of students intending to some extent to specialize in the teaching of the subject. All tutors in these departments were entitled to attend meetings of a Standing Sub-Committee in Art under the chairmanship of Clarence Waite, whose influence over the shaping of art teacher training in the whole of the London area therefore became immense.

In 1970, Dick Field, Waite's successor as head of the Institute's art department, published his valuable stocktaking account, *Change in Art Education*. This was followed in 1973 by *The Study of Education and Art*, which Field edited in collaboration with John Newick. By this time, these two had been instrumental in providing extended opportunities for qualified art teachers in the form of a course leading to the award of a diploma in art education. Prominent among the distinguished contributors from fields related to art education was the philosopher Louis Arnaud Reid, whose passionate opposition to the artificial segregation in education of the affective and the cognitive has animated his writing and teaching over the span of 60 years. Opportunities for research leading to MPhil and PhD degrees also began to be offered at this time and in 1976 the next incumbent, Stanislaw Frenkiel, gained approval for the establishment of a full- and part-time MA degree in art and design education, to the teaching of which Leslie Perry made a significant contribution over a period of 20 years. Other institutions developed similar courses and thus new opportunities for advanced study became available to teachers of art in many parts of the country.

Until quite recently, the structure of courses of initial art teacher education country-wide had remained much as it was in 1924 when instituted by the London Day Training College, that is, an art school training of usually four years, a one-year course comprising further development as an artist, some practical work undertaken with special reference to the classroom, some pedagogical theory and substantial practical teaching. The essential point is that the major part of the studio-based work reflected art school structures. This is hardly surprising, since most tutors had themselves been art school trained and were usually appointed on the basis of their art, craft or design specialism. So each department tended to have on its staff a painter, printmaker, textile designer, ceramicist and so on. In the interests of broadening students' experience, advice to develop a skill other than that attained at art school was frequently given. By and large, these arrangements were typical until the 1980s, by which time issues hitherto non-existent or at least overlooked had assumed a prominence that began to influence educational transaction at every level.

To begin with, the notion of art itself was changing. John Constable, early in the 19th century, had confidently told us that art was 'a branch of natural science'. However, the kaleidoscope of 20th-century experiments from fauvism, cubism and surrealism to conceptual art via abstract expressionism and pop art has brought us to a point where art may be seen as a branch of philosophical rumination – and all this has obviously had its effect on art school graduates in the sense that clear-cut demarcation of the traditional fine arts and the crafts has to a large extent been dissolved. Added to this the feminist movement, multiculturalism, and advances in information and communications technology all contributed in one way or another to a shift towards concept-based rather than skills-based workshops. Of course, it would be naïve to assume that working with materials in traditional ways need inhibit the forming of important pedagogical (as well as artistic) concepts, just as it would be naïve to suppose that concepts useful to the teaching of art can meaningfully be developed in the complete absence of handling and shaping materials.

By 1970, the BEd degree had been established across the country and, as a result, the colleges of education began to complement the supply of graduate specialist teachers of art. In the London colleges the BEd degree was validated by the University of London, which entailed the involvement of the university boards of studies: guardians of academic standards in their various subject fields. In the case of art, the relevant boards of studies were those in fine art and in history of art. The boards of studies were represented on the relevant examining boards, and this brought about an interesting, though uncomfortable, collision of the largely student-centred philosophy that had hitherto governed the colleges' attitude to examinations, and the discipline-centred philosophy of the boards of studies. With hindsight, this situation may be seen as having had a considerably salutary effect on the raising of standards and on the production of specialist teachers perhaps better prepared to proceed to advanced study.

Writing in 1970, Field makes the point that the nationally recognized specialist centres for the initial education of teachers of art, as represented by the influential Association of Centres of Art and Design Teacher Education (ACADTE), are 'among the more progressive institutions in art education'. By the early 1970s, with a membership of academic staff from 12 specialist centres, the objectives of the Association were:

to promote the effective education of teachers of art and design
to be a forum for consultation and discussion
to ensure the effective recruitment of students via the Clearing House for Postgraduate Courses in Art and Design Education.

Field goes on to say:

But probably their most persistent problem has been that of bringing together practical and theoretical studies.

One cannot conceive of a course concerned with the education of art teachers which does not include some practical art: for technical reasons, as preparation for practical teaching, as a workshop for the study of creative activity, and so on. Centres have devised a whole range of ways of integrating their courses; but this area of study seems to be the crucial point at which changing attitudes, changing methods and changing needs meet; there may always be flux here.

(Field, 1970: 100)

Since 1986 innovative developments within concept-based workshops that are central to the Institute's approach to the kinds of change to which Field refers have enabled students simultaneously to address subject knowledge and subject application. Workshops are defined as environments for enquiry into the making of, and response to, art and design and ways of teaching and learning. Activities explore ways of recording, ways of investigating, ways of developing and ways of presenting ideas. Thus workshops maximize opportunities for participants to engage in active learning. Their theoretical roots are embedded in ideas of personal construct theory (Kelly, 1955), experiential learning (Bruner, 1986; Salmon, 1995), creativity (Rogers, 1970; Claxton, 1997) and reflective practice (Schon, 1987). Activities are supported by a range of two- and three-dimensional materials and resources including information communications technology. Through a series of visual displays with accompanying written rationales, supported by critical evaluations and guided reading, students deepen and extend their understandings of the complex relationship between concepts and skills and visual and verbal modes of communication and expression. Every member of a workshop is a rich resource for learning and each workshop group consists of students from a wide range of art, craft and design backgrounds (a powerful argument for the continued involvement of universities in initial teacher education!). It is precisely this kind of opportunity for students to experience sustained engagement in academically rigorous, creative, subject-specific activities that has been reduced as a result of the government reform of teacher education.

The 1990s represented a period of increasing government intervention into and regulation of courses of initial teacher education (DfEE, 1998). For the first time, art teacher educators were required to respond to a succession of externally imposed directives related to student recruitment, course content and structure and assessment criteria. The combined impact of the ever-changing demands of the Teacher Training Agency and OFSTED inspection criteria has been far reaching. Less time is available for practical workshops – through which students' subject knowledge is extended and pedagogical skills are acquired – and subject-specific reading; organic course structures that fostered creative approaches to teaching and learning have been eroded by the mechanistic demands of managerial rationalism: the tick box and the audit. In short the overall climate in which those responsible for art teacher education are required to work offers students fewer opportunities to think deeply about the complex issues that inform a personal philosophy of art teaching.

Three additional factors influenced art education during this period. Firstly, in 1992 courses of art teacher education – most of which hitherto were located in polytechnics, with their roots in colleges of art – were absorbed into the university sector. The implications for such courses of the resultant changes in validation procedures, institutional ethos and funding arrangements are rarely acknowledged beyond the field of art. Secondly, at a time when teachers required specialist advice to support their implementation of the National Curriculum and to prepare them for the new challenges of school-based teacher education, most local education authorities continued to reduce their teams of subject advisers. Thirdly, and most significantly, a dramatic change occurred in higher education's involvement in art teacher education at secondary level. It is a reflection of the government's encouragement of alternative routes into teaching that between 1996 and 2000 the number of providers increased from 14 to over 30. Currently the range of provision includes both well-established, highly successful specialist courses of 90 or so students and newly established routes followed by as few as three students. The contrast in the available resources and the nature of student experience is vast.

As partnerships between higher education institutions and schools have evolved, closer and often highly productive working relationships between art tutors and teachers have frequently developed. Working from positions of strength a number of innovative approaches to the initial and continuing professional development of art teachers continue to be explored by committed course leaders. Opportunities have been grasped to develop the art curriculum and extend and enrich learning experiences for pupils, students and teachers through a variety of activities and projects including those with a research dimension. A DfEE-funded research project established in 2000 to investigate the nature of museum learning is grounded in the Institute's art and design PGCE course and long-standing collaboration with the education department of the Victoria and Albert Museum. As teacher education becomes increasingly school-based, art educators at the Institute and elsewhere recognize the growing responsibility of higher education tutors to address contemporary issues, challenge the status quo and identify future directions (Prentice, 1995; Addison and Burgess, 2000). At the primary stage of education undergraduate and postgraduate courses for intending teachers have become dominated by the demands of the National Literacy Strategy (1998) and the National Numeracy Strategy (1999). Within many primary teacher education courses the art presence is often minimal (Rogers, 1998). Prompted by a growing concern about this the Institute initiated a research project in 1999 now funded by the Teacher Training Agency to investigate the essential requirements for the teaching of art in primary schools.

Challenges and directions

The direction in which art education develops and the status it is likely to enjoy in the first decade of the new century will, to a large extent, be determined by responses to a number of challenges that confront art educators. While some challenges relate to the political, social, cultural and economic climate in which art and education exist, others reside within the subject field itself and relate to changing views about the nature of art education.

At the macro-level there are some fundamental inconsistencies and contradictions between policy, provision and practice. Underlying the government's declared commitment to creativity in education (Smith, 1998; NACCCE, 1999), a curriculum that reflects a new utilitarianism emphasizes conformity to standards and reinforces a narrow concept of what it means to be educated: rather there is a distrust of creativity (Hall, 1999). As Eisner (1998: 104) points out, 'when alternatives are suppressed or unavailable we tend to accept the accepted'. A major challenge for art educators is to challenge accepted forms of routinized thought and action through the promotion of a freshness of vision, cultural curiosity and constructive criticism. There is an urgent need for the intrinsic value of art in education to be reaffirmed in various mainstream debates about teaching and learning. The contribution of art to human functioning needs to be made explicit and informed by current ideas about multiple intelligences (Gardner, 1993) and emotional intelligence (Goelman, 1996).

There is also a need to co-ordinate at local and national levels initiatives that increasingly involve a range of stakeholders in collaborative enterprises: teachers, artists, business representatives, arts administrators, gallery and museum educators. In addition to greater coherence being achieved the effectiveness and distinctiveness of each partner's contribution would be maximized. New opportunities now exist for collaborative ventures to be encouraged and supported by the Arts and Humanities Research Board and the Council for Museums, Archives and Libraries. It is in primary schools that the most serious decline in art education has been witnessed as a result of the government's relentless pressure on teachers to raise standards of literacy and numeracy. After a two-year period of marginalization in most schools, teachers will require a huge amount of support from art co-ordinators and other external agencies in order to re-establish an art curriculum of quality.

For art teacher educators the continuing challenge is to find ways of engaging students in learning experiences of quality – particularly through practical workshops – in an ever more mechanistic and pressurized system of initial teacher education. The proliferation of providers of courses of initial art teacher education that has occurred in recent years is unlikely to serve the best long-term interests of art education (uncannily, echoes of the 1920s can be heard!). It is suggested that the time has come to re-establish clear criteria as a basis for the reorganization of a reduced number of viable, well-resourced, strategically located, specialist centres for the initial education and continuing professional development of art teachers. It is proposed that each centre would also have a clearly identified research strength and would be expected to demonstrate a sustained relationship between teaching and scholarship. Opportunities would exist for teachers to participate in relevant research activity and develop new research paradigms as members of project teams. Thus relationships between schools and universities, between theory and practice, and between art and education would be strengthened.

A national network of centres for art teacher education, plus the extended partnerships with schools and museums and galleries it would embrace, would play a major role in helping to influence the future direction of art teaching in schools. Its direction must be determined with great care. It is too simplistic to argue for the replacement of a modernist approach with a ready-made postmodern stance. A more appropriate way forward is likely to involve a 'fluid dialogue between different approaches' in acknowledgement of the multi-functional potential of art, craft and design in education (Addison and Burgess, 2000). Central to this position is a recognition of the need for art teachers to address critically a range of issues that relate to visual and material culture, to include the creative relationship between electronic technology and traditional materials and processes, between virtual reality and 'direct' sensory experience. In so doing: 'The past and the future should be in dialogue so that present practice can be negotiated rather than constituting a site where opposing ideologies battle out their differences' (Addison and Burgess, 2000: 2).

References

Addison, N and Burgess, L (2000) *Learning to Teach Art and Design in the Secondary School*, Routledge, London

Art Advisers Association (1979) *Learning Through Drawing*, Art Advisers Association

Barclay-Russell, A (1967) Great Britain: Training of artists and art teaching in general education, *Encyclopaedia Britannica*, Encyclopaedia Britannica International, Sutton

Bell, Q (1964) The fine arts, in *Crisis in the Humanities*, ed J H Plumb, Penguin, Harmondsworth

Brazier, P (1985) *Art History in Education*, Heinemann for the Institute of Education, University of London, London

Bruner, J (1986) *Actual Minds, Possible Worlds*, Harvard University Press, Cambridge, MA

Carline, R (1968) *Draw They Must*, Arnold, London

Central Advisory Council for Education (England) (CACE) (1967) *Children and their Primary Schools* (The Plowden Report), HMSO, London

Claxton, G (1997) *Hare Brain Tortoise Mind*, Fourth Estate, London

Department for Education and Employment (DfEE) (1998) *Teaching: High status, high standards*, Circular 4/98, DfEE, London

Department of Education and Science (DES) (1971) *Art in Schools*, Education Survey 11, HMSO, London

DES (1978a) *Primary Education in England*, HMSO, London

DES (1978b) *Art in Junior Education*, HMSO, London

DES (1983) *Art in Secondary Education 11–16*, HMSO, London

DES (1991) *National Curriculum Art Working Group: Interim report*, DES, London

Dewey, J (1934) *Art as Experience*, Putnam Capricorn Books, New York

Dyson, A (1981) *History of Art in Secondary Education*, Conference report, Institute of Education and Association of Art Historians, London

Dyson, A (1984) *Prospects for Art and Design History in Schools*, Conference report, Institute of Education and Association of Art Historians, London

Dyson, A (1991) The history of art and its uses in the school curriculum, in *Teaching the Humanities*, ed P Gordon, pp 108–26, Woburn Press, London

Eisner, E (1972) *Educating Artistic Vision*, Macmillan, New York

Eisner, E (1998) *The Kind of Schools We Need*, Heinemann, Portsmouth, NH

Eisner, E and Ecker, D (1966) *Readings in Art Education*, Xerox College Publishing, Massachusetts

Field, D (1970) *Change in Art Education*, Routledge & Kegan Paul, London

Field, D and Newick, J (eds) (1973) *The Study of Education and Art*, Routledge and Kegan Paul, London

Gardner, H (1993) *Frames of Mind: The theory of multiple intelligences*, 2nd edn, Fontana Press, London

Goelman, D (1996) *Emotional Intelligence*, Bloomsbury, London

Gulbenkian Foundation (1982, 1989) *The Arts in Schools*, Report, The Gulbenkian Foundation, London

Hall, P (1999) *Guardian* Debate 2, November, Institute of Education, University of London, London

Hughes, A (1998) Reconceptualising the art curriculum, *Journal of Art and Design Education*, **17** (2), pp 42–49

Institute of Education archives, University of London

Kelly, G (1955) *The Psychology of Personal Constructs*, Norton, New York

Lowenfeld, V and Brittain, W (1947) *Creative and Mental Growth*, 4th edn, Macmillan, New York

Macdonald, S (1970) *The History and Philosophy of Art Education*, University of London Press, London

National Advisory Committee on Creative and Cultural Education (NACCCE) (1999) *All Our Futures: Creativity, culture and education*, Report, DfEE, Sudbury

Office for Standards in Education (OFSTED) (1995) *A Review of Inspection Findings 1993/94*, OFSTED, London

OFSTED (1998) *The Arts Inspected*, Heinemann, Oxford

Prentice, R (ed) (1995) *Teaching Art and Design: Addressing issues, identifying directions*, Cassell, London

Puttnam, D (1998) Puttnam fears for arts, *Independent*, 10 April

Read, H (1943) *Education Through Art*, Faber & Faber, London

Richardson, M (1948) *Art and the Child*, University of London Press, London

Robinson, C (1995) The National Curriculum for art: translating it into practice, in *Teaching Art and Design: Addressing issues, identifying directions*, ed R Prentice, pp 124–33, Cassell, London

Rogers, C (1970) Towards a theory of creativity, in *Creativity*, ed P E Vernon, pp 137–51, Penguin, London

Rogers, R (1998) *The Disappearing Arts?*, Royal Society of Arts, London

Ruskin, J (1857) *The Elements of Drawing*, Smith, Elder & Co, London

Salmon, P (1995) Experiential learning, in *Teaching Art and Design: Addressing issues, identifying directions*, ed R Prentice, pp 22–28, Cassell, London

Sausmarez, de, M (1964) *Basic Design: The dynamics of visual form*, Studio Vista, London

Schon, D (1987) *Educating the Reflective Practitioner*, Jossey-Bass, San Francisco

Schools Council (1978) *Art 7–11*, Occasional Bulletin, Schools Council, London

Smith, C (1998) *Creative Britain*, Faber & Faber, London

Steers, J (1999) InSEA: past, present and future, unpublished paper, InSEA World Congress, Brisbane

Swift, J and Steers, J (1998) *A Manifesto for Art in Schools*, http://www.nsead.org/html/issues.html

Taylor, R (1986) *Educating for Art*, Longman, Essex

Tomlinson, R R (1944) *Children as Artists*, 1947 edn, King Penguin, Harmondsworth

Chapter 10

Business and economics: The challenge of curriculum recognition

David Lines

Introduction

The period from 1945 has been one of profound change in the British economy. In the half-century since then the industrial base has been transformed, the major importing and exporting markets have shifted and growth has brought about a massive increase in consumer wealth and purchasing power. There have been periods of full employment and of high unemployment, of rapidly rising inflation and slow price increases, of high growth and low growth; there have even been periods where growth, inflation and employment have juxtaposed bewilderingly within and between one another so that high inflation has sometimes accompanied high growth but at other times the opposite, and low inflation has seen high levels of unemployment but also, as now, few job vacancies. Alongside these changes we have seen trade union power wax and wane, the pound decimalized (perhaps soon to be euro-ized) and footloose multinational corporations wield financial muscle that compares with many countries' gross domestic product. Finally, a competing system as operated in the Soviet Union and other Eastern bloc countries has been defeated, leaving, apparently, only one way of doing business.

I mention these phenomena because they are essentially *economic* rather than social (though the two are arguably closely connected) and are very often the result of theories expounded by academics of whom most people have never heard. Thus it was Keynes's ideas that drove policy from 1945 until 1979, and then Friedman's up to the end of the 1980s. Where we are today is perhaps less certain, but with hindsight we may see the emergence of Polanyi, Etzioni and Sen as drivers of a new, more caring and environmentally aware economic system.

Given such profound change, whose speed is increasing exponentially via the Internet and e-commerce, surely we should be equipping our young people with the kind of knowledge of business and economic systems to ask the 'right' questions. These questions are, I would suggest, fundamentally to do with values, especially the assumption that the way we organize and distribute resources is 'given'. Yet where is the place of business and economics education in the school curriculum? Staggeringly, in my admittedly partisan view, still struggling for recognition and acceptance.

This chapter is in part a history of that struggle, but it is also a template for curriculum innovation and change in a wider context. For even when a subject is recognizably and self-evidently both 'useful' and relevant, even when it is popular with students and those who teach it, and even when as adults people say 'I wish we'd been taught that in school', it still doesn't guarantee it a place in the curriculum. For the inclusion of one inevitably means the exclusion of another and that substitution requires those with a stake in education (and who has not?) to make a judgement on the relative 'value' of each. It is perhaps instructive that there is no chapter in this book on the place of classics in the curriculum – that would have been as unthinkable 50 years ago as including one on business and economics. For those of us who advocate greater economic literacy, this movement at least gives grounds for hope, but progress is slow. It took 200 years for Latin, Greek and ancient history to fall from their pre-eminent position; one can only hope it does not take that time for the reverse to be true of business and economics education. I would argue that we do not have that long.

A note on terms

'The curriculum'

The curriculum, as a number of commentators have pointed out (Walsh, 1993; Aldrich, 1996; Chitty, 1996; Young, 1998), can be defined in a variety of different ways. However, because I believe the true focus of business education to be values, especially cultural values (Lines, 1999), it is appropriate to turn to Denis Lawton's definition of the curriculum: 'a selection from the culture of a society' (Lawton, 1996: 8). Lawton uses Linton's (1940) notion of culture: 'the sum total of the knowledge, attitudes and habitual behaviour patterns shared and transmitted by the members of a particular society', and shows how 'universals' are linked to and become part of the curriculum. Lawton argues that in complex, industrialized Western societies such as England's, it is impossible for the culture to be passed on solely through the 'family or by means of other face-to-face relations' (Lawton, 1996: 9). It is therefore necessary to delegate the responsibility of passing on some of this knowledge to schools, colleges and other educational institutions. This 'passing on' occurs in what could be called the 'formal' curriculum (Walsh, 1993; Aldrich, 1996) as well as the 'informal' one: in the playground, on the way to and from school, within homes and leisure centres, indeed wherever and whenever personal interaction takes place.

I would contend that the formal curriculum is likely to lag behind the informal one, but will be susceptible to what might be termed 'seepage', because the societal and cultural mores of the latter will ultimately influence the former. In the meantime, however, it is inevitable that the discussion of a topic such as the different prices of identical Sony PlayStations in the USA and the UK is more likely in the playground than it is in classrooms, which is unfortunate because, I contend, it is only where business and economics are taught that deeper and more telling questioning of the reasons behind and the implication of such pricing policies can be made.

'Academic' and 'vocational'

The terms 'academic' and 'vocational' have long been a source of dissatisfaction amongst educationalists because of what might be termed the 'baggage' that comes with them. *In extremis,* 'academic' was clearly superior, implying a Socratic methodology that resulted in cultural appreciation and well-roundedness, whilst 'vocational' implied craft training of an inferior mind. In *Qualifying for Success: A consultative paper on the future of post-16 qualifications* (DfEE, 1997) the terms 'general (academic), general vocational or vocational' are used in an attempt to remove any sense of predestiny. In this chapter I shall continue to use 'academic' and 'vocational', because those terms are the ones commonly understood. This does not impute a hierarchy.

'Business education'

Within what is termed 'business education' there are a number of distinct strands, from the highly abstract 'academic' subject of economics through GCSE and A level business studies and the General National Vocational Qualification (GNVQ) in business, to overtly and self-consciously vocational courses such as office practice, word processing, shorthand and so on. Each has a different lineage, often derived from either an 'academic' or a 'vocational' heritage. If they have one thing in common, however, it is that they are all 'examined' in some way or other, the vast majority by 'high stakes' external tests. This is because, despite the efforts of curriculum developers over the years, the infusion of business education below Key Stage 4, or in non-examined environments, has largely failed.

Business and economics: an overview and the challenge of vocationalism

Internal tensions and external hostility

Bundling business education 'subjects' together is a mistake, because the educational aims of each one are different. Nevertheless they often *are*, which is perhaps one of the reasons why gaining acceptance in the mainstream curriculum has been so hard. After all there is a long tradition in England and Wales of vocational training being 'voluntaristic' (Unwin, 1997) and containing 'no inherent connection with general education and schooling' (Green, 1997: 90).

Green's separation is perhaps no better exemplified than in the development of the major vocational awarding bodies, who until recently were quite distinct from the examination boards. Thus the City and Guild of London Institute and the Royal Society of Arts as well as, later, the Business and Technicians Education Council provided an alternative route for business students whose inclinations and aptitudes took them away from the 'academic' one. Furthermore these qualifications would only rarely be acquired in schools; they were, and arguably still are, seen as second class (see *inter alia* Green, Wolf and Leney, 1999) and any subject that carries even the hint of vocationalism appears in some way 'tainted' as far as the school curriculum is concerned. Indeed, even within business education generally the same rule applies, and school managers as well as some teachers see business studies as 'inferior' to economics, a view apparently confirmed by the Dearing Review, which identified the former as one of the 'easier' A levels and the latter as one of the 'harder' (Dearing, 1996: Appendix G3). As Barnes (1993) put it:

> The label 'Business Studies' in many ways expresses quite well the ambiguities inherent in a subject that many still regard as a dubious and upstart offspring of its legitimate parent 'Economics'. Does not the appendage 'Studies' in a subject name suggest some academic inadequacy in a subject itself? Can 'Business' be said to represent any kind of academic discipline? Is not Business an essentially practical affair concerned mainly with circumstantial and contin-

gent realities? Surely it is Economics that provides the real theoretical rationale for resources allocation decisions?

(Barnes 1993: 41)

In effect there remains an internal tension resulting from a desire to acquire academic respectability whilst simultaneously maintaining some element of vocationalism. As a result of such conflict it is perhaps unsurprising that economics and business have had such a difficult time establishing themselves, because they have rarely offered a united front. Furthermore, whilst the fight for legitimacy has been paramount, it has at best been guerrilla warfare against what might be termed the 'big battalions' of the curriculum (Goodson, 1985; Davies, 1996). These established subjects can call on historical precedence (including what Hirst (1993) termed the rationalist approach to the curriculum), large numbers teaching and studying their subjects at all levels, senior managers with the same background and even substantial financial resources. Crucially, there has also been a lack of political will to push economics and business into the curriculum, most notably in the original 10-subject National Curriculum of 1988, which pointedly ignored the large numbers of candidates (see Figure 10.3) entering business subjects at GCSE, instead choosing, belatedly and rather as an afterthought, the ultimately ill-fated cross-curricular theme: economic and industrial understanding (Graham with Tytler, 1993). Sadly, it seems nothing changes, for recent pronouncements about citizenship education in England and Wales – often the main vehicle for secondary economics education in other countries (Walstad, 1994) – appear largely to have ignored the possibility of business and economic themes, instead choosing a humanities approach, thereby once again demonstrating the power and influence of the 'big battalions'!

Teacher training and qualifications

Initial training

One of the reasons given for the lack of business and economics education below Key Stage 4 is a lack of suitably qualified teachers. 'Somewhat belatedly' (Whitehead, 1996: 198), specific training of teachers of economics started in 1972, when a course for postgraduate economists commenced at the Institute of Education, University of London, and this was followed in 1975, at the same institution, by one for teachers of business studies. Such courses are important because, as Dawson (1977) demonstrated, teachers trained to teach economics are more effective than those who are not. Yet the numbers trained to do so were, and still are, comparatively small compared to demand (see Table 10.1).

There have also been a number of modifications to the training itself, so that the Institute's course, for instance, is now a combined one, with equal emphasis placed on business and economics, a movement away from the tradition that saw very little crossover between teaching academic and vocational subjects. In this regard GNVQ has wrought significant change, with many teachers acquiring Training and Development Lead Body (TDLB) qualifications in addition to their degrees, as well as becoming familiar with the different styles and expectations of a more vocational approach.

There remain some anomalies, however. In 2000 the Teacher Training Agency announced that business studies would be removed from the 'other' category, and have initial training target numbers set for each institution (previously trainers could shift numbers between subjects within the 'other' category). This is a better reflection of the place of business studies in schools and colleges. At the same time economics remained separate, the result of earlier arrangements when it had been split from business studies, the latter being part of 'technology'.

The qualifications of business education teachers

As far as qualified staff of economics and business studies is concerned, Table 10.1 makes interesting comparisons.

The table reveals a number of trends. Over time the emphasis on older, part-time, female teachers of business studies has become less clear as more specifically qualified, younger staff enter the profession to teach the subject. The dominance of economics degree holders and the relatively sparse numbers of those with business studies degrees are worthy of note, though that has changed as more business degree courses have developed. For instance, for the PGCE economics and business course at the Institute of

Table 10.1 *The different profiles of economics and business studies teachers in English and Welsh schools*

	1988		1992		1996	
(%)	Economics teachers	Bus studies teachers	Economics teachers	Bus studies teachers	Economics teachers	Bus studies teachers
Female	28	74	34	68	n/a	59
Part-time	8	25	13	24	n/a	18
Aged>50	15	36	15	22	n/a	16
Degree in subject	47	3	49	4	n/a	16

Sources: DES, 1990; DfE, 1993; DfEE, 1997

Education, University of London, recent cohorts show around 40 per cent possessing economics degrees, another 40 per cent business or business-related degrees and the remainder either a professional qualification or degrees in related areas such as law or accounting.

Another significant point raised in the table is that the DfEE no longer collects the data on economics teachers, reflecting its declining importance within the curriculum. Table 10.2 offers further confirmation of this decline, the substitution of business studies for economics and the relatively small amount of time students are exposed to specialized business and economics education.

As far as those teaching the areas known as 'skills' – office practice, shorthand and keyboarding – are concerned, they generally possess either Pitman, City and Guilds or RSA qualifications as well as commercial experience (FEFC, 1997). Very often they also offer one of the business GCSE courses that are combined with IT, since the nature of such courses,

Table 10.2   *Percentage of secondary students' time spent studying economics and business studies*

	Age	1980	1984	1988	1992	1996
Economics	14	0.1	0.0	0.0	0.0	★
Economics	16	0.4	0.3	0.4	0.3	★
Economics	18	4.5	4.4	4.8	n/a	n/a
Bus studies	14	n/a	0.1	0.1	0.2	0.0
Bus studies	16	n/a	3.3	4.0	2.5	2.4
Bus studies	18	n/a	4.7	6.2	n/a	n/a

★ Not included in the survey
Sources: DES, 1986, 1990; DfEE, 1994, 1997

whilst based around the written word, places a strong emphasis on practical aspects of business and IT applications.

The history of business and economics in schools

Given the difficulties of defining business education outlined above, it is necessary to limit the discussion. I shall therefore concentrate on those business subjects that are the most popular in schools and colleges: GCSE and Advanced levels in economics and business studies and the GNVQ in business.

Economics

Examination entry numbers

Within schools, economics was a subject that blossomed after the Second World War, despite initial scepticism from the academic world (Robbins, 1955). Initially it was taught predominantly at Advanced level, from where it gained its academic credentials. This, it has been argued, is important if a subject wishes to make ground within the curriculum (Gilbert, 1984; Goodson, 1985, 1987; Davies, 1996). In 1954, 2,500 students offered economics at that level, a number that grew rapidly to more than 6,000 by 1961 and nearly 47,000 by 1989. From this peak it went into serious and rapid decline so that by 1999 only 18,377 sat the examination (see Figures 10.1 and 10.2).

Figure 10.1 not only shows the continuous expansion of economics over the 30-year period, it also illustrates how the subject was male-dominated in its early years, with females accounting for fewer than 10 per cent of the candidate entries. However, over time economics became more popular with girls, so that by the mid-1970s almost all the growth in the subject was accounted for by them. The data also suggests that the entry of business studies had no initial impact upon numbers taking economics, indicating no substitution at that time.

Figure 10.2 supplies the data for A level entries in both economics and business studies from 1989 to 1999. This show an apparent substitution of business studies for economics. In 1989, for instance, the total candidature for the two subjects was 56,176. In 1999 it was 56,303, suggesting only a slight increase. It should be noted, however, that the Nuffield Economics and Business Project (which we shall explore in more detail below, and which was first examined in 1996) is counted separately, and so the total is increased by 3,308 to 59,611 in 1999.

Business Studies at Advanced level continues to increase in popularity, despite the appearance of GNVQ business (see Figure 10.4). Although it is too soon to say with any certainty at this stage, economics appears to have halted the calamitous decline of the past 10 years or so. The influence of the new A/S, A2 Advanced level examinations is likely to have a significant and positive impact on both subjects in terms of candidate numbers, since they straddle the arts/science divide and can be seen therefore as a good way of broadening the curriculum.

Economics was studied at Ordinary level and CSE, and for a time was highly popular. In 1981, 43,000 students offered the O level and more than 100,000 at CSE (1976), when it was the eighth most popular subject. O level economics tended to have the strongest hold in independent schools

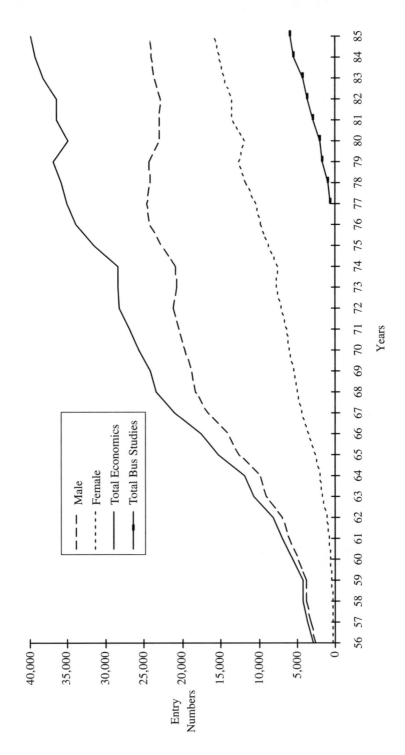

Figure 10.1 *GCE A level economics and business studies entries 1956–1985*

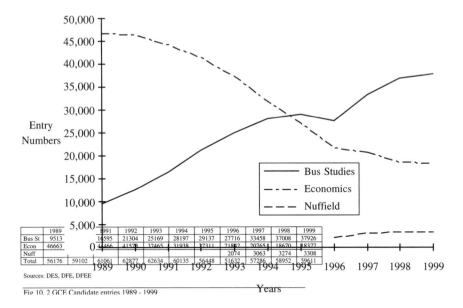

	1989		1991	1992	1993	1994	1995	1996	1997	1998	1999
Bus St	9513		16595	21304	25169	28197	29137	27716	33458	37008	37926
Econ	46663		44466	41578	37465	31938	27311	21882	20765	18670	18377
Nuff							2074	3063	3274	3308
Total	56176	59102	61061	62877	62634	60135	56448	51632	57286	58952	59611

Sources: DES, DFE, DFEE

Fig 10.2 GCE Candidate entries 1989 - 1999

Figure 10.2   *GCE A level candidate entries 1989–1999*

and was predominantly studied by boys (Parsons, 1996), but as Davies (1996) argues and Table 10.2 (above) shows, it never met the conditions necessary for high-status subjects: large departments, high resource allocation, more able pupils, promotion and incentive posts, headships and curriculum discrimination (Goodson, 1987).

Figure 10.3 shows GCSE candidate numbers from 1989 to 1999 in GCSE economics and business studies. It is interesting to observe the rapid growth of the latter, despite its exclusion from the 10-subject National Curriculum. There appear to be indications that it is now stabilizing at around 100,000 candidate entries per year (the 1999 figures are provisional). Economics, on the other hand, shows a seemingly inexorable decline.

The 'golden age' of school economics

In hindsight the period from around 1980 until 1988 was the 'golden age' for school economics. Examination numbers were growing and it appeared that the subject had reached such a momentum that it would not only become established in the sixth form but beyond that as well. In 1985 Ryba and Hodkinson were able to write confidently that:

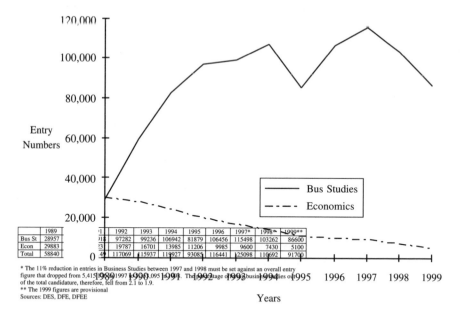

Figure 10.3 shows a line graph with the following embedded data table and axis labels:

	1989		1992	1993	1994	1995	1996	1997*	1998*	1999**
Bus St	28957		97282	99236	106942	81879	106456	115498	103262	86600
Econ	29883		19787	16701	13985	11206	9985	9600	7430	5100
Total	58840		117069	115937	118927	93085	116441	125098	110692	91700

Legend: —— Bus Studies   - - - Economics

Y-axis: Entry Numbers (20,000 to 120,000)
X-axis: Years

* The 11% reduction in entries in Business Studies between 1997 and 1998 must be set against an overall entry
figure that dropped from 5,415,095 to 5,427,000. The percentage of business studies out
of the total candidature, therefore, fell from 2.1 to 1.9.
** The 1999 figures are provisional
Sources: DES, DFE, DFEE

Figure 10.3 *GCSE candidate entries 1989–1999 (Figures for 1999 are provisional)*

> …numbers choosing to study economics as an O-level or CSE examination subject continue to grow and there are rapidly mounting pressures in favour of introducing at least an element of economics into the education of every young pupil within the context of compulsory schooling. These trends are likely to lead to an *explosion* of economics teaching in the 14–16 age range during the next decade.
>
> (Ryba and Hodkinson, 1985: 110, emphasis added)

For a time this prediction seemed likely to come true. In 1976 the then Prime Minister James Callaghan's Ruskin speech had emphasized the need for a more relevant curriculum, and a number of initiatives seemed to add weight to the argument. These included the development of the School Curriculum Industry Partnership (SCIP), the Industry Year (1986), the School Curriculum Development Committee's *Education for Economic Awareness* and a number of pronouncements from Her Majesty's Inspectors, the most significant of which was perhaps *Curriculum Matters 2* (DES, 1985), which made a strong case for the inclusion of economics within the curriculum. Finally, and importantly, the Training and Vocational Educational Initiative (TVEI) was set up by Lord Young at the Department of Employment with the explicit aim of bringing school and industry closer together.

The 'golden age' came to an abrupt halt with the original 10-subject National Curriculum, introduced in 1988. The new curriculum was so prescribed – largely at the personal whim of the then Secretary of State, Kenneth Baker (Davies, 1999a, 1999b, 1999c) – and teacher time so occupied, that any attempt to develop a *different* notion of what the curriculum might be simply could not be contemplated (White, 1998). Although the cross-curricular theme, economic and industrial understanding, was belatedly introduced in an attempt to fill one of the obvious gaps in the curriculum, it, like the other themes, was destined for oblivion (though of them all it was probably the most successful, see Dunnill, 1996): there was neither the time, the training nor the inclination on the part of teachers to engage in what was perceived as a 'peripheral' activity (Davies, 1996).

A crisis in economics

Despite the barrier that the original National Curriculum represented, business education and specifically business studies did not die, but for economics it had a lasting impact. The failure to establish a base at Key Stage 4 meant that the A level became isolated (Davies, 1996). Over time, and given other criticisms of the subject, fewer students chose to opt for it, so that today it is possible to talk in terms of a 'crisis' in economics. This crisis extends beyond England and Wales: not only are fewer students studying it in schools (SCAA, 1996), but numbers following degree courses are declining world-wide (Abelson, 1996; Brue, 1996; Pisanie, 1997; Green, 1998). I have argued elsewhere (Lines, 1997; Lines and Vertigan, 1997) that this response is a reflection of dissatisfaction with the subject, brought about by the feeling that economics is largely irrelevant to the values and development of the young people at whom it is aimed. This is because as it is currently configured, the subject fails to address crucially important ethical issues such as inequality, the arms trade, premature deaths, environmental degradation, female exploitation and so on (Hoogendijk, 1996; Ormerod, 1994; Lawson, 1997). The award of the 1998 Nobel prize for economics to Amartya Sen, who has been deeply concerned with such issues for many years, may indicate that a shift is imminent and certainly some of the examination specifications for Curriculum 2000 show promise of a more enlightened approach, but it is not before time and may have come too late.

Ironically, concerns over both the subject matter and the way economics is taught in schools have been in evidence for a considerable time. It is possible to detect a growing literature in *Economics*, the journal of the Economics Association and elsewhere (see Whitehead, 1994), which articulates this concern. The criticism starts in 1984, when A level candidate entries were still to reach their peak, in articles by Guratsky and Welford (1984), who presented a similar case in the same volume, arguing that syllabuses were both narrow and too theoretical.

Frank Livesey, a professor of economics as well as a highly successful A level textbook author, saw the root cause lying not so much within the school curriculum as with the economics taught in universities. Since school economics imitated that which emanated from higher education, any problems with the latter would inevitably infect the former (Livesey, 1986).

Rosalind Levacic (Levacic, 1987), herself an academic economist teaching in higher education, took Livesey's argument a stage further. She offered an interesting perspective by suggesting that a crude attempt to take the maturity of the learner into account would not work. By 'simplifying' the economic models used in higher education, they were rendered ineffective in terms of their ability to explain economic trends. But these very models, although apparently 'simplified', were nothing of the sort as far as the average A level candidate was concerned. They were both abstract and difficult to comprehend, as well as offering little insight into the world that the students themselves inhabited.

In 1986 and 1988 the debate on the future direction of A level economics was joined by two authors who were to become co-directors of the Nuffield Economics and Business Project (see below): Nancy Wall and myself. Wall argued that syllabuses were overloaded (1986), with the latest theoretical concept simply piled upon earlier ones, with little or no attempt to remove any to compensate. Thus, it was not enough, as in the 1960s and 1970s, to teach and learn about Keynesian theories of demand management – difficult enough in itself – but it was also necessary to add monetarism to the list of topics that had to be covered.

In my article, I took a more cognitive/pedagogic approach (Lines, 1988). I briefly described the work of Piaget, Bruner, Gagnè and Bloom and related it to the teaching of economics. I argued in favour of a new 'paradigm' for economics, writing that 'the micro-economics currently taught needs to be modified' (p 76); that 'International Trade should be reviewed' since 'the theoretical base for this area of study is chauvinistic, prescriptive and... tedious' (p 76) and that economists might have to 'call on the talents of other teachers in related disciplines such as Business Studies, Geography and History' (p 77).

At the same time as the critical literature was accumulating, the work of professors Linda Thomas and Steve Hodkinson, with other members of the Economic Awareness Teacher Training team (EcATT) at the Institute of Education, London and Manchester University's Department of Education, was also significant from a pedagogic perspective. Thomas and Hodkinson based much of their work on the theoretical underpinning supplied by phenomenography, that there is a unique description of a phenomenon (Dahlgren, 1984; Marton, 1989; Thomas, 1991). This theoretical position was not shared by all in the business and economics community, however, and as a result the work of Thomas and Hodkinson became somewhat divisive. Nevertheless it was important because it forged a link between the reality of students' lives and their learning in economics classrooms.

Economic awareness also entered previously uncharted curriculum waters, as exemplified by Ross's *Economic and Industrial Awareness in the Primary School*, published in 1990. This historically interesting book contained, amongst others, a chapter by Peter Mortimore, the immediate past Director of the Institute of Education, written just as the Education Reform Bill was being passed. As Mortimore so prophetically put it, 'But of course, schools will need time to do this, time that may be hard to find within the confines of the National Curriculum' (Mortimore, 1990: 22). As we now know, there was barely time to meet the statutory requirements of the curriculum, much less something optional like economic awareness.

For those interested, the journal *Economics Awareness* charts much of the work (sadly, and significantly, this publication is from 2000 no longer published).

Economics today and tomorrow

In the final analysis much of the EcATT material touched many teachers across the country, whether they were or were not economists, but the work was swamped by the demands of the National Curriculum, with its emphasis on particular subjects. These, as Aldrich has shown, were uncannily similar to ones that existed a century earlier (Aldrich, 1988), and which therefore excluded economics. Alongside these facts was the stubborn refusal to reinvent the subject at A level in line with the new realities of what students wanted and expected from a course. The consequence of these combined factors is that the subject has today slipped back into minority status, a long way from its 'golden age'.

There are grounds for hope, nevertheless. Some of the new examination specifications for 2000 are more enlightened than before; numbers taking the A level seem to have stabilized and a new AS level in economics may be an attractive alternative for students wishing to cross the arts/science divide. In addition, the government has decided that economics will offer the 'world-class test' beyond A level, something pointedly and significantly denied business studies, which may discourage the further substitution of the one by the other.

Business studies

Examination entries

Business studies at A level has been one of the success stories of the 1990s. As Figure 10.2 shows, there has been unprecedented growth throughout the decade, with a nearly fourfold increase in numbers. It now comes seventh in terms of numbers with 37,926 entries in 1999 and is now very close to major subjects such as history (38,482) and geography (42,181).

Similarly, despite the National Curriculum, business studies at GCSE continues to flourish, as we saw earlier, with around 100,000 entries per year. The freeing up of the curriculum at Key Stage 4, as well as the introduction of Part 1 GNVQ into schools, is likely to result in continued expansion, though as I shall discuss below, the relationship between business studies and GNVQ business is not as straightforward as might appear.

The roots of business studies

Business studies had a quite different pedigree to economics, being derived from both 'academic' and 'vocational' strands. The academic one was represented by the University of Cambridge Local Examinations Syndicate's (UCLES, now OCR) A level, which had its beginnings in the mid-1960s (see below), set firmly although not exclusively in the independent sector (Lines, 1987). UCLES' main rival in the business studies market was the Associated Examining Board's (AEB, now AQA) A level, which took a quite different and arguably more reflective slant, but which was perceived as 'easier', both to learn and to teach – perhaps because of its lower mathematical content.

UCLES also offered an O level syllabus but it never achieved wide popularity. There were three reasons for this lack of success. First, like economics, because it was developed from the UCLES A level it tended to be taught by those specialists in institutions offering the advanced course and this necessarily limited its range. Second, the UCLES A level was, by the time of its introduction, suffering from increasing competition from the AEB's syllabus. As a result there was less 'brand loyalty'; a teacher who had chosen to abandon the UCLES syllabus at A level would be unlikely to select the O level course, especially since there were close similarities in design and structure between the two. Third, in 11–16 comprehensive schools the O level faced competition from less 'academic' courses and those that were overtly vocational. Thus, for students who were predominantly of middle to lower attainment, commerce was a popular choice with boys, whilst the girls followed office practice, shorthand and typing (Kelsey and Lambert, 1988; Parsons, 1996; Chambers, 1991; Davies, 1996).

The factor that 'saved' business studies at Key Stage 4 was a happy juxtaposition of events. First, a significant curriculum development called business and information studies (BIS) was introduced (see below). This course built on the expertise that many 'skills' teachers already possessed, but updated them. As a result, in many schools IT was, and still often is, closely associated with business studies.

Second, TVEI not only provided computers, but more importantly it raised business studies' profile and the esteem of those teaching it across the whole school. For many business studies 'skills' teachers (office practice, typewriting and so on), this was a lifeline. It represented an opportunity to update their knowledge of information technology, as well as helping them to acquire a more academic approach to the subject.

Third, BIS as well as other business studies GCSE courses were stimulating and enjoyable. This was a fact emphasized by inspectors as well as teachers (Surkes, 1987; DES, 1987).

Together with GCSE and A levels, the business studies picture was further complicated by the existence of the Business Education Council's business studies courses (BEC, latterly BTEC), which were almost exclusively taught in further education (FE) establishments. BEC business studies was designed for post-16 students and was overtly pre-vocational, to cater for a clientele that tended to be those who had not done well enough to continue to A level in school and who planned to go out to work after college. Because of the training aspect of many FE courses, work-related facilities were often better, especially in the provision of computers but also in terms of links with employers. These aspects were reflected in the style of BEC courses.

General National Vocational Qualifications

A continued tradition from BTEC

GNVQ Advanced business was piloted in the academic year 1992/93 as one of the first cohort of subjects alongside health and social care, leisure and tourism, art and design, and manufacturing. Since it was widely seen as a substitute for BTEC qualifications (FEDA, 1994), which in the past had attracted large numbers of students, GNVQ Advanced business quickly established itself with the largest candidate entry (28,986 in 1999; the next biggest, leisure and tourism, attracted 14,039). As Figure 10.4 shows, its growth appears to have at least stabilized, and the question remains as to the extent of substitution with the dominance of modularization within the new AS/A2 changes from 2000 onwards.

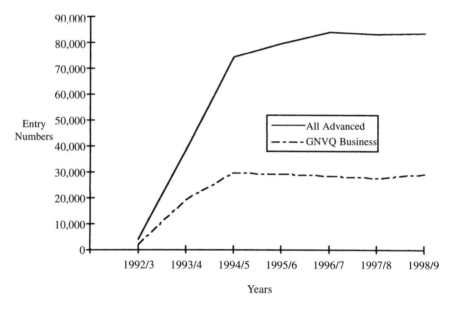

Notes:
- Registrations are students at the start of the two-year course.
- Data were collected at different times of the year and are therefore only indicative.
- GNVQ Advanced courses were introduced progressively, which explains much of the drop in the percentage of the total registering for business.
- The rate of converting registrations into a full award has been variable, at around half. For the year 1/8/95 to 31/7/96 there were 22,853 candidates tested. 59.8% achieved a full award. For year ending 31/7/97 of 28,415, 48.7% achieved a full award and for year ending 31/7/98, of 29,467 it was 51.9%. This makes GNVQ business considerably less important in terms of completions than A level business studies, although the two are not directly comparable, since GNVQ candidates can complete partial awards over a number of years. From 1997 these were known as 'active' candidates.

Source: QCA; Joint Council for National Vocational Awarding Bodies

Figure 10.4   *GNVQ Advanced business and total GNVQ Advanced registrations 1992–1999*

The background to GNVQ business

In 1991 the government introduced its White Paper: *Education and Training for the 21st Century*. It was wide-ranging and was 'designed to set the agenda for government policy on post-16 education and training for the next five years' (Hodgson and Spours, 1997). It established the principles of three pathways or tracks, which some commentators have seen as a way of 'protecting' the so-called Advanced level 'gold standard' (Hodgson and Spours, 1997; Young, 1998), especially by means of a new qualification, GNVQ. This qualification was designed to attract the 'new sixth former', ie those students who in the past would not have carried on at school or college beyond the age of 16, but who were doing so in ever greater numbers and being encouraged in this by governments who were increasingly concerned at the UK's low participation rates compared to other developed economies (Finegold *et al*, 1990; Raffe, 1992). In a sense, therefore, GNVQs were a 'reactive response' (Hodgson & Spours, 1997: 6), which is not the best way to inform curriculum development. It suggests superficial thinking, and as with the original 10-subject National Curriculum, GNVQs have been subject to constant criticism since their inception, especially with regard to their assessment, which has been seen as burdensome and inconsistent (OFSTED, 1993, 1994, 1995, 1996; FEFC, 1994; Capey, 1995; ICRA, 1995; Smithers, 1993; Wolf *et al*, 1994, Wolf, 1995) and which has led to a stream of revisions: a sure sign of inadequate and shallow planning.

Problems with assessment have, over the life of GNVQs, been partly responsible for GNVQ Advanced business moving away from the vocational towards a more 'academic' stance, which has called into question the need for both A level business studies and GNVQ business (Young and Leney, 1997; *Beeline*, 1997; Midgley, 1997; Taylor, 1998). The argument for dropping one of the two has added support given the desire to reduce the number of syllabuses on offer (Dearing, 1996), the fact that students increasingly see GNVQ Advanced subjects as substitutes for A levels (FEDA, 1994, 1997; DfEE, 1997) and the decision in early 2000 to rename GNVQs 'Vocational A levels', especially since A level business studies is often regarded, I believe falsely, as 'vocational'.

Therefore, for some within the business education community, GNVQ business is something of a Trojan horse. It was initially attractive because it offered a new route into the mainstream curriculum, offered job opportunities and raised the profile of business education nationally. This is even more the case today with the introduction of Part 1 GNVQs into Key Stage 4, where business is once again proving the most popular subject.

Unfortunately, like the Trojan horse, there is a danger of ambush. As I have already suggested, the most obvious is the possible loss of A level business studies. I have shown elsewhere (Lines, 1999) that GNVQ business and the A level started life being distinctly different – for instance the GNVQ competency model stresses process, whilst the A level is product-driven – but over time, as the criticisms of GNVQ have come to bear, the two are increasingly similar. This is especially true in the way each deals with values, to my mind a core theme in any valid business studies course. As GNVQ business has changed it has increasingly adopted a more reflective, critical stance, whilst the A level has, if anything, become more mechanistic. But it also applies to their assessment, where GNVQs now have a more vigorous external testing regime, whilst modularity allows Advanced level candidates to resit their examination, in the same way that GNVQ students are able to resubmit portfolio work.

On the other hand dropping the A level would be problematic. The large subject entries in both the A level and the GNVQ make them highly profitable for the awarding bodies, as well as demonstrably popular with students. Any attempt to remove either would inevitably meet strong resistance.

Curriculum initiatives

What follows is a brief outline, in chronological order, of the major initiatives in business studies and economics over the past 30 years. For readers who are interested, more detail can be found in my work 'Values and the curriculum: economics and business education at different stages in the development of young people' (Lines, 1999).

The Cambridge Business Studies Trust

As has been indicated above, business studies can itself be divided into 'academic' and 'vocational' (or 'general vocational') strands. The beginning of 'academic' business studies can be traced back to the 1960s when the Wolfson Foundation gave Marlborough College, an independent school in Wiltshire, a grant to create a new course. The result was a rigorous and intellectually demanding A level examined through the University of Cambridge Local Examinations Syndicate (UCLES), which even today forms the basis of what many see as the core of the subject in schools.

The relative success of the UCLES linear syllabus led to a number of imitators, the most successful of which was the Associated Examining Board's business studies version. This took a more reflective, less managerial and certainly less mathematical approach, and was perceived, consequently, as 'easier' (Barnes, 1993). Perhaps as a result (and also because it did not have a coursework component) it immediately attracted large numbers, which the UCLES syllabus never did (though its modular offshoot was competitive). As a result the AEB's syllabus is now by far the market leader whilst the original UCLES linear will, from 2000, no longer be offered.

The Cambridge Trust provided INSET and teacher training at the Institute of Education, University of London, from 1975 through to 1996. It continues with the former through the Trust's offices at Oakham in Rutland.

The Economics Association's 14–16 Project

In 1975 the Economics Association, with funding from the Esmée Fairburn Trust, embarked on a three-year project for 14–16-year-olds. The most tangible outcome of this work was three books, *The Young Person as Consumer*, *The Young Person as Producer* and *The Young Person as Citizen*, all published by Longman in 1985. Much of the material was highly innovative and moved economics away from its 'dismal scientism' (Whitehead, 1985) and into more exciting and relevant spheres that asked pertinent questions about development, distribution and resources, of the kind that would excite the interest of people of that age. Nevertheless, the failure of the project to associate itself with an examination board and a specific syllabus meant that the message was never likely to reach a wide audience (the same mistake was to be repeated with the Economics and Business Education Association's 16–19 Economics Project in the 1990s).

Business and information studies (BIS)

A far more successful innovation than the 14–16 Project, at least in terms of examination entries, was business and information studies. BIS was initiated within Hampshire LEA and involved a dual GCSE certification in business studies and information studies. It had a number of innovative features in terms of content, pedagogy, student learning, assessment and teacher support though it was sometimes criticized for lacking academic substance. It was aimed at pupils across the 14–16 ability range and was designed to be equally attractive to both sexes (before BIS, economics had been dominated by boys and vocational business studies by girls). The 1988 National Curriculum did have an effect, but the course was so successful it continued to grow. Indeed, as Figure 10.5 shows, BIS was a highly significant component of all GCSE business studies entries for a number of years, until competitors entered the market with similar and in some ways improved courses.

BIS also spawned an A level, though this course was far less successful.

The Ridgeway Project

The Ridgeway Project was named after the school in Wiltshire where it had originated. The courses, which covered a range of subjects in addition

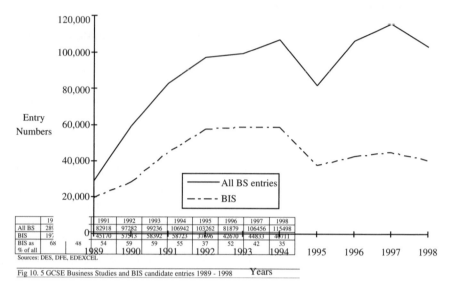

	19		1991	1992	1993	1994	1995	1996	1997	1998
All BS	285		82918	97282	99236	106942	103262	81879	106456	115498
BIS	197		45170	57913	58392	58723	37696	42670	44833	48711
BIS as % of all	68	48	54	59	59	55	37	52	42	35

Sources: DES, DFE, EDEXCEL

Fig 10. 5 GCSE Business Studies and BIS candidate entries 1989 - 1998

Figure 10.5 *GCSE business studies and BIS candidate entries 1989–1998*

to economics, were offered by London Examinations (now EdExcel) from 1989 until 1994.

The A level economics course contained six compulsory modules, some of which were innovative, certainly as far as economics was concerned. They included a problem-solving investigation of a real firm that required students to give an oral presentation of their results. There was also a coursework module that asked candidates to write a lengthy report on macroeconomic issues using both primary and secondary sources and data.

The Ridgeway Project offered lessons in terms of learning styles and assessment. The emphasis on investigation appeared to have a profound effect on student motivation (Wall, 1991) and brought students face to face with the real world, demanding that they relate their classroom learning to the issues faced by business. The very fact that a course entitled 'economics' required the application of such analysis to a small-scale business environment was itself important. This was the first manifestation of an attempt to bring together both economics and business studies, an idea further developed by the Nuffield Project (see below).

The Wessex Project

The Wessex product represented a more wholehearted attempt to bring together economics and business studies. It was the direct outcome of TVEI work in Somerset, but it was subsequently taken up by the LEAs in Dorset, Wiltshire, Avon and Gloucestershire (Leonard and Vidler, 1990). Like the Ridgeway scheme, Wessex covered a number of subject areas, with business/economics starting in 1989. The syllabuses were run by the Associated Examining Board (AEB) but, like Ridgeway, they were withdrawn early, in this case in 1994.

The Wessex business/economics course followed what came to be known as the 'Y front model' (Leonard & Vidler, 1990: 174), providing a common first year and then offering students the opportunity to proceed along either the 'economics option' or the 'business option' route. Although the Wessex Project pioneered the notion of bringing business and economics together, the common element was not heavily weighted in terms of the whole course. In addition, the very nature of the modules as they were constructed maintained a dichotomy between the two subjects. There was no attempt to integrate them in such a way as to encourage an intellectual synergy. Also their modular nature, introduced in order to increase flexibility for students and teachers alike, not only increased complexity in terms of assessment, but more seriously carried the danger of a lack of coherence (Wall, 1991). On the other hand, the Wessex pedagogic style was attractive and some of its lessons were adopted by the Nuffield Project.

The Nuffield Project

The Nuffield Economics and Business Project was funded by the Nuffield Foundation, initially to create a new A level course and then a GCSE. Latterly resources have been developed for GNVQ Part 1. The project started in 1991 and is due to end in 2000.

The Nuffield Economics and Business Project is innovative in a number of areas, including content (it is the first serious attempt to combine economics and business studies in a coherent form), pedagogy and philosophy (Wall *et al*, 1996). It takes seriously the notion of the development of the young person, and its impact in the post-16 curriculum has led to a modified version for the 14–16 age group.

Because the course has been taught for only a limited time, it is too early to say for certain how successful it has been. Initial candidate numbers were good, but growth rates from there have been somewhat disappointing (see Figure 10.2). Nevertheless the project has had an effect amongst teachers of economics who feel particularly threatened by declining numbers opting for their subject.

All the Nuffield courses are supported by wide-ranging and innovative student and teachers' resources. These range from textbooks, through photocopiables to databases and other IT materials. Teachers are supported through a national and regional network, INSET and conferences. In addition, support from BP Education for the GCSE has enabled relevant commercial and industrial information to inform the work of the project team.

Economics and Business Education Association's (EBEA) 16–19 Economics Project

By the early 1990s, as we have seen, economics in schools was in serious decline and so the EBEA (significantly renamed from the 'Economics Association') embarked on a project to create what was described as 'new economics'. The outcome was a textbook (EBEA, 1995), which contained some innovative ideas, but the impact of the project was relatively slight, almost certainly because there was no attempt to align with an examination board. A more detailed critique can be found in Lines and Vertigan, 1997.

Research issues and the international community

Given the difficulties of establishing economics and business studies in the school curriculum, it is perhaps unsurprising that the development of both research and an 'international community' has proceeded only fitfully.

The period that I referred to as the 'golden age' of school economics was reflected in a confident, outgoing international perspective, perhaps best exemplified by an international research seminar held at the Institute of Education in the summer of 1985. The book that resulted from these proceedings stands out, not only as an indicator of the strength of economics education internationally, but also as a signpost for research in the future (Hodkinson and Whitehead, 1986). Unfortunately, as we have seen, within three years a combination of the 10-subject National Curriculum and declining interest in A level economics had caused retrenchment, at least in England and Wales. This was perhaps no better exemplified than at the Institute itself, where a lecturing staff of six at the start of the 1990s was reduced to the equivalent of two by the end of the decade, and the initial training of postgraduate teachers of both economics and business had declined from almost 100 to 60 per year in the same period.

Despite this negative scenario, attempts were made to keep the international community alive, generally through the subject association and via personal contacts. In 1995 another conference was held, this time in Liverpool. It was co-sponsored by the Economics and Business Education Association as well as three US organizations – the National Council on Economic Education, the National Association for Economic Educators and the National Center for Research in Economic Education – and the Association of European Economics Education (AEEE). The resulting publication (Walstad, 1996) is noticeably more parochial and certainly more pessimistic, or perhaps realistic, than the one 10 years before (see, for example, contributions by Dunnill (1996) and Abbott and Huddleston (1996)), but at least there is a section on research from other nations, though this is dominated by US researchers.

Indeed, perhaps because of the difficulties experienced in the UK, it could be said that research leadership had passed to the other side of the Atlantic by the mid-1990s. Certainly Walstad's *An International Perspective on Economic Education* (Walstad, 1994) indicated that this might be the case, though a chapter by Whitehead (pp 137–56) at least put the UK case.

It would be wrong to overemphasize the North Atlantic link, however, since contact with other European countries has also been evident. The AEEE was formed in The Hague in 1990, although there had been earlier European conferences biennially since 1976. At The Hague it was agreed to publish a journal, but regrettably this lasted only until 1997. In the final edition the editor states that there was 'a growing feeling that the needs of European teachers is so varied that it is impossible to meet them in one English language publication' (1997, **7** (14), Winter).

Almost certainly this reflects a Europe with diverse educational systems, and different ways of approaching business and economics education. Nevertheless, whilst the journal no longer exists, the Association continues to hold its conferences in different European locations, and contacts continue to improve.

I used the word 'fitful' at the start of this section, and the past 15 or so years have seen some peaks and troughs in both the research and the international communities. It may be premature to write this, but I am of the view that we are now once again becoming more confident. Certainly at the 1999 international conference held in Glasgow, the mood was noticeably more optimistic.

The Glasgow conference was significant in a number of ways. First it was agreed that such conferences should become biennial, alternating between the UK and the USA, second that a book should be produced on research issues (this will be published in the Bedford Way Series in autumn 2000), and third, and perhaps most significantly of all from a domestic point of view, it reinforced a newly established research community of lecturers in higher education in England and Wales. This group, which first met in January 1999 at Staffordshire University, has subsequently held other meetings at Warwick University and the Institute of Education. The group is planning further twice-yearly meetings, as well as the creation of an academic journal to fill the gaps left by AEEE, *Economic Awareness* and the EBEA's journal, which has moved towards a more practical, classroom activity focus.

At a less 'organized' level, individuals and groups continue to work together across international boundaries. Indeed, whilst the business and economics education community is certainly quite small, it does at least have the advantage of being manageable, and the existence of the Internet in maintaining and developing contacts is as much a boon to academics as it is to the rest of the community.

Conclusion

It is possible to detect a pattern in the development of business and economics education. For economics there was a period of rapid growth up to the late 1980s, which in some sense was its 'golden age'. Then a combination of centrally inspired restriction on the curriculum, a failure to attract large numbers at Key Stage 4, as well as a resistance to change within the subject itself, resulted in a rapid decline in its popularity. This decline, at least in the post-16 curriculum, may be halted, but it is unlikely that economics will ever attain the position predicted for it 15 or so years ago.

In marked contrast to economics, business studies has flourished, at A level, GNVQ and GCSE. Its close connection with IT, as well as large numbers studying it at Key Stage 4, mean that it is now well established, and if the moves towards a 14–19 curriculum develop further, it is very likely that business studies will play a key role. However, because business studies takes many forms and does not possess the same academic pedigree as economics, its existence in at least one form remains under threat, though market forces are likely to resist any change.

Overall then, and despite the problems and the difficulties of curriculum recognition, business and economics education continues to survive in schools and colleges, and in many cases, to flourish. The academic community is also more optimistic than it has been for a decade or so, and this is important because a sound research base is, in my view, a prerequisite to successful curriculum innovation and change.

And what of the next decade? I am hesitant to predict 'success' after the experiences of the last 10 years; I suspect the challenge of recognition and acceptance will remain for some time. Nevertheless, if the curriculum really is about equipping young people with the tools required to face the particular demands of the 21st century, then surely business and economics education ought to have a secure place in that curriculum, not just for young people's but for all our sakes.

Acknowledgement

I would like to thank Dr Peter Davies of Staffordshire University and Dr David Whitehead for their comments on an early draft of this chapter.

References

Abbott, I and Huddleston, P (1996) The development of business education: change or decay?, in *Secondary Economics and Business Education: New developments in the United Kingdom*, United States and other nations, ed W B Walstad, Economics and Business Education Association, London

Ableson, P (1996) Declining enrolments in economics: the Australian experience, *Royal Economics Newsletter*, October

Aldrich, R (1988) The National Curriculum: an historical perspective, in *Bedford Way Papers 33: The National Curriculum*, ed D Lawton and C Chitty, Institute of Education, University of London, London

Aldrich, R (1996) *Education for the Nation*, Cassell, London

Barnes, S (1993) A-level courses in business studies, in *Economics and Business Education*, **1** (1), Spring

Beeline: The newsletter of the Economics and Business Education Association, (1), March 1997

Brue, S L (1996) Controversy and change in the American economics curriculum, Paper presented at the Pacific Rim Allied Economic Organisation Conference, Hong Kong

Capey, J (1995) *GNVQ Assessment Review*, NCVQ, London

Chambers, I (1991) GCSE business studies, in *New Developments in Economics and Business Education*, ed D Whitehead and D Dyer, Kogan Page, London

Chitty, C (1996) *Generating a National Curriculum, Block 4: Organising and control of schooling*, The Open University, Milton Keynes

Dahlgren, L O (1984) Outcomes of learning, in *The Experience of Learning*, ed F Marton, D Hounsell and D Entwistle, Scottish Academic Press, Edinburgh

Davies N (1999a) Schools in Crisis, Part 1, *Guardian*, 14 September, pp 1 and 4–5

Davies N (1999b) Schools in Crisis, Part 2, *Guardian*, 15 September, pp 1 and 4–5

Davies N (1999c) Schools in Crisis, Part 3, *Guardian*, 16 September, pp 1 and 4–5

Davies, P (1996) Economics and business studies: a subject in the curriculum?, in *Secondary Economics and Business Education: New developments in the United Kingdom, United States and other nations*, ed W B Walstad, Economics and Business Education Association, London

Dawson, G G (1977) Research in economic education at the precollege level, in *Perspectives on Economic Education*, ed D R Wentworth, W Hansen and S H Hawke, Joint Council on Economic Education, New York

Dearing, R (1996) *Review of Qualifications for 16–19 Year Olds*, SCAA

Department for Education and Employment (DfEE) (1997) *Qualifying for Success: A consultative paper on the future of post-16 qualifications*, DfEE Publications, London

Department of Education and Science (DES) (1985) *The Curriculum from 5 to 16*, DES Inspectorate of Schools

Department of Education and Science (DES) (1987) *Report by H M Inspectors on the Hampshire Business and Information Project*, HMSO, London

Dunnill, R (1996) Managing economics and business education in schools, in *Secondary Economics and Business Education: New developments in the United Kingdom, United States and other nations*, ed W B Walstad, Economics and Business Education Association, London

Economics and Business Education Association (EBEA) (1995) *Core Economics*, Heinemann Educational Books, Oxford

Finegold, D et al (1990) *A British Baccalaureate: Overcoming divisions between education and training*, Institute for Public Policy Research, London

Further Education Development Agency (FEDA), Institute of Education and The Nuffield Foundation (1994) *GNVQs 1993–97: A national survey report – interim*, FEDA, London

FEDA, Institute of Education and The Nuffield Foundation (1997) *GNVQs 1993–97: A national survey report*, FEDA, London

Further Education Funding Council (FEFC) (1994) *General National Vocational Qualifications in the Further Education Sector in England*, FEFC, Coventry

Further Education Funding Council (FEFC) (1997) *Standards and their Assurance in Vocational Qualifications: National survey report*, FEFC, Coventry

Gilbert, R (1984) *The Impotent Image: Reflections on ideology in the secondary curriculum*, The Falmer Press, London

Goodson, I F (ed) (1985) *Social Histories of the Secondary Curriculum*, The Falmer Press, London

Goodson, I F (1987) *School Subjects and Curriculum Change*, The Falmer Press, London

Graham, D with Tytler, D (1993) *A Lesson for Us All*, Routledge, London

Green, A (1997) Core skills, general education and unification in post-16 education, in *Dearing and Beyond*, ed A Hodgson and K Spours, Kogan Page, London

Green, A, Wolf, A and Leney, T (1999) *Convergence and Divergence in European Education and Training Systems*, Bedford Way Papers, Institute of Education, University of London, London

Green, F (1998) Can economics stem a drop in interest rates?, *Times Higher Educational Supplement*, 30 October, p 4

Guratsky, S (1984) The adequacy of A-level syllabuses, *Economics*, **20** (2), Summer

Hirst, P (1993) The foundations of the National Curriculum: why subjects, in *Assessing the National Curriculum*, ed P O'Hear and J White, Paul Chapman Publishing, London

Hodgson, A and Spours, K (eds) (1997) *Dearing and Beyond*, Kogan Page, London

Hodkinson, S and Whitehead, D (eds) (1986) *Economics Education: Research and development issues*, Longman, Harlow

Hoogendijk, W (1996) *The Economic Revolution*, Jon Carpenter Publishing, Oxford

International Centre for Research on Assessment (ICRA), Institute of Education and the Centre for Curriculum and Assessment Studies, University of Bristol

(1995) *Evaluation of the Use of Set Assignments in GNVQ (SAGE Project)*, Manpower Services Commission

Kelsey, B and Lambert, P (1988) Business metamorphosis, *Times Educational Supplement*, 26 February

Lawson, T (1997) *Economics and Reality*, Routledge, London

Lawton, D (1996) The changing context: the National Curriculum, in *Teaching Economics and Business*, ed S Hodkinson and M Jephcote, Heinemann, Oxford

Leonard, C and Vidler, C (1990) Wessex modular business/economics, *Economics*, **26** (4), Winter

Levacic, R (1987) What changes should be made to the A-level syllabuses for the 1990s?, *Economics*, **24** (4), Winter

Lines, D (1999) Values and the curriculum: economics and business education at different stages in the development of young people, unpublished PhD thesis, ULIE, London

Lines, D and Vertigan, S (1997) Ethics, economics and economics education, in *Education, Environment and Economy: Research issues*, ed S Slater, D Lambert and D Lines, Institute of Education, University of London, London

Lines, D R (1987) Business studies: the search for a paradigm, unpublished MA dissertation, ULIE, London

Lines, D R (1988) The future direction of Advanced level economics, *Economics*, **24**, Part 2, (102), Summer

Lines, D R (1997) What's the big idea, *Times Educational Supplement*, Economics and Business Supplement, **11**, 4 April

Linton, R (ed) (1940) *Acculturation*, Appleton-Century-Crofts, New York

Livesey, F (1986) Whatever happened to economics, *Economics*, **23** (2), Summer

Marton, F (1989) Phenomenography and the art of teaching all things to all men, Paper presented to the annual meeting of the American Research Association, New Orleans

Midgley, S (1997) Choice threatened as the future of A-level hangs in the balance, *TES Extra*, I, 4 April

Mortimore, P (1990) The primary curriculum: issues and priorities, in *Economic and Industrial Awareness in the Primary School*, ed A Ross, SCIP, Polytechnic of North London, London

Office for Standards in Education (OFSTED) (1993, 1994, 1995, 1996) *GNVQs in Schools: Quality and standards of General National Vocational Qualifications*, Annual reports, HMSO, London

Ormerod, P (1994) *The Death of Economics*, Faber & Faber, London

Parsons, C (1996) Economics and business in the curriculum: their changing roles, in *Teaching Economics and Business*, ed S Hodkinson and M Jephcote, Heinemann, Oxford

Pisanie, J A (1997) Declining enrolments in economics, in *Royal Economics Society Newsletter*, March

Raffe, D (1992) *Participation of 16–18 Year-Olds in Education and Training*, NCE Briefing Paper No 3, National Commission on Education

Robbins, L (1955) *Economics*, **65** (260), December

Ross, A (ed) (1990) *Economic and Industrial Awareness in the Primary School*, SCIP, Polytechnic of North London, London

Ryba, R and Hodkinson, S (1985) Economics for the 14–16 year-old, in *Teaching Economics*, ed G Atkinson, Heinemann, London

School Curriculum and Assessment Authority (SCAA) (1996) *GCE Results Analysis*, SCAA, London

Smithers, A (1993) All our futures: Britain's educational revolution, *Dispatches*, Channel 4 Television

Surkes, S (1987) Business studies flagship course could founder, *Times Educational Supplement*, **11**, December, p 10

Taylor, R (1998) Qualifying for success: a consultation on the future of post-16 qualifications, in *GNVQ Today*, ed R Dransfield, (7), Summer, Peacock Press, Hebden Bridge

Thomas, L (1991) A new perspective on learning – what does it mean for economics?, *Economics*, **27** (2), Summer

Unwin, L (1997) Reforming the work-based route: problems and potential for change, in *Dearing and Beyond*, ed A Hodgson and K Spours, Kogan Page, London

Wall, N (1986) Drawing a line: what are the limits at A-level?, *Economics*, **22** (3), Autumn

Wall, N (1991) The 16–19 economics curriculum, in *New Developments in Economics and Business Education*, ed D Whitehead and D Dyer, Kogan Page, London

Wall, N *et al* (1996) Economics and business at A-level: an integrated approach, in *Teaching Economics and Business*, ed S Hodkinson and M Jephcote, Heinemann, Oxford

Walsh, P (1993) *Education and Meaning: Philosophy in practice*, Cassell, London

Walstad, W B (ed) (1994) *An International Perspective on Economic Education*, Kluwer Academic Publishers, Norwell, MA

Walstad, W B (ed) (1996) *Secondary Economics and Business Education: New developments in the United Kingdom, United States and other nations*, Economics and Business Education Association, London

Welford, R (1984) Broadening the A-level syllabuses, *Economics*, **20** (2), Summer

White, J (1998) New aims for a new National Curriculum, in *The National Curriculum beyond 2000: The QCA and the aims of education*, ed R Aldrich and J White, Institute of Education, University of London, London

Whitehead, D (1985) Values in economics teaching, in *Teaching Economics*, ed G B J Atkinson, Heinemann, London

Whitehead, D (1994) Economic understanding in the United Kingdom, in *An International Perspective on Economic Education*, ed W B Walstad, Kluwer Academic Publishers, Norwell, MA

Whitehead, D (1996) Economics and business education, in *A Guide to Educational Research*, ed P Gordon, Woburn Press, London

Wolf, A (1995) *An Assessment-Driven System: Education and training in England and Wales*, ICRA Research Monograph No 3, ULIE, London

Wolf, A *et al* (1994) *GNVQ Assessment Review Project: Final report*, Technical Report No 23, R and D Series, Employment Department Learning Methods Branch

Young, M and Leney, T (1997) From A-levels to an advanced level curriculum for the future, in *Dearing and Beyond*, ed A Hodgson and K Spours, Kogan Page, London

Young, M F D (1998) *The Curriculum of the Future*, Falmer Press, London

Postscript

Denis Lawton

I have been asked to write an overview of this book from the point of view of the school curriculum as a whole rather than individual subjects. I enjoyed reading the contributions although I had an uneasy feeling that the existing list of subjects might give a misleading impression of the Institute's views of knowledge and the curriculum. This is so for at least three reasons. First, no serious educationist would now pretend that a list of subjects on its own can produce a satisfactory whole curriculum. Second, the list of subjects is unfortunately incomplete: it was planned to have a chapter devoted to social studies or social science subjects – sociology, social anthropology, psychology and politics – but the relevant member of staff left for another university where he became too busy to write his chapter. It is also the case that one important school subject, physical education, is not a subject at present taught at the Institute of Education. Third, the Institute of Education has for many years put forward various views advocating a reformed curriculum. For example, after the Second World War a group of educationists centred on the Institute of Education were disappointed that the 1944 Education Act had almost nothing to say about the curriculum. They formed themselves into 'The Council for Curriculum Reform' and produced a remarkable report *The Content of Education*, edited by a young lecturer at the Institute, Joseph Lauwerys (later its distinguished Professor of Comparative Education). The Report recommended, *inter alia*, that there should be a planned curriculum with a common core that would include the social sciences. The whole of Chapter X of the Report was devoted to the social sciences and recommended specifically that:

> The principles underlying this book – that education must help young people develop themselves and become responsible members of a democratic society – emphasize the need to give an important place in the core curriculum to the

social studies... The main advantages of both economics and politics as school subjects are that they give training in clear, accurate and objective thinking.

(Lauwerys, 1945: 170–71)

Another occasion when the Institute intervened in National Curriculum planning was in 1988 when Secretary of State for Education, Kenneth Baker, put forward a compulsory National Curriculum as part of the Education Reform Act 1988. A group of Institute staff regretted that an opportunity had been missed to reform the curriculum rather than to fossilize the traditional grammar school curriculum as a mixture of core and foundation subjects. The result was that Kenneth Baker stuck to his model of the National Curriculum, but the National Curriculum Council (NCC), which had been set up to implement and supervise the development of the curriculum, immediately tried to move away from the subjects-only model by introducing a series of cross-curricular themes such as citizenship and the environment.

In other words, the NCC also wanted to persuade schools that a curriculum based only on traditional subjects left obvious gaps. But in the event the cross-curricular themes were optional whereas core and foundation subjects were compulsory. Few schools found it possible to give themes such as citizenship the attention they deserved. It was left until David Blunkett's Curriculum 2000 was planned to promote citizenship to the status of a subject.

In anticipation of that reform, the Curriculum Studies Academic Group at the Institute organized a conference in 1999 at which both David Blunkett and Bernard Crick spoke. (See Cairns *et al*, 2000, for some of the proceedings of that conference.)

There are other ways in which the Institute has from time to time invited those concerned mainly with single subjects to look at the whole curriculum. For example, in 1997 the Archbishop of Canterbury, Dr George Carey, opened a conference concerned with values in education to which many members of staff contributed (see Lawton, Cairns and Gardner, 1999).

In his Preface to this book Ashley Kent is right to emphasize the fact that one of the great strengths of the Institute, especially at PGCE level, is in those groups responsible for teaching curriculum subjects. Over the years we have built up strong traditions of teaching and research in those subjects, which are quite outstanding. Yet there has always existed a tension between the 'chalk-face' work of PGCE tutoring and the sometimes more fundamental approaches of those concerned, for example, with philosophy, psychology, sociology and – more recently – curriculum studies. The Institute has learnt to manage the tension very well, even creatively, as this book frequently illustrates.

It would, however, be misleading to overstate the tension between subjects and the whole curriculum. The chapter by Tony Burgess and John Hardcastle on English is an admirable explanation of a subject that essentially permeates the whole curriculum in a highly creative way. It is also gratifying to note that all subjects were treated as an aspect of culture rather than as a form of knowledge in the traditional way. In fact one of the most interesting features of the book is the discussion of how subjects have all changed over the years: the accounts of science and history were particularly enlightening from this point of view. Alaric Dickinson's history story is also fascinating as an illustration of the political debate about the curriculum. (The curriculum is, of course, always a political matter, but rarely has the conflict been as explicit as it was after the Education Reform Act 1988 raised the question of 'what should history be?'.)

Another subject that has changed dramatically over the years is religious education. This chapter, aptly subtitled 'Soul-searching in an era of supercomplexity', not only provides a splendid historical account, but also faces up to the cultural and multicultural questions involved.

I do not have sufficient space to discuss every chapter, but each one makes a contribution to the debate about the whole curriculum. The final chapter is different in another way: it is less concerned with how economics and business have changed and more concerned with how the case was made for innovation. In this way we are provided with a case study of curriculum change that is extremely valuable even if the story is unfinished.

Many years ago, Peter Gordon and I attempted to write a brief history of the curriculum in England, covering the 19th and 20th centuries (Gordon and Lawton, 1978, but long out of print). The book was difficult to write partly because so little had at that time been recorded about the history of individual subjects. This volume has certainly gone a long way towards filling that gap – but the whole book is much more than that. I have stressed the development of the whole curriculum, but there is a wealth of material here about, and many insights into, the development of teacher education.

References

Cairns, J et al (2000) *Education for Citizenship*, Cassell, London

Gordon, P and Lawton, D (1978) *Curriculum Change in the Nineteenth and Twentieth Centuries*, Hodder & Stoughton, London

Lauwerys, J A (ed) (1945) *The Content of Education*, The Council for Curriculum Reform/ULP, London

Lawton, D, Cairns, J and Gardner, R (eds) (1999) *Values and the Curriculum: The school context*, Institute of Education, University of London, London
Lawton, D and Chitty, C (1988) *The National Curriculum*, Institute of Education, University of London, London

Index

Page references in italics indicate tables or figures